797,885 Books
are available to read at

Forgotten Books

www.ForgottenBooks.com

Forgotten Books' App
Available for mobile, tablet & eReader

ISBN 978-1-330-57689-2
PIBN 10006338

This book is a reproduction of an important historical work. Forgotten Books uses state-of-the-art technology to digitally reconstruct the work, preserving the original format whilst repairing imperfections present in the aged copy. In rare cases, an imperfection in the original, such as a blemish or missing page, may be replicated in our edition. We do, however, repair the vast majority of imperfections successfully; any imperfections that remain are intentionally left to preserve the state of such historical works.

Forgotten Books is a registered trademark of FB &c Ltd.
Copyright © 2015 FB &c Ltd.
FB &c Ltd, Dalton House, 60 Windsor Avenue, London, SW19 2RR.
Company number 08720141. Registered in England and Wales.

For support please visit www.forgottenbooks.com

1 MONTH OF FREE READING

at
www.ForgottenBooks.com

By purchasing this book you are eligible for one month membership to ForgottenBooks.com, giving you unlimited access to our entire collection of over 700,000 titles via our web site and mobile apps.

To claim your free month visit:
www.forgottenbooks.com/free6338

* Offer is valid for 45 days from date of purchase. Terms and conditions apply.

Similar Books Are Available from
www.forgottenbooks.com

The Dance
Historic Illustrations of Dancing from 3300 B.C. to 1911 A.D., by An Antiquary

Dancing in All Ages
by Edward Scott

Dancing, Ancient and Modern
by Ethel L. Urlin

A History of Dancing from the Earliest Ages to Our Own Times
by Gaston Vuillier

Folk Dancing
by Grace Imogene Fox

Dancing and Dancers of Today
The Modern Revival of Dancing as an Art, by Caroline Caffin

Grammar of the Art of Dancing, Theoretical and Practical
Lessons in the Arts of Dancing and Dance Writing (Choregraphy), by Friedrich Albert Zorn

The Chalif Text Book of Dancing, Vol. 1
by Louis H. Chalif

Dancing Made Easy
by Charles J. Coll

The Morris Book
With a Description of Dances As Performed By the Morris Men, by Cecil J. Sharp

Æsthetic Dancing
by Emil Rath

Dancing Without an Instructor
by Professor Wilkinson

Swedish Folk Dances
by Nils William Berquist

American Country-Dances, Vol. 1
by Elizabeth Burchenal

The Russian Ballet
by Ellen Terry

The Theory of Theatrical Dancing
With a Chapter on Pantomime, by Carlo Blasis

A Handbook of Irish Dances
With an Essay on Their Origin and History, by J. C. O'Keeffe

The Japanese Dance
by Marcelle Azra Hincks

Modern Dance for the Youth of America
A Text for High School and College Teachers, by Ruth Anderson Radir

Newman Catechism on Classical Dancing
by Albert W. Newman

Plate I, a.

Plate I, b.

The Antique Greek Dance

after sculptured and painted figures

> ἐστὶ δὲ καὶ τὰ τῶν ἀρχαίων
> δημιουργῶν ἀγάλματα τῆς
> παλαιᾶς ὀρχήσεως λείψανα.
> ATHÉNÉE, 629, b.

BY

Maurice Emmanuel

Docteur ès Lettres
et Lauréat du Conservatoire

TRANSLATED
BY
Harriet Jean Beauley

WITH DRAWINGS
BY
A. COLLOMBAR AND THE AUTHOR

NEW YORK: JOHN LANE COMPANY
LONDON: JOHN LANE, THE BODLEY HEAD
MCMXVI

Copyright, 1916,
By Harriet Jean Beauley

Press of
J. J. Little & Ives Company
New York, U.S A.

M. Marmontel*
of the Conservatoire

and

M. Th. Dubois
Member of the Institute

In affectionate homage

M. E.

349627

FOREWORD

Without the assistance of Dr. Marey, member of the Institute, and of M. Hansen, Master of the Ballet of the Opera, I should have lacked much of the material for this work. M. Hansen, who unites great learning with a charming personality, consented to give me his opinion of each of the representations of movements shown on the vases and bas-reliefs which I have used; he even went further,— he gave me the benefit of his experience in the analysis of these movements by photography. To Dr. Marey I am indebted for help in my arrangement of the series of figures which form the basis of this work. I beg them to accept my profound thanks.

With my whole heart I thank M. Croiset, member of the Institute, whose advice was most valuable; M. Collignon, member of the Institute, who permitted me to ask his assistance in classifying the paintings and sculptures; M. Pottier, of the Louvre Museum, who not only opened the glass cases there, but who gave me the benefit of his erudition; M. Müntz, member of the Institute, archivist of the School of the Beaux-Arts; M. de Chantepie, administrator of the Library of the Sorbonne, and his collaborators, MM. Chatelain, Lehot, Mortet, who, in their great kindness, made themselves as the instruments of toil in my hands; M. Nuitter, archivist of the Opera, who put me in communication with many interesting manuscripts; M. Babelon, curator of the Cabinet of Medals, through whom I am enabled to publish some hitherto unpublished types of antique dancers.

I express my gratitude to M. Havet, member of the Institute, who made me welcome at all times when I was in need of his advice.

I would testify to the inspiration which I received from M. Bourgault-Ducoudray's lessons on the history of music.

TRANSLATOR'S FOREWORD

The Antique Greek Dance *was written by one who loved both Greek art and the dance with a deep and understanding love,— Maurice Emmanuel, of the Paris Conservatoire.*

The result of his study was this book, published some years ago. The edition was soon exhausted, and, in order to obtain a copy of this authoritative work the translator was obliged to search the old book shops of Paris.

Believing that the world-wide reawakened interest in all phases of the dance makes imperative the publication of this remarkable book in a form and a language that will make it available to students and artists, it has been translated.

In France the copies were eagerly bought and treasured by artists, dancers, and teachers of dancing. Painters, sculptors and actors were also quick to see its worth, as all of the expressional arts have a common foundation. One who has felt in his own awakened mind and body the harmony that comes with freedom from constraint, through training in rhythm and expression gained from the natural dance, is better equipped to show forth the same quality in his work, whether his medium be brush, violin or voice.

Emmanuel's theory is that, while the anatomy of the body remains the same, the method of movements cannot alter, so that, fundamentally, the modern dance must obey the same laws as the antique dance.

Long and patient study of thousands of figures of Greek painting and sculpture enabled him to so far reconstruct the ancient dance that he could compare it with the modern ballet and follow the likenesses and differences between them.

The special qualities of the modern French dance are precision and rhythm, with the mimetic almost entirely absent.

The special qualities of the Greek dance are a very keen sense of mimetic value, joined to perfect rhythm, but somewhat lacking in precision.

The author has compared these, holding in his mind a picture of the ideal dance which should have all the excellences of each, without any of the defects.

He has taken up the positions of the legs and their movements, the positions and movements of the arms; and those of the head and torso, as used in the modern classic dance and depicted upon ancient vases, high and low reliefs, and upon the frescoes of Pompeii. He has searched Greek poetry for that quality common to all of the musical arts,—the quality of rhythm. From the poetic rhythms he has reconstructed the music-rhythm, and from both, the dance-rhythm. He found that Greek poetry, correctly enunciated, indicated the music to which it was originally declaimed, thus giving the clue to the dance-rhythm, making due allowance for the fact that the poetry of the dance is not as closely bound by the formal rules as the more stately measures. He found that comment on the subject by Greek authors, far from contradicting his conclusions, confirmed them in most details. But, in the end, the painted and sculptured figures furnished most of the information he sought; the rhythms of the poets and the descriptions by various Greek writers giving only the footnotes for the true documents.

Like all investigators, he followed many paths that led nowhere before discovering the authentic source of information. Patiently he searched the writings of many authors of the post-classic period, but found them undependable, not only because of their ignorance of the subject, but because they did not even write with an understanding of their own language. Baffled there, he searched the Greek plays, from those of Aristophanes to those of Sophocles, to discover what the characters might say regarding the art. The reader may gain some idea of the amount of labor required for this research by remembering that he was working in a foreign language and one no longer spoken. He modestly remarks that "the information so gained has a certain value." Eventually, he concluded that most of the knowledge must be acquired from the sculptured and painted figures. Of these he examined thousands, and, with the help of the most famous archæologists in France, who were eager to assist him, he classified them in chronological order, beginning with those of the fifteenth century B. C. Next, he separated the different kinds of dances belonging to each period; then he followed the changes and modifications of each dance from one period to another. Lastly, he critically compares the reconstructed Greek dance with the modern ballet. From all of the representations he selected about five-hundred-and-seventy-five to illustrate his book. He begins with the vases of Mycenæan style, which Perrot prefers to call "Vases in the Ægean style" because they are found throughout the Ægean basin. These date back to the fifteenth century B. C. In them, the artists confined their designs to shells and flowers, not yet daring to attempt to depict the human figure. They are to be noted as the precursors of the geometric style of the vases of Dipylon, in which the form and decoration is of geometrical character, in straight lines. The human figures, here introduced for the first time, would seem to partake, in a slight degree, of the curved lines of the earlier period. These first representations of dancing figures are very important. There are dances by warriors, funeral dances, and dances by the citizens.

In the seventh century B. C., the style becomes Orientalized. At this period the first incised decoration is noted, the vase being first painted all over in the same color, the design being then cut through to the natural color of the clay.

The figures have, by this time, become more flexible; the geometric stiffness begins to disappear.

In the sixth century B. C. the artists chose a very red clay, painting the figure in black, touched up with white. These paintings represent the funeral dances, the Pyrrhics, and the merry dances of Komas. But new ones are introduced,—dances in honor of the gods and those in which the gods take part; also, the dance-games of leaping, running, throwing the discus, etc. It must be borne in mind that all of these exercises were done to a musical accompaniment, and are, therefore, to be considered dances in the Greek meaning of the word. The freer movements of the dancers may bear some relation to the change in the manner of decorating the vases; the ceramists painted the background black, leaving the figure in the natural red clay.

But not until the fourth century B. C. did the painters attain that *perfection of detail which is scientifically correct and at the same time a source of illumination. The movements become more complicated and varied; the dances more fantastic. This period marks the high tide, as far as representations of the dance are concerned.*

In the third century B. C. the designs are stiff, clumsy, and overornamented; at this time the Bacchanalian scenes are favored; the dances become freer but less rhythmic.

The funeral vases of the fifth and fourth centuries B. C. are the most beautiful of all; the profile figures are simple and perfect in drawing.

Greek sculpture developed more slowly than painting, though in the seventh century B. C. the reliefs give more information regarding the dance than do the paintings, but they are very rigid.

The golden age of Greek sculpture, the fifth century B. C., is the richest of all in really scientific representations of the dance, the figures attaining a splendid freedom of movement. From that time forward, art becomes more sensuous, though it is still far from the decadent Græco-Roman period.

The succeeding century saw the creation of the marvelous little dancing figures of Tanagra. These lithe dancers have little in common with the stately figures of Phidias. The workers in clay filled their figures with a spirit of gayety and charm.

There are few dancers to be found among the more pretentious works of the second century B. C., but the great sculptures of that period show a complex rhythm which should be carefully studied. There are a multitude of little clay figures of dancers. This is the period when great prominence is given to the worship of Dionysos and Aphrodite.

The first century B. C. sees a return to the archaic forms which is artificial and deliberate. With these figures, Greek art may be said to end.

Maurice Emmanuel's task was not ended when he had examined all these things in many museums; there is a wide margin for speculation afforded by the fact that many of the ancient pieces are in very imperfect condition. Deterioration due to atmospheric conditions, wanton destruction, and, what the author considers worst of all, ignorant "restorations," were some of the problems that confronted him.

The technique of the Greek dance is proved to be very simple, as was necessary in an art in which every one participated, but, in order to understand the movements, it is necessary to take into account the limitations imposed upon decorators of vases and kindred ornamental work. It is often the case that they must depart from facts in order to make the figures conform to a design, the paramount thing being the pattern, rather than a record of the dance as it actually is. Thus equilibrium is often sacrificed; perspective destroyed. In many cases the figures are placed on the same plane, though their positions would indicate the contrary. Often there are two rows of them, with no floor indicated, so that those in the upper row appear to be leaping to an unheard-of height. All these conventions made the interpreter's work more difficult. The torso is often represented in face, with the legs profile. This, however, is not an indication of the artist's ignorance; the convention is intentional and has a meaning. During a long period the figures all advance on the left leg. Later, this convention disappears; the archaic bas-reliefs escape it altogether by taking refuge in another, viz., the leg carried forward is the left when the marcher is turned to the right of the spectator, and the right when he is turned to the left of the spectator, thus keeping both legs in view. This convention persists in the works of Phidias and his contemporaries.

Notwithstanding these set forms, the Greek artists were able to fix the fleeting "moment" of a movement, and they observed much more accurately than we do, as may be proved by contrasting our impression of the same "moment" with the result of an instantaneous photograph, and noting the perfect correspondence of the photograph with the Greek conception. This keen vision of the ceramists and sculptors enables us to get a very clear idea of the Greek dance, though the author sometimes selects examples less good from an artistic standpoint as being the best of all when considered as relating to the dance.

The first part of the study will be given to the gymnastics of the dance, as far as the pictures allow them to be discovered. That is, to arrive at an understanding of the result by examining the processes leading to it. The pupil must not fall into the error of regarding this preparatory work as an end in itself. Moderns have separated the arts of dancing and acting; with the Greeks it was not so; dancing was pantomime as well as rhythmic movement, and the only way to get the spirit of the Greek dance is to take this attitude toward it.

But it is first necessary to consider the gymnastics of the art; the sculptors studied the poses of the dancers, and the dancers, in turn, copied the poses of the statues. It is not always easy to separate the mimetic from the purely dancing movements in these representations, as at first glance they appear very much alike.

Greek art is, like all things that progress, subject to change, but the fundamentals remain the same. The changes are less notable in the pictures of religious dances, because the ritual was a very definite thing and prescribed certain poses and gestures from which there could be no deflection. Outside the limits of religious formalism the changes are greater,—the Greeks were not without a very modern love of novelty.

All of the gestures originally had a concrete significance, becoming symbolic with the passing of time. Few of the more ancient ones were discarded, but new ones were added. They may be divided into three groups:

Gestures of ritualism and symbolism,
Gestures of every-day life,
Gestures of concrete type becoming decorative motifs.

The mimetic funeral, for instance, is an example of a decorative movement evolving from a concrete gesture. In most remote times the hired mourners scratched their faces and tore their hair as an extravagant demonstration of grief. These practices were forbidden by Solon, and, from his time, became merely symbolic gestures, the mourners placing the hands over the face or on the head.

The gesture of the veil is so beautiful that it has never fallen into disuse, dancers in all times recognizing its decorative value, even after the meaning has been lost. In the decadent period of Greek art the veil gestures were used as they have been by certain modern dancers, more to emphasize nudity than to conceal it, thus perverting the original expression, which was one of modesty.

The gymnastics of the Greek dance were founded on natural, instinctive movements, like the walk, the run, and the leap, movements upon which was built the superstructure of the dance. By placing a thought back of the instinctive movement, it becomes a gesture, an expression. The dance thus becomes more than a mechanical exercise, it is an expressional movement to an accompaniment of song and instrumental music. The primitive dances of all peoples are expressive; the separation between gymnastics and acting comes only with a more complex civilization. This separation, so marked in our time, was unknown to the Greeks, yet the author has been able to trace in the statues and paintings the same steps used to-day. Some of the dances are made up of walking and running steps set to music, with the head, torso and arms in repose. The Greeks used the natural oppositions of members in the same way that was taught by the great Noverre in the eighteenth century. This element may have been prominent in Greek dancing long before the artists acquired sufficient skill to depict it and also before they were emancipated from the old conventions, but it finds its highest expression in the Parthenon frieze, where the whole aspect of the marchers shows that they are taking part in a solemn religious ceremony, yet the lightness of their movements shows that they are at the same time taking part in a dance. The variety of pose, the rhythmic opposition of arm and leg, head and torso, is limited only by the conditions imposed by the set forms of representation of a religious ceremony. Even in the case of these stately dancers, the spectator is impressed instantly with the fact that the Greeks did not dance with the feet and legs alone, but with the whole body. When the torso, head, arms and hands were eliminated as dancing members, the dance lost all of its expressional value and became artificial. This has been carried to the farthest limit in the modern ballet, which, retaining the steps of the Greeks, has lost everything else.

No modern steps are here considered except those which were also used in ancient Greece. The technical expressions have been retained, but are so carefully explained that they are clear to the non-professional reader.

First are considered positions and movements of the modern dance, which must serve as the standard of comparison in order to *make the work intelligible. The Five Fundamental Positions of the legs are taken up; these are all on the soles of the feet. From them are derived the principal Positions of the II and IV. Reference is made to paintings and reliefs to show that the Greeks used these Positions, a point necessary to establish, since movements must begin and end with Positions and are determined by Positions. ·Often the successive "moments" of a step are represented by paintings and reliefs widely separated geographically, but which, unmistakably, form a true series when placed in proper order. In this way it is proved that the Greeks used the Pirouette, the Entrechat, and many other steps that are an integral part of the modern French ballet.*

So much for the likenesses between the two kinds of dance.

The differences become more apparent when the movements of the head, arms and torso are considered. In the modern ballet the arms may fall motionless at the sides, may be raised over the head in certain positions that are carefully calculated so that they may not affect the stability of the foot-position, causing the dancer to lose balance, the hands may pick up the flower-like full skirt;—this is about all the arms are allowed to do, and even this must follow hard-and-fast rules. The movements of the head are even more restricted; the torso almost ceases to live. The body above the hips becomes merely a decorative adjunct to the dance. All this may show forth the dancer's agility and skill, but, at best, such a dance is nothing more than a beautiful gymnastic of the acrobatic order.

The Greek dancer, on the contrary, having due regard for mimetic values, employs movements of the torso, head and arms as a part of the dance, vivifying it and raising it out of the class of gymnastic exercises.

The Greek dancers did not, like ours, regard curving movements of the arms as the only kind permissible; they did not hesitate to speak in abrupt angles if the exigencies of the dance-drama demanded it, though the more stately dances always show the elegant curved positions. The hands might be hidden in the cloak, but the pose of the arm carried expression. The hand continued the expression of the arm, completing the gesture. The hand gesture of the Bacchantes is characteristic,—the hand held back, wrist turned so that the palm is seen, thumb held high. *This pose is confined to the comic phases of Bacchanalian dances, like those of the Komastia, as is the step in which the foot is lifted so that the whole sole is seen.* The play of the hands is second in importance to the foot-movements.

In the modern dance there are few positions of the hand taught, and these have no dramatic value, the hand being regarded as simply a finish for the arm.

When the Greek dancer's arm becomes passive, it takes much the same position as the one habitual with ballet dancers,—arm hanging, fingers separated, the middle finger opposed to the thumb.

The ballet recognizes five Positions of the torso, between which there are two that may be taken with the body bent toward either side. Body positions being limited by the anatomy, are much alike among dancers of all time. The predominant poses in the Greek dance is the forward or backward bending of the torso. Neither pose is exaggerated in the noble dances, but is characteristic of the dances of the Bacchantes. In the orgiastic dances all movements are exaggerated, as is natural when it is remembered that the dancers are in a state of frenzy akin to insanity. It has been suggested, and the idea is plausible, that there was a pathological reason for the Bacchic frenzy that sent devotees dancing over the mountains on cold winter nights, screaming an accompaniment to their wild steps. Little wonder that the body bent far forward or far backward became a symbolic movement in the Dionysian celebrations, where wine and flowers, torches and song, had their part in the worship.

The head is nearly motionless in most ballet work; with the Greeks it was, expressionally, as important as the torso. In the Dionysian dances it followed the direction of the bending body. In other dances it moves in opposition to the torso.

The different members, having been considered separately, must next be studied in the infinite combinations of which they are capable. More than 95,000 such combinations have been proved possible, but in actual practice many of them would be ugly, expressionless, and useless.

Opposition between the different parts of the body is defined by Emmanuel as a constant readjustment of weight among the members to maintain perfect equilibrium, and was so used by Noverre. It is nature's means of keeping the body balanced. This law of Opposition, as used in the dance, lifts a natural, instinctive act up into the domain of esthetics.

As to the ways in which the members may be combined, no book can answer the question: "Which are good combinations and which are not?" Only the education of the members themselves can give the dancer the power to decide unerringly. This is better than a set of rules on the subject, because hard-and-fast rules destroy spontaneity. A few of the combinations most used are taught, and from these others may be derived, according to the dancer's skill and inventiveness. Among the ones most in vogue are the Arabesque and the Attitude, two complicated poses minutely described in this book, both suggesting lightness to such an extent that the dancer scarcely appears to rest on the earth. The Tanagra figurines possess the same quality. Both the ancient and modern dancers attain this expression by observing the laws of Opposition. This law is often disregarded by the Greeks, but there is a very definite reason for it;—when they wanted to suggest the instability of a drunken Satyr, they knew no better way to do it than by parallelism of movement, advancing the right arm and leg at the same time, and letting the head follow the same direction as the torso. In all serious work the law of Opposition is observed. Noverre and Blasis did not copy antique vases, but they were scientific artists, who knew that the opposition of members resulted in stability as well as grace, and, avoiding an uneasy appearance, was pleasing to the eye.

Having treated the members separately and as a whole, the body has, up to this time, been considered as though in a series of poses. Motion has not been considered.

But, with the body in a given position, it can move only from that position, taking its initial movement from the point at which each member is placed. It follows that, having studied the poses of the antique statues, in their relation to modern dances, the movement can be predicated from the position. In this way the whole dance can be reconstructed.

At this point the gymnastics of the dance are taken up, to render the body supple. Few American students will envy the little ballet *students of Paris the tedious and often painful hours of practice which fits them for the stage. Most will sigh with relief at the knowledge that the Greek system depended more upon all-around training of the body that fitted it to become an agent of expression rather than to exploit it in unusual kinds of motion. The result may have been, and doubtless was, less precision than ours; but, in the modern classic dance, too much that is valuable has been sacrificed to precision.*

Many of the exercises used by us were, without doubt, used by the Greeks, such as Bending, Separating, Striking, Circles of the Legs. These movements are all natural ones. These lead to complicated ones beginning or ending with such poses as the Attitude and the Arabesque, which were in use in ancient Greece, showing that they had a system of training that was fundamentally the same as ours.

A great part of the book will be found to treat of the modern ballet steps and tempos, giving minute descriptions of them, and from them reconstructing the Greek steps. Often the sculptures represent a step at its characteristic moment, a moment so individual that it could belong to no other step; therefore, if the same moment is to be found in a modern movement, the inference is plain.

Thus it is demonstrated that they employed turning movements of which the most conspicuous example is the Pirouette. The whirling draperies shown in the paintings prove the rapidity of motion. The "turn by stamping" was a graceful movement not used now. The Greek figures even show, by the skill exhibited in the Pirouette and the turn by stamping, whether the dancer was a highly trained professional or an amateur.

Investigators less scientific than Emmanuel have made one great mistake in translating these antique figures into modern dances, or rather into imitations of Greek dances; they have ignored, or been ignorant of the fact that the early artists were unable to suggest a figure in the act of leaping, and so contented themselves with a representation of the moment preceding or following the leap, when the knees were still bent. These imitators of the Greek dance have evolved what might be called the cult of the bent knee, not realizing that it is, expressionally, the pose of bodily instability or mental indecision, where the pose is at all prolonged. Later, when the artists became more sure of their technique, this symbol of the leap was discarded, and the actual moment in the air was represented.

When a movement presents no characteristic moment the tempo or step is not so easy to reconstruct. But, if two or more figures can be found which, to one versed in the dance, appear to represent "moments" of some step in the modern ballet, it can be demonstrated by photographing a living dancer at each movement, and in this manner much knowledge may be gained.

It must not be forgotten that the Greeks attached a wide significance to the word "dance." Every movement executed to music was considered a dance, the combats of the Pyrrhics, and the stately processions of the temple choruses. The Greek made his oracles speak in numbers; the orator timed his utterances to the flute; fortifications were built or torn down to the rhythm of the double flute. At last, the nation went mad on the subject. But the essence of rhythm permeated to the very center of Attic existence. Rhythm must manifest its presence in bodily movement whether the result was obtained easily or with difficulty. The perfection of rhythm they called "eurhythmy," a word the very sense of which is not understood to-day.

To correctly interpret the dances represented in Greek art, it is necessary to know who are the persons who dance. The high gods descended from Olympus to preside at the dances of their worshipers; they even took part in the dances, stately and dignified dances, often simplified to a cadenced walk, as gods should move. Victory dances; Eros dances; Hermes and Dionysos dance.

The Dionysian dances are those most often spoken of,—and most misunderstood. As the god of the vintage, he is the god who presides over joy and folly. Music accompanies him over the hills; he is nature personified. His companions are the Satyrs and Nymphs, Naiades and Menades, Pan and Silenus. In the early times these beings were, many of them, of repulsive aspect and their dances clumsy. But these characteristics were softened with the centuries, though, in the Hellenistic period, the Dionysian cult became so obscene that a description of the dances would be out of the question.

Frenzy was not confined to the Dionysian dances, but had its place in those of Orpheus. All steps and tempos were exaggerated out of all resemblance to their original form. Disorder was the only recognized order.

In Greece, as in our own time, amateurs danced for their own amusement and enjoyment of rhythmic motion. These dances were of widely differing types, from those of the Komastai (who went about in noisy bands, serenading sober and respectable citizens who were so foolish as to be caught by one of these rowdy groups) to the groups of young girls who dance as lightly as butterflies, and for the same reason, for joy in being alive.

The Greek dance is a singular mixture of steps of different character, from the Steps on the Toes, the Pirouette, which can be learned only by long study, and the more rudimentary movements; their dance differed from the modern ballet in that it was an unfettered expression. The unexpected was sure to happen. The Greek dancer speaks with his whole body; he is at once dancer and actor. Being less conventional than ours, the Greek dance was, at the same time, lacking in precision.

It has remained for the twentieth century A.D. to discover that the union of music, dance, and song, as practiced in the fifth century B.C. contained something too precious to be lost. Emmanuel devoted years of study to proving it, and the translator offers his work to English-speaking students with the firm conviction that the time has come for a general acceptance of these facts, and a full faith that the dance-drama is about to assume the same importance in modern life that it held in ancient Greece.

ABRIDGED ANALYSIS

THE SCULPTURED AND PAINTED FIGURES

SOURCES: 1. Historical sources of the Greek dance. — 2. The Painted and Sculptured Figures. — 3. The Rhythms. — 4. The Texts. — 5. Methods applied to the study of the dance. — 6. The figures treated in chronological order.

PAINTED VASES: 7. Vases in the Mycenæan style. — 8. Vases in the geometric style, called Vases of Dipylon. — 9. Vases in Oriental style,—made by the incised process. — 10. Vases with figures painted in black on a red clay ground. Sixth century. — 11-12. Vases with red figures on a black ground. (Fifth, fourth, and third centuries B. C.) — 13. Painted ceramics on a white ground (Lecythes), funeral vases.

HIGH AND LOW RELIEFS: 14. Archaic art. (Seventh and sixth centuries B. C.) — 15. Fifth century B. C. — 16. Fourth century B. C. Tanagra. — 17. The period known as the Hellenistic. (Third and second centuries B. C.) — 18. First century B. C. Art of Greece and Rome. Archaic art. Bas-reliefs of terracotta.

INTERPRETATION OF THE SCULPTURED AND PAINTED FIGURES: 19-20. The "restorations." — 21. Terra-cotta forgeries. — 22-23. Errors and conventions in painting and perspective. — 24. Absence of any line indicating terra-firma in the paintings on the vases. — 25-28. Head and legs in profile, body full-face. Necessary corrections. — 29. Conventions proper to bas-reliefs applied to the positions of persons walking. — 30. Unnatural movements. Exact movements. Persistence of certain kinds of movements throughout the entire series of paintings and bas-reliefs. — 30-31. Limitations of the study of dancing-movements by the Greeks.

THE TRADITIONAL GESTURES OF THE FIGURES ON THE PAINTINGS AND BAS-RELIEFS: 34. Confusion possible between certain traditional gestures, symbolic acting, and pure dance-movements.—35-36. Creation, repetition, variations on the theme, according to Greek art. — 37. Three classes of traditional gestures:

I. SYMBOLIC OR RITUALISTIC GESTURES: 38. Gestures of the divinities who dance.
39. Gesture of the chaste Venus. — 40. Gestures of worshipers. — 41. Gestures of mourners. — 42. Gesture of tying on the sandal. — 43. Gesture with the veil.

II. GESTURES OF THE CUSTOMARY KIND: 44. Gestures with the tunic. — 45. Masculine gestures of the arm with the cloak. — 46. Gesture of the hand on the hip. — 47. Gesture of the athlete pouring oil over his body. — 48. Gesture of the athlete rubbing with a strigil. — 49. Gesture of the athlete binding his forehead with a fillet.

III. GESTURES THAT ARE CONCRETE BECOMING DECORATIVE: 50. Gesture of the arm curved above the head. — 51. Gesture of the Venus Anadyomene. — 52. Gesture of Aquarius. — 53. The dancers make use of the traditional gestures and transform them to meet their needs.

THE MOVEMENTS IN GENERAL

Natural Movements: Walking and Running

54. Mechanical movements. — 55-56. Expressive movements or gestures. — 57. Dancing movements. — 58. Mimetic type of Greek dances. — 59. The wider significance of the Greek word which means singer and actor as well as dancer.

THE WALK: 60. Dances which appear to be modifications of the movements of running and walking. — 61-62. Mechanism of the walk. — 63. Opposition of the arm and leg in walking. Opposition in dancing. — 64. Representations of walking taken from the sculptured and painted figures. The walk on the soles of the feet. — 65. Varieties of the walk on the soles of the feet. — 66. Development of the correct form. — 67. Representation of the march from the Parthenon frieze. — 68. Persistence of the walk on the soles of the feet.

THE RUN: 69. Mechanism of the run. — 70. Instinctive opposition between the arm and leg while running. — 71. Many aspects of running at different moments. — 72. The run is a succession of leaps. — 73. The figures appear never to leap without first bending the knee sharply. — 74. Principles of the leap stated.

75. Representations of the run from the sculptured and painted figures. 76. Runner;—leg-movement. — 77. Runner kneeling. — 78. Runner, one leg raised in opposition to the other. — 79. Runner setting out. — 80. Showing runner at the moment when the whole body hangs suspended. — 81. Runner following the modern method. — 82. Conventional method, academic pose. — 83. Runner following the archaic method.

84. The dance—steps growing out of the transformations and alternations of the walk and the normal run.

TECHNIQUE OF THE DANCE

I. The Positions

(All sentences in italics relate to the modern dance; the others treat of the Greek dance.)

85-86. *Positions and movements.*—87. *Positions of the Legs; Positions of the Arms; Positions of the Body; Positions of the Head.*—88. *Importance of the Positions of the Legs.*

LEGS: 89-96. *The Feet in the fundamental Positions. The five Positions: I, II, III, IV, V.*—97. *Holding out one foot.*—98. *The five Positions give sufficient variety.*—99-101. *The principal positions: The Second and Fourth principal Posi-*

tions.—102-103. *Positions on the half-toe; Positions on the toe.*—104. *Feet turning outward.*—105-111. *Examples of the different Positions.*

ARMS: 112. *Varieties of the Pose of the Arms. Positions of the Arms.*—113. *Extending the arm and hand.*—144. *Symmetrical Positions of the two Arms.*—115. *Contrasting Positions of the two Arms.*—116. *Arms employed; arms free.*—117. In the Greek dance the Positions of the Arms are not symmetrically arranged, as in ours.—118. Arms often rigid, or bent at abrupt angles.—119. Hand always active.—120-131. Symmetrical Positions of the Arms.—132-143. Contrasting Positions of the two Arms.

HANDS: 144. The palm.—145. Hand active.—146. Hand flat.—147. Index finger separated from the other digits.—148. Hand raised in front of the eyes.—149. Exceptional positions of the hand and fingers in "character" and grotesque dances.

BODY: 150. *Positions of the Body.*—151-156. *Positions of the Body.*—157. Positions used by only the Bacchic dancers.

HEAD: 158. *Positions of the Head.*—159-163. Positions of the Head.—164. Groups of three dancers, illustrating classic positions.

165. Positions of the Legs, the Body, and the Head, used more by the Greek dancers than by us.

166. *Combinations of positions between them. Their theoretical number.*—167. *Oppositions of the dance.*—168-170. *Remarkable combinations; the Arabesque Attitude.*—171. Opposition; the Tanagran Eros.—172. Absence of intentional Opposition; drunken dancers.—173. Opposition in dancing affecting drawing and sculptural design.—174. *The Attitude.*

II. Preparatory Exercises

175. *Connection between the positions and the movements.*—176. *Statics and changes of the dance; preparatory exercises.*

LEGS: 177. *Bending and holding.*—178. *Bending.*—179. *Separating.*—180. *Toe down.*—181. *Separating.*—182. *Toe down.*—183. *Battement.*—184. *Battement the ground.*—185. *Battement held.*—186. *Great Battement.*—187. *Transmission of movement from the leg which rises and lowers.*—188. *Different forms of the Great Battement.*—189-190. *Restoration of the Great Battement.*—191. *Circles with the legs.*—192. *Circles with the legs on the ground.*—193. *Circles of the legs held.*—194. *Grand circle of the leg.*—195. *Circles with the legs.*—196. *First exercises.*

ARMS: 197. *Movements of the arms; transmission of the movement from the arm which is raised and lowered, which opens and closes.*—198. *Realistic representations of the arms in curves. Movements of the arms of our dancers largely decorative.*—199. Movements of the arms. In the dance the arms and the hands interpret by their gestures, and they have a dramatic value.

BODY AND HEAD: 200. *Movements of the Body and Head.*—201. Movements of the Body and Head.

202. *Combinations of movements in Opposition.*—203. Combinations **of movements**. Eurhythmy.—204. Arrhythmic dances.

III. Tempos and Steps

GENERALITIES: 205. *Directions according to which the dancer places himself.*—206. *The Step determines the Tempo.*—207. *Tempo signifies Movement.*—208. *Time the feet remain on the ground, Time they remain in the air, Time of their return.*—210. Gradation of the exercises.

POSTURES OF THE FEET: 211. *The step and the posture of the feet, and length of the step in the dance.*—212. *The three forms of posture for the feet.*—213. Shoes without heels.—214. *The three forms of posture for the feet.*—215. Position of the feet on the half-toe.—216. Position of the feet on the toe.—217. Flexible sole.

DESCRIPTION OF SOME TEMPOS AND STEPS: 218. *The Slide.*—219. *The Chassé.*—220. *The Coupé.*—221. *The Fouetté.*—222-223. *Jeté.*—224. *Observations relating to the preceding movements.*—225. Representation of such movements as the Chassé and the Coupé impossible in one figure.—226. The Slide.—The Slide made on both feet at the same time.—227-228. Fouetté.—229-230. Jeté.

231. *Tempos increasing Ballonnes.*—232. Tempo Ballonnes.—233. *Balance steps.*—234-235. Balance steps.

236. *Tempos and Steps on the toe.*—237. *Leaving the Fifth for the Second, on the toes.*—238. *Rising on the toes.*—239. *Steps on the toe.*—240. Tempos on the toe.—241. Small steps on the toes.—242. Running-steps on the toes.

243-244. *The Assemblé.*—245-246. *Mutation of the feet.*—247. *Beating-step (Battus).*—248-249. *The Cut (Entrechat).*—250. *Three cuts.*—251. *Four cuts.*

252. *Isochronism of the movements which are similar, consecutive.*—253. *Steps of the Entrechat.*—254. The Assemblé and the Mutation of the Feet.—255. Beating-steps. Entrechat.

256. *Turning movements on the ground and in the air.*—257. *Whirling steps.*—258. Pirouette.—259. *Pirouette outward and Pirouette inward.*—260. *Preparation for the Pirouette.*—261. *Execution of the Pirouette.*—262. *Pirouette on the instep.*—263. *Varieties of the Pirouette.*—264. *Turning in the air.*—265. Turning movements.—266. Turning by stamping.—267. Turning by stamping in Fourth crossed.—268. How to determine the direction of the rotation of the figures represented in the paintings and reliefs.—269. Pirouette.—270. Pirouette outward and Pirouette inward.—271. Pirouette on the instep.

RECONSTRUCTION OF THE TEMPOS AND THE STEPS

from the Antique Figures

COORDINATION OF THE MOVEMENTS: 272. Superposition of movements.—273. Succession of movements.—274. Repeated movements.—275. Alternated movements.—276. Enchainments alternated.—277. Movement oppositions,—

278. Opposition of movement of the arms and legs—279. Opposition of movements of the body and head.—280. Relation between opposing movements.—281. Résumé.

IDENTIFICATION OF THE MOVEMENTS BY MEANS OF THE SCULPTURES AND PAINTINGS: 282. The moments of the movements.—283. Characteristic moments.—284. Essential moments.—285-286. Number of figures necessary to determine the movements of the dance.

RECONSTRUCTION OF THE TEMPO: 287. One image may furnish a representation of a characteristic moment.—288. Images showing two characteristic moments.—289. Figures in Series.—290. Cat-leap.—291. Statues and paintings showing the two supreme moments.—292. Incomplete series: interpolations.—293. Series of statues and paintings which are widely separated.—294. Résumé.

RECONSTRUCTION OF THE STEP: 295. Composition of the Steps.—296. Steps which had fallen into disrepute before this time.—297-298. Examples of restorations. Vertical axis line of equilibrium.—299. Steps made by leaping directly upward and alighting in the same place.—300. Knees flexed from Antique vases.—301-302. Leg raised.—303-304. Springing in place, leg raised.—305. Bacchic steps a special form.—306. Sidewise wheeling.—307. "Little Russian" dances.—308. Dances with body bent backward.—309. Backward bending maintained.—310. Intermittent bending.—311. Body alternately bending backward and forward.—312. The backward bend made as a part of the step.—313. Objective point of movement.—314. Body bent forward all through the steps.—315. Dancers who crouch or kneel.—316. Dances with the mantle.—317. The veil dancers of Pompeii.—318. Managing the veil.—319-323. Dances with the joined hands. Different forms.

STUDIES OF THE DANCER

324. *The dance properly so-called.*—325. *The Bar.*—326. *Gradation of exercises.*—327. *The ballet-masters.*—328. Dancing lessons.—329. Gymnastics of the dance.—330. List of exercises.—331. Choregraphy. The master of the dance.—332. Traces of the Greek choregraphy which have been preserved.

THE CHOREGRAPHY

The mimic funeral.—The rhythmic games

STEPS FOR TWO: 333. Decorative contrasts.—334. Two men.—335. The dance of the Wine Press.—336. Two women.—337. Man and woman.—338. Man and woman with arms about each other's necks or holding each other by the hand. 339. Repugnance of the Greeks against dancing of couples interlaced.

STEPS FOR THREE: 340. Three women.—341. One man and two women.—342. One woman between two men.

THREE DANCERS AND A LEADER: 343. Traditional groups.—344. The god who leads precedes three women, without holding their hands.—345. The god who leads holds the hand of one of the women.—346. Three women without a leader.—347. Dances held in groups.

CHORUS OF THE DANCE: 348. Absence of perspective from the representations of choral dances, consequences.—349-352. Choral choruses in which the dancers hold one another by the hand.—353. The ring.—354. The choruses in which the dancers in file do not hold hands.—355. Dancers in ranks, facing front. —356. The chorus of the theatre.—357. The "Tratta."—358. Dances in armor.— 359. Pyrrhic for one.—360. Pyrrhic for two.—361-362. Pyrrhic en masse.

MOURNING DANCES: 363. Attic funeral rites.—364. The mourners of Dipylon. Primitive gestures of sorrow.—365-370. Evolution and persistence of the gestures of mourning.—371. Funerals of modern Greece.

THE PLAY RHYTHMS: 372-373. Application of rhythm to play.—374. The Kubistétères.—375. The dances on vases Cottabe.—376. The rope-dancers of Pompeii.—377. The games of exaggerations.—378-380. Play rhythms.

THE DANCERS

THE GODS WHO DANCE: 381-382. The greater and the lesser gods.—383. Victory a dancer.—384. Eros the dancer.—385. Atys dancer.—386. The Curetes (Clashers) as dancers.—387. Pyrrhic and dances of the Curetes.—388. Dionysos and the Dionysian dances.—389. The Silenes and the Satyrs.—390. Pan.—391. The Menades.—392. The Bacchants.—393-394. Accessories of the Bacchants.—395. Bacchanalian feasts and their ritual of disorder.—396. Groupings of the dances of the Bacchanales.—397. Mimetic dances and mimetic scenes.—398. Presence at the Bacchanal of persons who were strangers to the Dionysian period.—399. Dionysian dances of the Hellenistic period.

DANCES IN HONOR OF THE GODS: 400. The fantastical ritual; the orgies.—401. Dances in honor of Rhea.—402. Orphic dances.—403. Phallic dances. —404. Altar of sacrifice in the center of the circle of dancing Bacchants.— 405. Character of the movements in the orgiastic dances.—406. Religious dances not orgiastic.—407. Hierodules wearing the kalathos; their dance.—408. Religious processions.—409. Procession to the temple of the Harpies, from the Parthenon frieze.—410. The Parthenon frieze.—411. Religious processions on the painted vases.—412. Conventional decoration from the representations of the processions and the *rule of the same step.*

PRIVATE OR SOCIAL DANCES: 413-414. Professional dancers and dances by free citizens.—415. The Komos dances.—416. Amateurs who were clever in the art of dancing.

CONCLUSION

417. Results acquired.—418. Technique and Esthetics.—419. Esthetics of the dance.—420. Eurhythmy.—421. Arrhythmy.—422. The conventions.—423. The imitation of the Greek dances.—424-425. Greek Tempo and Step.

THE SCULPTURED AND PAINTED FIGURES

SOURCES

1. In the study of the antique Greek dance, information comes from three sources, as follows:

The *Figures* (painted vases, bas-reliefs, etc.).

The *Rhythms* of the poets—lyrics, tragedies, comedies, ballads, etc.; therefore, the works appertaining to this period in which the three musical arts—poetry, music, and dancing—are closely related, furnish the foundation of the rhythms of the dance.

The *Writings* of different authors which treat of questions relating to the dance, and which, with the exception of a few scattered pamphlets, are all that remain in Greek literature on this subject.

2. It is, perhaps, unnecessary to call attention to the relative importance of the <u>sculptured figures</u>, which, indubitably, belong at the head of the list. If this much can be established, our study of the steps has no other object; for notwithstanding the aberrations of the fancy of artists who were inexperienced, the movements of the dance, as depicted on the vases and reliefs are often good and accurate renditions of the scenes of the dance, and may be considered the most valuable documents upon which we may draw for consultation.

3. The poetic *rhythm* itself bears out the idea gained from the study of the figures on the painted vases and reliefs. With the poetic accompaniment of song and dance, the rhythm becomes the bond which unites the three arts. With the ancients this union is so complete that, if we arrive at an understanding of their poetry, we shall, at the same time, discover the secret of their music-rhythm and their dance-rhythm. This result has been difficult to obtain. Until lately we could not differentiate with precision between the formal rhythms and the more simple ones. The versification, correctly enunciated, enables us to analyse the metres, the successions in tempo, the heavy and the light, the law of their alternation, and their relative duration, when the movement of the verse is uniform, repeating in long passages the systems of strope-construction of the model agreed upon, as the alcaic strope, the Saphic strope, etc. Unhappily, the true poetry of the dance has a movement much more free from restraint of the set metrical type than the poetry of the choruses of Æschylus, Pindar, or Aristophanes, so that we cannot make an exact analysis of it.

But, from the one it is possible to surmise the other, its order and its structure, with fewer and fewer deflections from the regular metres, resulting in confusion. But, considering the part played by conjecture, it is impossible to discover from the restorations the elements necessary to make a plausible comparison with the figures on the monuments. It is admitted that, elsewhere, the rhythm takes on a form quite different from this. The metres follow more closely the grammatical, and to some extent, the pedagogical laws. They do not take into account the particular exigencies of music and the dance.

It is not, therefore, out of place to deduce from their methods certain modifications which apply equally to the set forms of the three musical arts.

Despite the lacunæ which are difficult to fill up, the Greek rhythm of the poetry of revel is a direct source of information, and, from it the historian of the dance can gain a great deal.

4. The *texts* of the authors do, in a great measure, establish the indications furnished by the painted and 'sculptured figures and by the *rhythms*. Not that the agreement is always easy to find, but only that it is possible of accomplishment. In default of a methodical treatise, which appears to never have been written, it is permitted one to learn for oneself the Greek idea of dancing and the domain of that art. It is for us to point out that which is singularly great and beautiful in it, and it is for us to teach, however badly, the processes of the gymnastics of the dance; it is for us to learn that it is a divine art, and that it plays no small rôle in the education of man. It is, likewise, made possible for us to make a long list of the dances which were practiced in ancient Greece, during different periods, and this will be somewhat to our advantage. Of these dances we know little except their names and some similar data, under which they will be broadly catalogued.

The compilation made by J. Meursius in 1618, is a laborious enumeration, made in alphabetical order, of all the expressions used by a philologist of Holland relating to the dance. It would be useless to search in this work or that of Krause (*Gymnastics and Agonistics of Hellas*) for the elements of a restoration of the antique Greek dance, or any approach to it. The pamphlets of Buchholtz, of Kirchhoff, and of Flach are not more explicit. To place much reliance on their writings is to plunge oneself into uncertainty and confusion. The *Dialogue of the Dance* of Lucien is a caprice, replete with gaiety, and describes the Roman pantomimes with the freshness of an eye-witness. The discourse of Libanius, *Concerning Dances*, is of the earliest period, the fourth century B. C. The compilers and lexicographers, Athenatus, Pollux, Proclus, Hephestion, Hezechius, Suidas, etc., all of whom wrote after the classic period, wrote with so little understanding of the subject that their works are full of contradictions. They are nothing short of a plague with their primitive philology. To seek among them for the key to the Greek dance is to forever block one's path to discovery. They are ignorant of even the language; they give the most diverse meanings to the same words, choosing as seems good to them. Is it too much to expect Plato, Xenophon, or Aristotle to volunteer some dissertation on the dignity of the dance and its gracious beauty, when they were in a position to know so much about it? Better to hunt in the comedies or in the tragedies, where the characters themselves dance, and, now and then, make some comment regarding dancing. All of the information furnished by the texts has value, and is interesting. Upon surveying the whole situation, it is plainly to be seen that, in order to get any real knowledge of the philosophy of the dance, the figures on the monuments must be recognized as their own best commentary.

5. The method which I shall suggest for the study of the antique Greek dance is quite different from any that has been used. It is from the dances depicted upon the vases that we shall ask our first dancing-lessons. From the images we shall learn the reasons why the Greek dance occupied certain spaces; then we shall use the *rhythms* to discover why they used certain tempos; the *texts*

shall tell us *why* they danced and what ethical value they placed on the dance. Many mistakes have been made by an effort of synthesis, and a seeking to reconcile, evidence so abundant and orders so diverse, carrying the movements, the rhythms, and the esthetics of the art all together to a harmonious ensemble. In order to obtain this result, it will be well to separate the difficulties into groups. Suppose that, in the beginning, we ignore, for the moment, all sources of information except the figures.

What are these paintings and sculptures, and how are we to interpret them? What is the value of the information they give? How far do they themselves agree?

6. The figures used in this study cover a long period of time. From the vases of Dipylon to the art objects of the Gallo-Roman period, many of which were copied from Hellenistic work, there pass more than twelve centuries. The changes in technique, and, much more, the subjects represented, make it possible to assign with some exactness the date of the vases and reliefs. From them we have taken a small number, of the chronological sequence of which it is possible to speak definitely; all of the others belong to a series, the duration of which is uncertain. The archæologists, through systematic interpretation, have, in the past few years, established the chronology of a number, but, through the new discoveries being made all the time, they are often obliged to modify their statements. However, the combined results show enough in common so that they may be considered a useful frame for the picture.

PAINTED VASES

XV to X B. C.
7. **Vases in the Mycenæn Style.**—These vases, which M. Perrot has done more than any one else to classify, he calls "Vases in the Ægean Style,"—because they have been found throughout the whole basin of the Ægean Sea. They are decorated with figures of animals and plants, but show no human figures. They will not, therefore, receive much attention in this book. It was the flora and fauna that inspired these artists, and

they drew the seaweed and molluscs with remarkable ability. To their brushes we owe much that is lovely in line and curve. M. Pottier has thrown much light upon our understanding of curvilineal decoration of vases belonging to this category.

8. **Vases in the Geometric Style, Called the Vases of Dipylon.**—Like the vases called Mycenæan, these are of Greek origin, but they are fundamentally different from them. A product of evolution, their origin is most obscure, and their decoration wholly different from any others. The straight line is substituted for the curved one, and the ornamentation is geometrical; the plants and animals present a rigid appearance, and the drawing is primitive. The human figure, it would seem, has escaped the odd geometricalization of form; these personages are detached as opaque silhouettes from the clear ground-work of the vase, a sort of hieroglyph of sharp angles and grotesque heads. (Figs. 515, 516, 541, 542.) 〔XI to VII B. C.〕

The representations of the dancing movements exist in great numbers. In order to write of the dance in its earlier manner, and preserve accuracy, it is necessary to note carefully the work of these ceramists. The funeral scenes are the evolution of the great vases of Dipylon, apparently, by a direct representation of the personages and the ritualistic dance that accompanied the burial of the dead, the same ranks of armed warriors, who advance with the same steps. There are three kinds of dances represented, *funeral dances, dances by warriors,* and *dances by the populace;* these constitute almost the whole repertoire of the ceramists of Dipylon, which deal with the human figure.

9. **Vases in the Oriental Style.**—Regarding the discoveries on the Islands of the Archipelago, of Ionia, and of Greece proper, the principal centers of manufacture were Rhodes, Milo and Corinth. The Oriental 〔VII B. C.〕

influence is evident in the choice of motifs of ornamentation. The human figures are framed in plants, interspersed with animals, borrowed, no doubt, from the textiles made in Oriental countries. A coat of white, spread on the surface of the vase forms the foundation upon which were superposed the ornaments, which were often arranged in parallel rows.

From the middle of the seventh century B. C., a new process is to be noted in the decoration; this is *incision*. It consists in cutting the contours of the figures with a sharp-pointed instrument; the point cuts through the painted surface, and the clay foundation is revealed. The relation of this kind of technique to metallurgy is evident. The presence of this incised decoration on the vases is of great importance in establishing the chronology of ceramics, as this style of work is not found prior to the date given.

The list of colors, which is very conventional, is reduced to red, black and white. These colors, combined, give to the work an atmosphere of lightness and gaiety.

The movements of the dance represented show also figures more flexible, less rigid. The walk on the ball of the foot (102), the running bend (77), the leap, are marked by a flexion of the knees, becoming less formal (300). The burlesque dances of Komos (415) were greatly favored as subjects by the ceramic painters of the seventh century B. C. The ranks of warriors in armour, of the preceding series, which are not wholly unlike them, are often engaged in singular combats; two heroes in helmets, facing each other, occasionally take part in the simple Pyrrhic dance (358), threatening with their lances. Always, these gentlemen were quite enough for the simpletons who confronted them. Although their individuality is strongly marked, the type is already changing from the geometric style.

10. **Vases with Figures Painted in Black on a Red Clay Ground.**—The workmanship and the style show the Attic traits predominant; the decorations of plants and animals disappear. The strict manner and the too great exclusiveness of the painters of vases eliminates the quality of picturesqueness; they are not as interesting when the animals and flowers are sacrificed to make way for the human figures alone. The personages are detached from the ground, and the decoration does not so completely cover the foundation. The white covering is abandoned; the clay paste, colored red with oxide of iron, shows a foundation tawny and smooth; the figures, painted in black, come out sharply. The process of incision (9) is the same in all cases. The painters touched up the parts intended to represent the flesh of women with white, while men were represented entirely with black, (Figs. 504-505.) In the same manner the Egyptian artists differentiated the colors for the sexes.

VI B. C.

The technical fineness and the excellence of the design, while showing something of the stiffer archaic, becomes more liberal; the artists do not step aside from forms which are simple and therefore suited to the subject. Indeed, they laid more and more stress upon simplicity.

The funeral dances, the military dances, and the dances of Komos continue to enjoy great favor, but new dances appear upon the scene; processions of the gods, preceded by players upon the lyre and players upon the flute to whose rhythms step the Immortal Ones; Satyrs and Menades of the circle of Dionysos dance in honor of their superior, who, now and then, appears among them; choruses from the theatre, in ranks and in files, etc. There may be mentioned also the *Amphores Panathenaiques,* showing the prize-winning conquerors in the gymnastic games, the palestrian scenes, leaping, running, throwing the discus, throwing the javelin, etc., which, together with the characteristic dances already spoken of, held some traits in common. (372.)

V B. C.

11. **Vases with Red Figures on a Black Ground.**—From about 410 B. C. the technique of the painters is entirely changed; they use a method directly opposite to that of the sixth century B. C. It is the figure which is kept in the red clay with the background painted black. The incision remains the same. On the bodies of the figures the details were worked out with black paint, lightly sketched in with a brush. The design becomes free, the archaic rigidity giving way to a perfection of elegance. (See Plate I, Figs. 481–552.) The designs remain simple. All of the representations of dancers are marked by an upward tendency on the vases of the fifth century B. C. The mimic funeral takes on a greater importance from the wonderful funeral vases called *loutrophores*, and on the *lecythes*, on a white ground, which were ritualistic objects in the cult of the dead.

The *character dances* were not rare, if one may judge from the ceramic paintings of the fifth century B. C.

IV and III B. C.

12. **Series of Vases with Red Figures.**—These vases establish the evidence that many technical peculiarities persisted until the end of the third century B. C., a period which apparently ends the making of painted vases in Greece. But it is quite possible to distinguish, from their style, the work of the ceramists of the third and fourth centuries B. C.

Fourth Century B. C.—The skill of the painters is minutely perfect. The movements become really interpretive coupled with scientific correctness. They float and are fashioned amply. At the same time, the scenes represented are complicated; the persons are disposed in many differing designs. The brush of the artist acquires a surprising virtuosity; the dancers revolve:

the dancers whirl and fling their veils in the air. The more fantastic dances are the ones they prefer.

It is needless to remark that it is not enough to consider the foregoing works in order to arrive at a knowledge of the Greek traditions.

Third Century B. C.—The designs become heavy, the style debased. The retouching with white increases. Confusion results from the great number of figures introduced into the scenes. The floral decoration overflows until but little of the groundwork shows. The whole effect is at once rich and clumsy.

Among the scenes, the Bacchanalian predominate. There is a veritable inundation of Satyrs and Menades, whose dances exhibit the more movement as they become less eurhythmic; they move to the music of tambourine and castanets. Often, Eros Hermaphrodite whirls in their midst, marking by his presence the union of the cycles of Dionysos and those of Aphrodite.

13. Notwithstanding the greater simplicity, they did not neglect the important details, as is seen in the *paintings on a white ground* on the vases of the seventh century B. C. (9), and which form the point of departure. The sixth century B. C. and the ones following do not give up the same technique; they develop a parallel series, and one must be very careful not to confuse the two.

The *lecythes*, funeral vases, of the fifth and fourth centuries B.C. are by far the most beautiful of the Attic wares. The figures are painted in profile, of simple design, and transparent, and the work shows a lightness and sureness of touch which is marvelous.

HIGH AND LOW RELIEFS—TERRA-COTTA FIGURINES

14. **Archaic Art.**—The sculpture of Greece developed more slowly than the art of painting, which advances with comparative rapidity. In the seventh century B. C. the plastic arts give more information

VII and VI B. C.

on the subject under consideration than do the ceramic paintings; and there is no doubt that the frescoes, their models, lost to us, were their masterpieces. The characteristic common to the early period of Greek is the rigidity, often the awkwardness, of the movements of the figures. Of the antique wooden statues, rigid idols, there are great numbers remaining. These were succeeded by the gods of marble, which present an appearance of greater suppleness. Only in the sixth century B. C. did the sculptors begin to detach the arms from the body and show a space between the legs to indicate that the figure was walking. At the commencement of the fifth century B. C. the technique is already studied, and takes on the character of the work of the first years of the succeeding century. Though the name *Archaic* has fastened itself to these statues, they are as truly masterpieces as the works of the period following.

Of the sculptured figures of which this study will have occasion to speak are the following types:

The statues of men who step on the left foot.
The metopes of Selinonte.
The small bronzes of Dodone.
The colored statues of women from the Acropolis.
The temple of the Harpies.
The bas-reliefs of Thasos.
The Ægean pediments.

The movements of the figures are generally simple, but the themes are many; there are different types of the walk and the run; poses and gestures that are conventional (gestures with the veil and gestures with the tunic, for example), which become the true formulas which persist throughout all Greek art (43, 44); files of persons, scenes of combat, etc., these are the principal motifs of archaic art. The dance is not directly related to these movements, but its forms are affected by them.

At the end of the sixth century B. C. and at the beginning of the fifth, there appear *plaques of terra-cotta* which are true reliefs and are not to be confounded with the painted ones of the same period. The scenes are the mimic funeral, the dances executed by the courtesans, who shake the castanets, and which bear witness to the advance made by the artists who work in clay; this advance was due to the ease with which the medium could be handled. But the *figurines of terra-cotta* remain always the coarser.

15. Kalamis, Myron, Polycletus, Pæonios, and Phidias.—The fifth century B. C., when art reached its highest point, was a time of deep religious sentiment.

V . B. C.

The principal works were:

The pediments, metopes, and friezes of the Parthenon.

The pediments, metopes, of Olympia.

The Phigalian frieze.

The Nike of Pæonios.

The frieze of Victory at Athens.

The dancers of Herculaneum.

The technique had by that time attained perfection, and the movements became more daring; they always preserve a certain nobility of which it would be difficult to speak too strongly. The corteges slowly file past, the plastic dances executed by beautiful young women—but these are not the only dance-movements interpreted by the sculptors of the fifth century B. C. Sometimes the dancers whirl about, flinging their tunics into the air, so that they take on the gracious curves of a *swallow in flight*. (268.) Pæonios makes his Victory dart into the air with a freedom that has never been surpassed.

The terra-cotta figurines of the fifth century B. C. reflect the severe style of the great statues.

16. Scopas, Praxiteles, and Lysippus.—Art becomes more sensuous, more realistic. Grace has been substi-

IV B. C,

tuted for the noble severity of the preceding century. The style is modified, though there is no question, as yet, of decadence. In Greece art changed with the years, ceaselessly transforming itself.

Principal works:
Frieze and statues of the tomb of Halicarnassus.
The Menade of Scopas.
The Aphrodite of Praxiteles.
The Apoxyomene of Lysippus.
The Venus of Milo.
The Victory of Samothrace.
The choraic monument of Lysicratus.

The disorderly movements of the Bacchic dances are absent from the work of the masters of the fourth century B. C., and are held in less and less esteem by the sculptors and bronze-workers.

The series of Tanagra figurines of terra-cotta of the fourth century occupy a conspicuous place in the history of plastic art. Beyond a doubt the dancing figures of Tanagra reflect the influence of the great sculptors of the same period, it is also evident that they are original creations. They are objects with which the public is so familiar that it is unnecessary to speak at length regarding them,—the daintiness of their treatment is proof enough that they were not copies of more pretentious works. Also, the little figures of baked clay show that their makers took advantage of the ductility of the material to escape the limits otherwise imposed upon sculptors. It is to be noted that the sculptures of the third century B. C., while fanciful, never go too far, but that their modelers aimed to arrest one perfect moment, to fix and hold the charm of its spirit. These moments are existent in a thousand and one scenes,—young girls playing ball, coquettes who turn backward as though looking at some one, veiled women who lightly fling their tunics in the air. Nothing could be more elegant or more chaste than these refined dancers, whose movements have no sensual qualities. They are just young women who dance because they are gay at heart.

17. **Hellenistic Period.**—In the fourth century B. C. the movement is sober and restrained; in the third it is slightly exaggerated, and virtuosity is the latest art term. The school of Athens strives to preserve the classic forms, but the Asiatic schools, Rhodes, Pergamus, are suspected of too novel tendencies. The art of Alexandria, though more eclectic, is less violent; Alexandria is a city of learning. The picturesque bas-reliefs, the decorative pictures, possess an elaboration of detail, pushed to the extreme, which is the keynote of the art of Alexandria.   *III and II B. C.*

The principal works:
The frieze of Pergamus.
Laocoön.
The Farnese Bull.

The greatest pieces of sculpture now in existence include but few examples of dance-movements, but the complex rhythm of gesture suggests, in a manner, the gymnastic of the dancers.

On the other hand, in the terra-cotta figurines made in Myrina, Smyrna, Tarsus, Ephesus, Milos, Alexandria, and Cyrene, dance subjects abound. Nike dances, Satyrs, Bacchants, Eros-bacchants; dancers turning and twisting their veils; figures swaying, etc. It is a sensual dance, in a period given over to the cult of Aphrodite and Dionysos, which takes the place of the cult of the higher gods of the fifth century B. C.

18. In the first century B. C. there is a reaction, a return to the classic tradition of the Athenian school. There appears a genius named Praxiteles, whose work has all the nobleness of the earlier Greek work. But he and his followers are not content to be inspired by the spirit of the ancients, they would themselves originate a form of art. So much do they admire the   *I B. C.*

antique that they elaborately copy the stiffness and archaic quaintness; but theirs is only a pretense. It is not always easy to distinguish between the old and the new.

There is, however, one peculiarity by which, in many cases, the archaic work can be known. The persons all walk on the half-toe in the copies. This pose is seldom seen in the more ancient art.

The terra-cotta figurines disappear with the second century B. C., but the industry of the modelers reappears in another form in the first century B. C. The bas-reliefs made in Italy, and quite often in the "archaisant" style, furnish some beautiful examples of dancers; Satyrs and Menades go wild with Bacchic frenzy, the *clashers* dance in armour, vine-growers tread out the grapes to cadences.

INTERPRETATION OF THE FIGURES

19. The Restorations.—Of all the Greek art relics, only a few of these fragile vases and terra-cottas remain, most of these more or less defaced by time and the hand of man, and they are to be highly prized. From them it is possible to reconstruct the Greek funeral, even as they themselves have been buried in the earth. They are historical documents as well as objects of art which call on us to admire them. The methodical excavations already fruitful, give us reason to believe that many questions will be answered as they proceed; it may be that the Greek funeral ceremonies will be revealed in full.

The statues have suffered, though they were solid and resistant; exposed to the air, they rapidly disintegrate, because of atmospheric conditions. In the confined air of the temples they have more often been broken by being thrown down from their places. But the worst outrages are due to an ignorant population, which had destroyed the things it could not appreciate, and was incapable of making; the worst mutilations of the antiques have been the intentional work of man. To-day, the fragments exhumed, are, some of them, proved to be forgeries. It is an absolute rule among archæologists that a forgery *must* be detected, and every new acquisition is vouched for as far as the honesty of the savant can determine it. Formerly, the "broken pots" did not appeal to the amateurs of antiques any more than the statues without heads or the heads minus noses.

Demand, then, that the galleries of sculpture in the Louvre give up their secrets of the antique Greek dance. Discover for yourself, not at some far-off place, the glorious goddess who, alas! has lost both her arms,—the two laughing Satyrs who express joy in every line. They dance, their feet are clad in strange shoes, their heads are posed forward, and they look on the ground, as dancers often do, one of them plays upon cymbals. Behold these two precious moments of the Greek dance: movements of the legs, of the head, the arms, the torso, all to the accompaniment of instruments. The presence of the *kroupezia*, enormous sandals of wood and barbed with iron, is clearly revealed by the pose of the dancers; these odd shoes were used to mark the divisions of the step and interest the ear as well as the eye of the spectator.

It will be well to make a list of these works. The dancing Satyrs have already been mentioned.

A beautiful marble statue of Parian marble.

Head badly posed, the chin, the lips, the nose, and part of the front of the neck, the left arm, both legs and trunk are modern, but the right arm is antique.

Of the other Satyr, Parian marble, it is said:

Head, antique, approaching and yet seeming to retreat, a strange and bewildering attitude to find in a statue. The modern parts are the right forearm, the hands, the right foot, the left foot and part of the leg.

You will learn little from the Satyrs, and that little will be from the torsos.

20. In this manner were the "restorations" of the museums carried into effect! In this condition is "antique art" offered to the public for its admiration! Since that time they have renounced the falsifications which the Renaissance declared proper and necessary. While it is a matter for regret that those who destroyed the

statues were inspired by a sort of sacrilegious courage, is it not, even more, a matter for sorrow that these antique fragments have served as the pretext for so many fantastic "restorations" on the part of modern sculptors? A parallel effect has made our national museum a vast necropolis.

Here are a few facts regarding the manner of making these restorations. They mould plaster casts of the antique fragments, add whatever new parts they see fit, just as long as they can get a rib of one great statue or a foot of another, or even a piece of drapery, using this as a motif to indicate what they imagine the rest to have been!

Dr. Treu, conservator of the Museum of Sculpture in Dresden, has not hesitated to undertake a work so delicate, but his results have been much better. He has the statues reconstructed by pure hypothesis, but is careful to leave the fragments of ancient work loose, so that they can be removed, thus leaving the relic in exactly the state it was before the restoration was made.

But in other museums the works are denatured by the additions. The curators have awakened to this deplorable state of affairs, but, up to this time, they have seen no way to better them.

21. The closest attention is necessary when reading an essay on antiques or studying them at first hand. That which is at hand is all too likely to be accepted. The industry of making forgeries has been going on for years, and the first task of an archæologist is to watch carefully for "discoveries" made by the merchants of terra-cotta figurines. It is quite easy to fabricate a vase or figurine, but the specialist in antiques must watch for differences in the color of the patina, the glaze, etc. Terra-cotta figures can be made very nearly perfect, and it is not always possible to convict the fraud.

Some of the vases of the Campana collection have been retouched, and it is difficult to remedy these mistakes without danger of spoiling the whole painting. Respecting some of the other terra-cottas shown in the galleries, they challenge examination, each and every one showing that it is, beyond a doubt, authentic and original. These things have been catalogued in such a way that no attention has been paid to periods.

The era of "restorations" is over, but it lasted long enough, and it was fruitful enough.

22. Errors and Conventions of Design.—It is not sufficient to be assured of the authenticity of the sculptures, there was faulty work in the past, and it is of value as indicating the fancy of the decorators, and it furnishes exact pictures of the *Positions* and the *Movements*,—in truth, they speak more loudly than words.

In ancient Greece, all the world danced, although all the world were not dancers. The technique of the dance was very simple, otherwise it would not have been acquired by any except the initiates. To understand and translate the dancing movements it is not enough to note the management of pencil and clay, as that would still leave the student wanting in practical knowledge. The conditions imposed upon the ceramists made it impossible for them to reproduce certain points with exactness. Often, therefore, they mixed their own fancies with the facts before them, partly to cover their ignorance of perspective. Also, the object was to make a decorative design, not an exact copy of the scene before their eyes. Still, there were traditions which were, for canonical reasons, always respected. The artists disliked absolute symmetry, and, in all ages, they sacrificed equilibrium to decorative design.

The more they respect the traditions of the dance the less likely they are to give an exact copy of what they see.

23. They are equally at fault in certain conventions of perspective, which often leads the modern spectator astray regarding the movement depicted. These conventions may be put down to the inexperience of the artists.

24. On the greater number of the vases the floor, or ground, upon which the figures stand, is not indicated; the figures approach one another as though they were all on the same plane, though their positions show that they are not. Thus it comes that the painters disposed the figures as though they were on two floors, one above the other; the result is that some appear to be leaping higher than human beings possibly could leap, but are still poised on the soles of their feet.

25. The paintings never show the human face in full-face view, but always in profile. The legs are also in profile, one behind the other, as in the Egyptian statues and pictures. Often the body is presented in full-face, as is also the Egyptian custom. Fig. 111 exhibits these characteristics. The direction of the run is clearly indicated.

To correctly interpret the relative position of each part of the body, consider that the torso, the arms and the head belong to a person who is running in the direction of the observer, with the torso, arms, and head all carried as one toward the left, having made a quarter-circle. A proposed image, substituted as an ideal representation, would be as follows:

Torso seen from the right side, in profile.

Arms extended, palms to the right, and fore-shortened.

Head full-face, seen from above, and fore-shortened.

Legs at rest.

26. Not to generalize too much as to the preceding figure, or to carry too far the kind of correction of which it is an example, let it be said that it is no result of total ignorance of drawing that made this artist pose it just as it stands. It is the result of careful observation. On a very celebrated antique vase with black figures, known as the François vase, one may note a similar convention. The subject is a dance of Theseus around the Minotaur. Young men and young women, intermingled, are formed in file, holding each other by the hand. While the leader of the dance, who is independent of the chain, is presented entirely in profile, all of the other dancers, from the necessity of their relative position, are in full-face. This painting is a perfect example of the twists imposed on these personages. (350 and Fig. 571.)

27. The Bacchants often have the head hanging forward or bent backward; this is a sign of the frenzy of the ritual (400). Sometimes the painter intentionally makes the torsos of Menades or Satyrs face the spectator, while the head is bent backward, which may seem a hard blow to perspective, and, though they are fore-shortened, the head is reversed in profile. (Figs. 118, 119, B.)

When the head is hung forward the painter eludes the difficulty by hiding the face, allowing only the top of the head to be seen, the head being abruptly pitched forward on the chest at about a quarter-circle, and the profile bent downward. (Fig. 111.)

28. That certain statuettes show this exceptional position, proves that it was not adopted by the painters merely through bad designing. (Fig. 136.)

29. The bas-reliefs, both archaic and the later copies, often present the same conventions as the vases, torso facing, arms extended, right and left, head and legs in contrasting profile view. There is one other convention which persists in appearing on all the bas-reliefs of the sixth to the third centuries B. C.

In the sixth century B. C. the statues in the round walk on the left leg. This cannot be always by accident of design; the constant use of the pose points to intention. Much later, this convention is lost, and the figure advances sometimes on one leg, sometimes on the other. The bas-relief of archaic date escapes the formula of the sinister; there is a sort of rule adopted for bas-reliefs of the fifth century B. C.: *the leg carried forward is always the left when the marcher is turned toward the right of the spectator, and always the right when he is turned toward the left.* There are exceptions, but these are readily explained by the technical requirements. It would seem that the sculptor's logic impelled him to show the personages in an equilibrium which changed its form according to the direction of the walk, so as to keep both the legs in sight. The examples furnished by the frieze of the Parthenon are characteristic. (Figs. 21, 596.)

The same conventional treatment is found to be applied to the figures of the Victory Aptere, of Phagalias, of Trysa, of Pergamus. Only at the end of the Hellenistic period and in the Roman epoch do the sculptors break away from a tradition which had the force of authority, to show their figures in a pose that permitted them to turn their backs to the spectator.

30. It is really far from easy to make this matter clear in a lecture. If the interpreter is to be accurate, it becomes necessary to note the causes of deterioration to which the movements are exposed, whenever the Greek artists resorted to artifices to transform them for decorative purposes. In default of a rule that will hold good at all times, the only safe way is to reserve decision.

31. The proof of these deductions lies in the figures themselves. The Greek artists used their eyes. With a bit of clay and a few theories they fixed the most elusive moments. Compare their work with the photographs of modern dancers, and see how correctly they expressed the things before their eyes.

It thus becomes possible to draw true conclusions as to the Steps and Tempos, through the great numbers of representations. It is quite possible to get a very clear idea of what the Greek dance was like, in its grammar and traditions.

32. It would not be possible to make a complete catalogue of the ancient figures in dancing positions. By selection and elimination, choosing sometimes the painted vases and sometimes the reliefs, sometimes the ones that are less good from an artistic standpoint, we may gain most precious knowledge of the dances.

From the point of view of this study, it is not permitted to proceed with too close adherence to chronology, through the diverse scenes of Greek art with any hope of following the transformations through which the dance passed. To get any true vision of the whole, they must be considered en masse, and then separated into groups, each containing figures of certain marked characteristics. How else, when there are six centuries of painting and sculpture? The student may ask if there be not danger of confusion in using a common title for arts so different. This is unlikely, and, in default of a better system, it will be adopted. Without invoking the continuity and persistence of the antique traditions, of which this modest essay furnishes some new examples, we find remarkable details, by following the history of the movements of the Greek dance.

The search will be, not so much to follow the changes in the type of the dances as to arrive at an understanding of the gymnastics used in their preparation.

The first part of this study will be to obtain an answer to this question:

What were the methods used in the dances of the Greeks?

33. Evidently, this is not the point of the entire dance. With us modern people, the art of the dance and the art of acting are separated, which was not the case with the Greeks. With them, the association was constant. Dancing was not merely a pretext to move to a certain rhythm, to fall into elegant poses connected by beautiful movements. The dance was more than a pretty gymnastic; it was a language. They created a pantomime that is properly so

called, in that it possessed mimetic meaning; by symbolic gestures, the dance conveyed a meaning, though, in some instances, the movements appeared to have no order. To penetrate to the spirit of the Greek dance, we must look at it with their eyes.

The modern dance is our term of comparison. Reduce the Greek dance, for purposes of simplification, to the same limits. In a sense, this is to belittle it,—to deprive it of its mimetic character. But by this means we get a better idea of its gymnastics. From this point of view, it escapes the changes wrought by time; the mechanism is seen to be always the same. All through the ages, they use the same kind of mechanics; on this ground alone dare we consider the Greek dance as a whole, and consider, one by one, the diverse elements introduced by time.

THE TRADITIONAL GESTURES AS SHOWN BY THE FIGURES OF THE PAINTINGS AND SCULPTURES

34. One searching through the relics of Greek art for traces of the Greek dance is exposed to the dangers that await all investigators; he discovers too many objects suitable for study. Granted that it would be a mistake to class all of these figures as dancers; Plato, Lucien, Athennus,—to cite the three authors most useful to a student of the history of the dance,—all speak of it as *the art of speech by means of gesture*. It follows that the scenes shown often do represent dances, at least in the broader meaning which the Greeks gave the word. When the figures are isolated, as in many pieces of sculpture, they often show that they were directly inspired by the dance. The sculptors went to the public exhibitions, and there studied the attitudes of the dancers, and, later, reproduced them in their masterpieces. Afterward, the dancers, in their turn, copied the poses of the statues. To this mutual exchange, then, we owe the vast number of dancing figures that appear in sculpture.

But, as already stated, the study of the gymnastics of the dance must be kept separate from the mimetic and gestural side of the subject. Between the two it is not always easy to distinguish the difference, as the superficial aspect of the purely gymnastic movement may be the same, to all intents and purposes, as the movement that has mimetic value. It will be well to compare the figures 1 to 10. In order to avoid mistakes a dividing line should be drawn by making a list of the traditional gestures which persist throughout all Greek art.

35. Greek art is, above all else, a thing of change. It ceaselessly renews itself, transforming its technique by means of new themes. Political revolutions and religious innovations as much as progress in art itself, serve to modify it. Accordingly, the force of tradition, while permitting many changes in the course of seven or eight centuries, yet holds as far as fundamentals are concerned. This is to be attributed in part to the formalism of religious ritual, as, in the antique religion, each gesture had its own meaning which was piously preserved. The customs were of too ancient origin to remain always the same, but in private life the change was less than in the more public ceremonies. Despite political commotions, the Greeks did not break with the past, that is, the soul of Hellenistic thought. Art advances, step by step, always curious to find something new, but always retaining the old. Are the copies made by one artist after another surprising? The efforts of each profited all. Each masterpiece was the common good fortune, and, changed, repeated, transformed, it added to the glory of all. Was it not enough for an artist to contribute some delicate nuance to the art which belonged to all alike? This spirit is found throughout all centuries, and accounts for the endless repetitions and minor changes.

36. All of the gestures have, primarily, a concrete significance. Some of these meanings are always retained; others change; still others lose their identity, continuing in use merely as decorative motifs. But the essential character, however varied or hidden, can be discovered in the initial theme. It is not easy to determine the exact period at which each gesture makes its first appearance.

37. The traditional gestures may be divided into three groups:
Gestures that are ritual and symbolic.
Gestures of every-day life.
Gestures of the concrete type becoming mere decorative motifs.

TRADITIONAL GESTURES SHOWN BY PAINTINGS AND SCULPTURES 25

Ritualistic and symbolic gestures

38. Gestures of the Divinities Who Dance.—These are very ancient, and are of Oriental origin. The naked goddess who, with her hand, makes the milk gush forth, the whole gesture being coarse, is, in the Greek version, transformed into the chaste Aphrodite. Heuzey (see "Catalogue of the Terra-cotta Figurines in the Louvre," Vol. I) discovered the evolution, and his analysis is often cited.

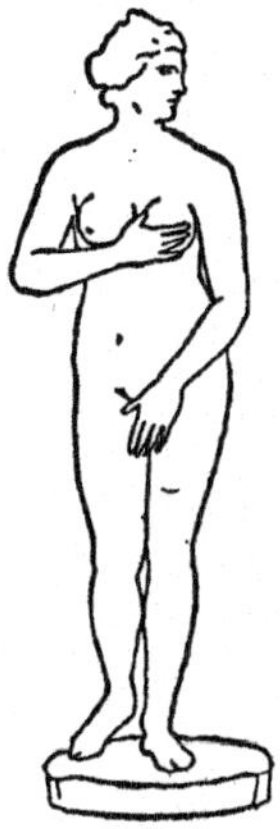

39. Gesture of the Chaste Aphrodite.—Praxiteles shows, in the Aphrodite, the same form of gesture as the Venus de Medici and the Venus of the Vatican; are they copies of the famous lost masterpiece? The gesture is alike in all three cases and the statues are nude. In the Roman period, when the 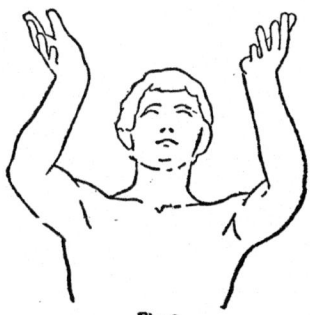 figures, though draped, hold to the original significance of the movement, there is found one singular defect to be noted, especially in the "Dancer" of the Vatican, which is a mediocre work.

Fig. 1.

Fig. 2.

40. Gestures of the Worshipers.—This is one of the most common forms of gesture, and consists of holding the arms out with the palms up. The praying child in the Museum of Berlin (Fig. 2) is of this type.

41. Gesture of the Mimetic Funeral.—This is a striking example of the transformation of an abstract movement, purely decorative, consequently, a dance-movement, becoming a concrete gesture. In the most remote times (vases of Dipylon, vases of Corinth) the mourners tore the hair and scratched the face as a sign of sorrow, during the ceremonies of exposition of the dead and the burial. Little by little, the gesticulation became less violent. In the fifth century B. C. there remains only the imitation of the customs against which Solon issued an edict. Here is proof that the funeral gestures were governed by ritual and that a study was made of them. (363 to 370.)

42. **Gesture of Untying the Sandal.**—Type: the figure (bas-relief) of the Victory Aptere. The Nike gesture goes beyond that of the Aphrodite. There are many variants of it. One is that of *taking off the sandal*. Whether this gesture be symbolic or concrete, it marks the highest tide of Greek art. The goddess rests on one leg, the other being lifted to enable her to put her hand on the sandal. The boldness of the pose suggests that the painters designed it and that the sculptors learned it from them.

Fig. 3.

43. **Gesture of the Veil.**—The ample Greek dress permitted a woman wearing it to make of it, at pleasure, a dress, a cloak, or a veil, because it was simply a long piece of cloth. The gesture of the veil is made by turning the head to the side while covering the head and shoulders with the fabric. In the fifth and fourth centuries, the intention of the gesture is, above all, to express modesty; the veil is a mobile wall behind which a woman takes refuge. The gesture with which a bride removes her veil is called *the nuptial gesture,* an admirable example is on one of the metopes of Heraion (14). Facing Zeus, who sits upon a rock, the divine bride stands "with opened veil held with exquisite modesty. It is an attitude of retreat; the chaste gesture of the young wife who unveils in the bridal chamber" (Collignon). The gesture of Latona "archaisant," in the Louvre, bears the imprint of great nobility, but it is nothing more than a decorative motif (Fig. 3). Graceful enough in itself, it is, at the same time, absolutely inexpressive.

The Aphrodite Genitrix of Myrina (17) is a fourth century B. C. type, and shows an early concept of the veil-gesture; she is a chaste goddess, who protects herself from too close scrutiny (Fig. 4). But in the third century B. C. the veil ceased to be a barricade behind which to hide; the drapery of the Hellenistic Aphrodite is most of it removed,—it is only used to emphasize the nudity.

The expression of the gesture is that of going forward and returning (E. Pottier). The great days of the dance-repertoire passed, and the significance of the motion suffered the same metamorphosis as the arts of design. Grave and chaste in the fifth and sixth centuries B. C. the dancers who used the veil in the third and second centuries B. C. made it an accessory of lascivious steps.

Gestures of every-day life

44. Gesture of the Tunic.—This motif is many times repeated in the paintings and sculptures, and is one of the earliest, but it is used down to the latest period. It is a gesture that is instinctive when a woman is wearing a long robe. It consists in lightly lifting the drapery with the hand, thereby leaving the feet at liberty. The Greek woman made the gesture with great elegance, gathering up a handful of the fabric at the back to keep it from touching the ground and thus becoming soiled. The gesture is not one of coquetry, used to make the walk more attractive, but it introduces a kind of eurhythmy, so that, when it ceases to be a gesture of utility, it is frankly a dance-movement (Fig. 33, Par. 50).

Fig. 4.

Sometimes the arms lift the plaits laterally, sometimes forward, occasionally backward, now and then they are held close to the body. At last, the movement is joined to a turning motion of the torso, when it loses all its original meaning and becomes merely an artifice of the dance (Fig. 105). Fig. 104 is a rare combination of the turning with the gesture of the tunic.

(Many types of the gesture of the tunic are to be found in the first volume of "Greek Sculpture" by Collignon; reproductions of the archaic statues of the Acropolis, among others, Plate I; figures illustrating the text, pages 343 and 366. They are of the same character as Figs. 33, 50, 102, 103, 104, 105, 106, 501, etc., in this volume.)

It will be seen that it is difficult to mark the limit and separate the gesture of every-day life from the one which is purely a dance-movement.

45. The Masculine Gesture of the Arm with the Cloak.—In the fifth and fourth centuries B. C. this gesture was used to suggest repose. The orators of the tribune expressed their professional dignity by means of it. At the opening of the third century B. C. it lost its solemnity· the roguish Eros of Myrina often folds his mantle about him with a great pretense of gravity. The gesture becomes one of the more frolicsome kind of dancing movements. The noble is transformed into the playful.

Fig. 5.

46. Gesture of the Hand on the Hip.—The arm is more or less retired. More recently, the action takes on an appearance of rapidity, but an examination of the Tanagra figurines will show the student that that period is characterized by a dreamy immobility. It is a gesture at once noble and familiar, which allows great elegance in the gathering and holding of the drapery (Fig. 5). The dancer takes a gesture of utility and imparts to it a high degree of beauty; the hand on the hip lifts the tunic, holds the dress, and, by the tension of the material, reveals the feminine form through its veils (Fig. 452).

47. Gesture of the Athlete Pouring Oil Over His Body.—One arm is raised and curved above the shoulder; the hand holds a vase containing oil; the other hand, close to the body, is held as though to prevent the escape of the liquid (Fig. 6). This gesture is not to be confused with that of the "Pourer" (52). This being wholly realistic in treatment, the Pourer being more decorative in effect.

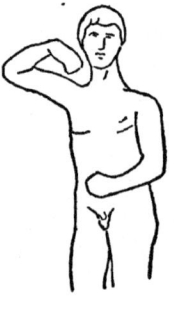
Fig. 6.

48. Gesture of the Athlete Who Rubs His Body with a Strigil. Covered with the dust and perspiration of the conflict, and the oil used to make the body supple, the athlete, who has just come from the exercises of the palestra, rubs his skin with a strigil. This gesture, which Lysippus appears to have introduced into art in the fourth century B. C., is not easy to recognize; the fact that the small scraper cannot be seen, and that this instrument is the only thing that explains the movement to modern eyes causes uncertainty.

Fig. 7.

49. Gesture of the Athlete Who Binds a Fillet About His Head.—Here the gesture is also made without the accessory that explains it. Fig. 7 has all the air of a dancer.

Concrete gestures becoming decorative gestures

50. Gesture of the Arm Bent Above the Head.—Pottier says of this gesture, that, in the fifth and fourth centuries B. C., it expresses energy of the combative kind (metopes of Olympia, Parthenon, Tomb of Halicarnassus, etc.); and, as it degenerates from its primitive meaning, becomes, in the Hellenistic period, the gesture of abandon, of complete repose. It is not yet a mere decorative convention, but is full of elegance, though somewhat lacking in logic, because the person seems to be asleep with one arm supporting the head, a most unstable position. Of the same kind is the Faun of Munich, who is heavy with wine, like the Satyr of Naples. The Ariadne of the Vatican has better equilibrium, although the gesture of the lovely sleeper is rather affected. The Niobe at Florence is more sincere; here the hands are held in a manner that suggests dramatic truth.

Fig. 8.

The gesture of the wounded Amazon resembles the preceding, as a conventional expression of suffering (Fig. 8); but, by an inversion, the same thing becomes a gesture of energy in the primitive concrete phase.

51. The Gesture of the Aphrodite Anadyomene.—The goddess wrings her hair to get the water out of it (Fig. 9). Although this is essentially a concrete gesture, it may become, according to the nature of the subject to which it is applied, a conventional decorative motif. In this case it is not merely a woman drying her hair, but a goddess coquetting in a lackadaisical manner with her arms.

52. Gesture of Pouring.—One hand, holding a vase, is lifted in order to make the contents of the bottle flow forcibly; the other hand is held as low as possible in opposition: this allows the liquid to fall through space with a beautiful curve

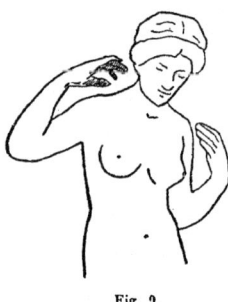

Fig. 9.

Fig. 10.

(Fig. 10, Par. 151). The gesture can be recognized many times where it is used as a mere decorative form, having quite lost its original concrete signification and become a dance-movement (Figs. 152, 584, 590).

The paintings from Pompeii often show a modified form of the same gesture combined with a play with the veil where it becomes a convention.

53. This list, while incomplete, suffices to make clear the part played by the dancers in the development of the traditional gestures. With regard to the mimetics, the gestures were the same as those of the dance, because the Greek dance recognized the art of acting as a part of the art which comprised dancing, acting, and music, as well as poetry; without this knowledge, dancing becomes merely a series of gymnastic movements.

THE MOVEMENTS IN GENERAL
Natural movements. The walk and the run

54. Mechanical Movements.—Among the movements of the body that depend on voluntary action and which, while purely *mechanical*, have a definite aim, there are—walking, running, leaping, vaulting, etc. These movements are instinctive, and always retain the same form, except in small details which each person varies according to his own individuality.

55. Expressive Movements: Gestures.—Depending upon the coöperation of the mind are the movements which interpret the thoughts,—which are the medium of communication with other persons. These are, properly speaking, *gestures*. They constitute a language of infinite variety; they are less hide-bound than words, for they are manufactured in the most appropriate form by the user, according to the needs of the moment. These motions are called *expressions*, as opposed to mechanical movements. A change of thought will at once affect the bodily position; to prove this, do not take the studied gesture of the orator, but that of the simple peasant. You will be struck by the sobriety, and, many times, by the mobility, of their gestures. If they are lacking in precision, they express the ideas of the every-day man. Gesture is a sort of physical-ideograph of the figure in the mind.

56. It may be well to note here that conventions are, little by little, introduced into gesture. It is clear that primitive peoples, who have only simple ideas to express, do not possess the riches of gesture of the more intellectual races, with whom it becomes a complex language made up of nuances. Like spoken language, it has recourse to figures. For expressions of sudden and violent explosion, do we not bend the arm with fist clenched, and strike a blow in the air? This is one kind of metaphor. What does the spectator at a comedy understand when one of the characters rubs the back of his hand? It is a metonymy. Therefore, gesture becomes an intellectual instrument by which the person impresses his mark upon the mind of another: it is to be determined which gestures are instinctive and imitative, and which are influenced by tradition and custom. For instance, the famous actors of Rome, Pylade and Bathyelle, being pantomimists, used only the gestures that all of their audience would understand, and these gestures have remained unchanged to this day.

57. Dance Movements.—The mechanical movements and the expressive movements or gestures are clearly separated, in our time, as far as they concern dancing, but this was not the case with the Greeks, with whom the *dance-movements* were neither entirely mechanical nor wholly imitative. The young animal, says Plato, does not remain in repose, it leaps, it runs; its activity never ceases, nor does its pleasure in it; it even expends its superabundant energy in the most useless movements. In this there is a resemblance to man in the dance. But while, with the animal, the motion is due only to vitality, with man there is also an enjoyment in the sense of rhythm, of *harmonious movement*. This was recognized by the directors of the dance, and the same Greek word is used to signify "joy" and "dance." Though this etymology suggested by Plato may be at fault, there is no mistake in the fact. The dance is more than play, it is an exercise of the body which is embellished by art and by music, in their rhythmic elements, and they are its indispensable auxiliaries.

58. That all the dances of primitive humanity were, in their inception, mimetic would seem to be proved. The purely gymnastic dances are a later development. The separation is complete, even in our own day, between the dramatic and the dance-movement, between the gesture and the mechanical movement. We attach the same value to the same signs; their reason for existing is the same, to manifest a special activity. In our ballets the dance-scenes are not to be confused with the dramatic scenes; their dramatic action belongs to the department of pantomime; the others, characterized by rhythm and the precision of the steps, and the momentary suspension of dramatic action, are intended to exhibit the talents of the dancers and to show the public a brilliant spectacle.

The separation did not exist in the Greek dance in the same degree as in ours. But it is possible to discover from the painted and sculptured figures the *steps of the dance* which are analogous to ours, and, like ours, devoid of mimetic meaning. The ritualistic symbolism is, of course, there, partly hidden, for the Greeks did not permit their dances to become mere muscular exercises. Properly speaking, the mimetic interposes itself into every movement of the Greek dancer.

59. The same word which means dance and ball-play is also used to designate the Pyrrhics, which were the reproduction of the evolutions of the phases of combat. It was used to describe the worthy citizen who celebrated Komos, and the professional "who spoke mutely, and expressed everything with his hands." With the Greeks the dance was an art much more highly regarded than with us. The philosophers attributed to it a moral influence; they said that "the dance is, of all the musical arts, the one that most influences the soul. The arts of poetry, music, and dancing are divine in their nature and are the gifts of the gods." They are not intended alone to give pleasure, they are a cult, in which the god are honored. Therefore, it is impossible to study one of these without the others. Instead of isolating the gymnastic movements it is better to look for the bond, of which Plato said: "It is the intermediary between the bodily rhythm and the soul, and it is the dance-gymnastic which teaches eurhythmy."—This is proof that they had a dance-gymnastic, and it is no less certain that it is possible to discover it.

THE WALK

60. Many dances, of different periods and different localities, are based on the modifications of the walk and the run. Sometimes the dancer follows a certain rhythm which makes the walk or the run in itself a dance; thus a simple gymnastic of the natural order becomes an art.

These are the kinds of movement most used by the Greek dancers. It is not rare to find the legs employed in the common walking or running steps while the arms, torso, and head are in repose. All this contrary to the accepted modern ideas of dancing.

Natural, instinctive movements are the foundation of the Greek dance, as of all dances.

61. **Mechanism of the Walk.**—The mechanism of the walk is

36 THE MOVEMENTS IN GENERAL

complex. Reduced to its external manifestation, it consists of movements of extension and flexion by each leg in turn, so managed as to hold the body over the center of gravity. When modern painters and sculptors represent a man walking they show one leg bent and the other held more or less straight, this being the im-

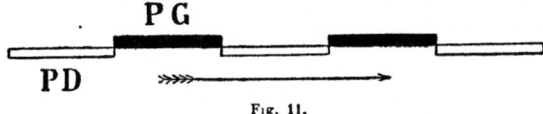

Fig. 11.

pression produced on the eye—a combination of many movements. In reality, the phases of the walk are less simple; the eye is deceived. Modern photography proves that the Greeks saw more correctly than modern people do.

62. I. In the normal walk, on level ground, *the two feet are placed on the ground alternately;* at the moment when the rear foot is raised, the forward one rests flat on the ground. The diagram, arranged by Marey, shows clearly how the feet alternate.

II. The foot is posed on the ground only at the heel, the toe being in the air (Fig. 12, 2). But the toe is immediately lowered and the sole of the foot rests on the ground. As the body is pro-

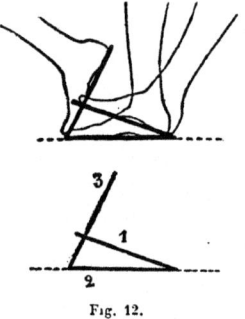

Fig. 12.

pelled forward, the heel is lifted, describes a quarter-circle from low to high, the foot not touching except at the toe (Fig. 12, 3), and the same leg is then lifted and swung forward. In two words, *the foot is posed on the ground at the heel and quits it at the toe.* It is a sort of see-saw movement, as is indicated in Fig. 12, which was made by superposing three images corresponding to the three principal movements, and taken from the series of photographs shown in Fig. 14.

III. Consequently, the two feet of the walker are never placed on the ground at the same moment, neither are the heels, neither are the toes. *The movements of the legs are symmetrical successions.*

THE WALK 37

IV. There is one instant when the two feet touch the ground, that is when the foot forward is posed ready to take the weight, and before the rear foot is lifted. The position is one of extreme instability, as may be seen from Fig. 13. The left foot, advanced, rests the heel on the ground (Fig. 12, 1), when the right foot, not touching except at the toe, is also lifted (Fig. 12, 3).

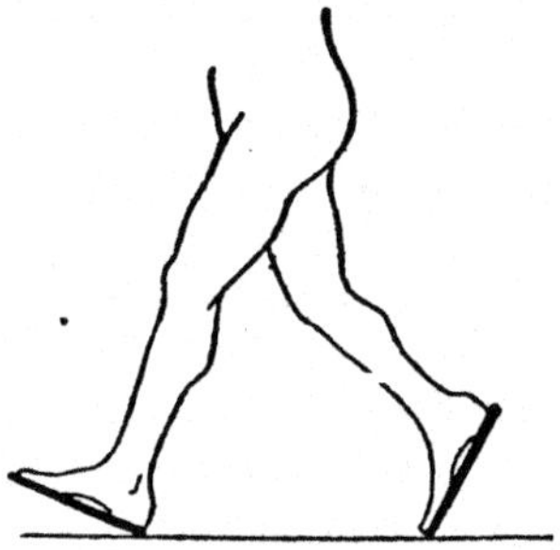

63. Opposition of the Arms and Legs in Walking.—While walking, the arms swing freely, the general condition of equilibrium in movement keeps arms and legs in opposition, as per these two formulas.

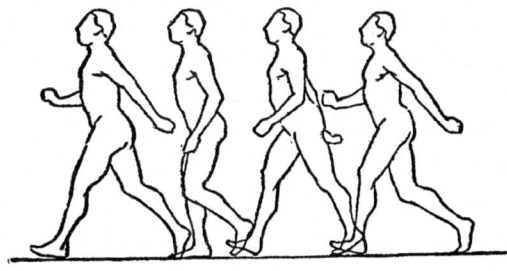

Fig. 13.

When the left foot is advanced the left arm swings backward.

When the right foot is advanced the right arm swings backward.

In other terms, the left foot and the right arm, the right foot and the left arm: Fig. 14 makes clear the association and the opposition in movements of arms and legs. It is from photographs made at different moments, showing successive motions; Fig. 12 shows the same thing in another manner.

Fig. 14.

The ancient ballet masters knew and used the law of *opposition* of the arms and legs in the walk. Noverre (eighteenth century) shows in a wonderful manner the natural interplay and combination of movement in the dance. The word Opposition is used to indicate different members of the body directed toward different points, rather than moving in symmetry.

64. Representation of the Walk in Greek Painting and Sculpture.—On the more ancient vases and reliefs the walkers are presented in one particular aspect, which is a simplification of the aspect affected by primitive artists everywhere; all are shown in profile, more or less stiff, and with the feet flat on the ground. This convention, which is also seen in Egyptian art, possesses the awkwardness common to all archaic work. The Greeks retained it until it became a tradition; it is to be seen in sculpture of the best period, even the frieze of the Parthenon. Experiment proves that a person can get no elasticity when walking on the *soles of the feet*.

Some of the archaic artists appear to have intentionally rejected this convention and substituted one of their own fabrication, which gives a better appearance to the walker. It is used on the famous vase of Aristonophos, in the Capitoline Museum, which dates from the commencement of the seventh century B. C., according to Pottier. Ulyssus and his companions seem to be working out the steps of a dance. Springing on the tips of the toes, they advance, legs lifted high, as though they were about to kick out the eye of Cyclops. It must be admitted that the scene is not strictly a dance-scene, but it is not to be questioned that when a comic scene is exhibited it is a part of a satyric drama. Therefore, the captives of Polyphemus are not dancing. The Rhodian ceramists of the seventh century B. C. (9) painted bold warriors, who advance on the toe, making grimaces. It is more than likely that the artists who were bold enough to use this most strange innovation borrowed the form from the dance. More, the walk on the toes, notwithstanding its instability, is easier to draw, because its mechanism is less complicated than the normal walk. It became, in the hands of primitive artists, a formula to be applied without discrimination. It is curious to find that two monuments of nearly the same date should show, one, dancers who walk heavily on the whole sole of the foot, and other persons in armour advancing lightly on the toes, though it is quite evident that they are *not* dancing. It is confusing.

Nearly all of the artists, both painters and sculptors, previous to the sixth century B. C. present their figures walking on the soles of both feet (Figs. 515, 541, 542).

65. What are the variants of this form, and in what way are they modified?

Sometimes a file of persons advance, holding one another's hands, their steps being, of necessity alike, but differing in length of stride.

Fig. 15.   Fig. 16.

This is not accident, it is part of the design. On the François vase the chain of dancers who execute a farandole present this peculiarity (Figs. 15, 517). The men, wearing short chalmys which do not impede their movements, walk with longer steps than the women, who alternate with them. These, by reason of the gorgeous tunics which enfold them with sheath-like closeness, appear to be the victims of fashion, and move with difficulty.

Elsewhere this same discord in the length of step is to be noticed in dancing groups, and it is not always a matter of difference in sex.

Fig. 16 is an example of this. The two are, perhaps, Menades: they advance rapidly, one in front of the

Fig. 17.   Fig. 18.

other. The longer step makes for speed, and gives an effect of great energy.

In Fig. 17 one can see that an effort is made to render the legs more supple; the walker still steps on the soles of the feet, but there is a little less stiffness, because the knees bend.

The dancing figures all appear to suffer from this defect,—see

Fig. 18, cut from a bronze plaque (64); the carver was not willing to make his figure walk on the soles of the feet at the same moment, nor could he lift both toes at the same time, so, one of the good fellow's feet follows one convention while an entirely different one is used for the other; he lifts the heel of the right foot, but the whole of the left one remains fixed to the ground.

66. Fig. 19 is very interesting; it shows perfectly the antique idea of the walk. It is taken from a votive bas-relief found on the Acropolis, and belongs to the second half of the sixth century B. C. Hermes, followed by three Kharites who hold one another's hands, walks on the soles of the feet, as do the first and third women.

Fig. 19.

But the second Kharite lifts the left heel, presenting an appearance altogether novel. It is curious to see how the artist, fearing to go too far in the matter of innovations, clung to the old custom in the case of three figures, trying the new method on only one. Once introduced, the new form became popular. The vases of the sixth century B. C. furnish examples (Fig. 20). In the fifth century B. C. it became general, though the work of that period retained much of the stiffness which characterized the paintings in red of the severe period (Fig. 461). But the tendency was toward better work and progress was not slow (Fig. 106).

This is not to say that the walk on the soles of the feet was wholly abandoned; most artists held piously to the traditions of the past, though, little by little, they discarded them.

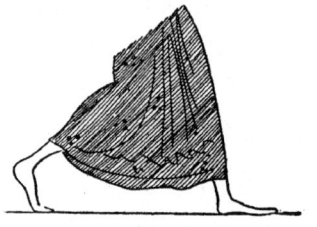

Fig. 20.

67. Representation of the Walk on the Frieze of the Parthenon (15).—As far as the condition of the bas-reliefs permits us to judge, nearly all of the persons walk on the soles of the feet. Some of the figures are isolated, some walk two-by-two (Figs. 21, 22).

These groups may be compared to certain groups on the vases with black-painted figures of the period of the sixth century B. C.

A great number of the black-figured vases are ornamented with processions in which Hermes or Apollo take part. The god who conducts is followed by women who are grouped in different ways. The gestures are nearly always symmetrical; the profiles, from head to feet, are parallel, the feet of each figure projecting beyond those of the figure preceding. Thus the painter indicated a great number of persons (Figs. 23, 24).

It is certain that in every period the ceramics reflect the great paintings.

Fig. 21.

Fig. 22.

It is, therefore, interesting to ascertain from the work of Phidias that the perspective used in his time was not different from that of the painters of the sixth century B. C. There is the same parallelism of profile, the same symmetry of gesture, the same disposition of the feet, one in advance of the other, the same walk on the soles. Only, in the Parthenon figures, the stiffness gives place to a marvelous suppleness. The weight of the body is supported on one foot; the other leg bends lightly at the knee as the step is taken.

Fig. 23.

Fig. 24.

One thinks, at first glance, that the procession has halted. The aspect of these beautiful persons is that of immobility; there is little in it that suggests the walk, which, as Marey says, is an expression of perpetual instability. Without question, the young women who carry the libation vases show, by their slow step and quiet air, that it is a sacred procession; the same may be said of the flute-players. At the side of the cortege there are a number of persons, indubitably motionless, who appear to be spectators. They seem to be interposed between the ranks of the marchers; only on this supposition can one get a correct idea of the perspective which is indicated on the bas-relief. There is a great variety in the pose of the persons who are not marching. Compare these with the fragment in the Louvre, where two men face the women who turn to the left; one holds a basket, the other, who seems to be the director of the company, surveys the deployment. These two, who are seen in three-quarters view, rest on their left legs; the right legs are bent at the knee, and only the toes touch the ground. The right heel, which is hidden from sight, must, necessarily, be lifted. The same observation applies to the second woman carrying a vase on the north frieze; this woman, who is seen in profile, has stopped to aid a companion who faces her. She rests on the right leg which permits the knee to bend and the heel to raise.

It is seen that the marchers keep their heels on the ground while the spectators rest the weight on one leg, leaving the other free, with only the toe touching the ground. Here there is no question of inexperienced artists; this is the ritualistic pose for a religious procession. The old convention of the walk on the soles expressed the hieratic character of the ceremony; with this convention there is another to be noted, and that is the peculiar perspective of the walk on the archaic bas-reliefs (29) showing all of the persons advancing in the same time and with the same step.

It would be foolish to pretend to interpret with exactness all of the details, many of which are essentially decorative; their creator cared more for beauty and for the religious expression of the work than for realism. The only faults are those imposed by religious tradition.

68. To show the persistence of the walk on the soles of the feet, the following examples are noted.

A bas-relief of the fourth century B. C. shows a chorus of seven persons, divided into two groups; they are preceded by a dancer. They walk with short steps, and their hands are hidden in their mantles (Fig. 526).

A painting taken from a Greek tomb, not anterior to the third century B. C., represents a dance executed by twenty-seven figures distributed in two groups (Fig. 530). Twenty-six of them are running rather than walking, on the soles of the feet. Only the leaders lift the heel.

Of the first century B. C. there are many "archaisant" figures, among others the mediocre bas-relief called the Kharites of Socrates, in the Vatican.

THE RUN

69. Mechanism of the Run.—The run is not a rapid walk. It differs from the walk, which is, more or less, *on the ground*, in that it is a movement *in the air*, the body being lifted more or less high above the ground.

Compare the diagram of the walk with this one of the run.

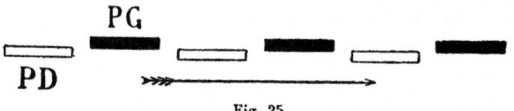

Fig. 25.

Observe that, in the run, there is a *period of suspension, during which both feet are above the ground* (Marey).

In other words, *the run is a series of leaps from one foot to the other* (74).

Fig. 26 is a reproduction of a series of instantaneous photographs of the same runner, showing the advance from one leg to the other.

Image 2 corresponds to the moment of suspension.

The figures 27, 28, and 29–30, present the runner during the three first leaps of the run.

Fig. 27 corresponds to the moment of departure; in this he carries the weight of the body forward and at the same time flexes the right knee in order to get the necessary spring to throw the left leg forward.

Fig. 28: the moment of suspension which corresponds to the leap. The left leg begins to descend as the body darts through the air.

Fig. 29: the second period of suspension, corresponding to the second leap from the left leg to the right.

Fig. 30: preparation, by holding the weight on the right leg, foot lifted high, for the third leap, from the right leg to the left.

70. In the run, even more than in the walk, there is an instinctive *opposition* of the arm and leg (63). The photographs prove that without any argument.

71. It is sufficient to briefly mention these few of the many aspects of the run. Images 1 and 3 of Fig. 26 and Fig. 30 show a singular difference between some of the antique representations and the modern. The form, which never varies and of which the funda-

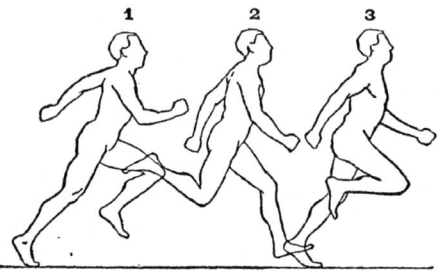

Fig. 26.

mental type is shown in Fig. 27, is not inexact. It represents a true *moment* of the run, but it is not natural in all its details. The monotonous repetition of the same pose tends to prove that the artists did not see all of the *moments* (282) of the run.

The ancients observed very closely. The education of their eyes was carried to a high state of development. Marey points out a remarkable resemblance between the runners painted on the Athenian amphoræ of the fifth and fourth centuries B. C. and the runners whose movements are here analyzed.

72. **The Leap.**—The three photographs, taken at successive moments, are sufficient proof of the relation between the run and the

leap. The Figs. 31 and 32 represent,—the first (Fig. 31) the moment when the body is flung forward, the second (Fig. 32) the same leap during the period of suspension (69). Fig. 38 also represents the moment of suspension.

The effective leap is the leap that is high and long, and this is the same when it is a part of the run. It will be seen that the two moments of the leap, fixed by the images 31 and 32, correspond exactly to the moments (282) of the run represented by images 1 and 2 of Fig. 26 and by the analogous Figs. 30 and 28, without taking into account the fact that in one the right leg and in the other the left leg is the active one.

73. Attention must be called to this point: when the leap is used in running, the body is passive, the legs alone being active; in the dance it is different,— "no leap without bending."

74. The principal forms of the leap are—*the long leap; the high leap; leap forward; leap backward; leap to the side; leap in place; leap from one foot to the other; leap, coming down on the same foot; leap on the joints of the feet, etc.*

75. **Representations of the Run in Painting and Sculpture.**—It may be taken for granted that in the more ancient sculptures the simpler forms of movement will prevail. On the reliefs, there is a sense that the artists are feeling their way, there is a hesitation in the technique, but always logical development. Art became freer as time passed. Taking a series of vases of different periods this is noticeable. Design is perfected as the centuries pass,—it shows more grace and energy. The brush becomes more discreet, the movements lighter. On the vases with black figures (10) and on the first vases with red figures (11) the motion is bolder and more rapid.

76. It is not always easy to know which of the figures are running and which are walking. Though the mechanism of the two are so unlike, the primitive artists hesitated a long time before adopting a style of drawing that would indicate the difference.

They were contented to make only the legs active. The two
feet rest solidly on the ground
(16); progress can be discovered
when the heel of the rear foot is
lifted (Fig. 33); much later, the
rear foot touches only at the toe
(Fig. 34).

A form of running that is most
gross and wholly artificial is where
the legs drag along the ground
this is found on some of the vases of
the degenerate period (Fig. 518).

77. Archaic art employed one
form more awkward in appearance
even than the preceding, but of
which the expressional value is great. Some of the ceramists launch
their runners into space (Figs. 35, 36)
flinging their legs widely in a sort of kneeling posture. This type of runner is also
found on the bas-reliefs. But here, in order
to give the figure the necessary stability, the
sculptor is obliged to pose him on the sole
of the forward foot and the knee of the rear
foot, giving the body a crouching position. This is the case of the
Nike of Delos (sixth century B. C.) of which Fig. 37 shows a part,

Fig. 33.

Fig. 34.

Fig. 35.

Fig. 36.

and of a small bronze of archaic type found on the Acropolis, also
a Nike.

The goddess of victory, later imagined as a being of the air, is here shown settled as heavily on the sole of her foot as though she were riveted to the earth. Detached in part though it may be, it is necessary that a statue should have a base. The Perseus (Fig. 35) and the strange winged genius (Fig. 36) and the Nike of Delos are all leaping. This expresses rapidity of motion.

78. On a bas-relief of Assos, now in the Louvre, is shown a type of runner essentially of the Greek type. Hercules and the

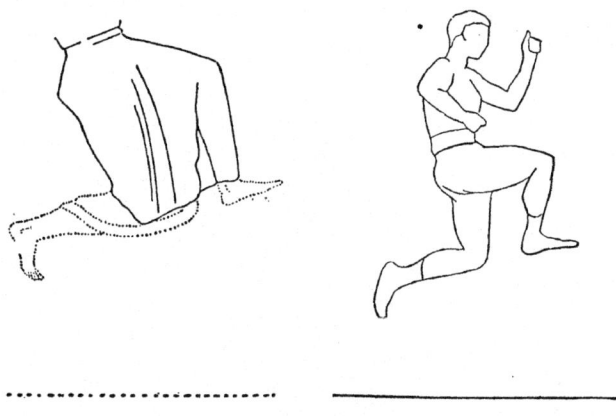

Fig. 37.   Fig. 38.

Triton put the Nereides to flight. To be sure, they look more as though they were walking than running; but the artist has naïvely suggested a rapid pace. Compare them with the lightly-moving Nereides of the verse of Homer or Sophocles! They follow in file with hands extended in a gesture of fright, legs set wide apart, as though the girls were paralyzed with terror. The sculptor's intention is quite plain (Fig. 39). The *will* to run is clear. One of the most ancient masters of bas-relief caught a *moment* of the run which had escaped modern artists until instantaneous photography proved the artist of the past correct. See Fig. 30.

In the same period, the sixth century B. C., the painters of the vases began to grow more daring. The technique is more free, they follow more closely the natural movements which are fugitive. It is sufficient to refer to Fig. 30, or to Fig. 26, 1, which is analogous,

Fig. 39.

to get an idea of the manner of the run as depicted on the vases with black figures. The line of the ground on which the feet rest is more clearly indicated in Fig. 40 than in most, though the same thing marks Fig. 528. The Athenian runners (Fig. 41) are the most exact of the series, and are repeated many times on the amphoræ of the fifth and fourth centuries B. C. The form of run in which the runner lifts the leg which is forward and just touches the toe of the rear foot to the ground is not appreciated as it should be. The painters of the red-figured vases would reject the modern manner.

79. A comparison of Figs. 42 and 43 with the photographic reproductions in Fig. 27 discloses a startling resemblance. They might almost have been superposed, the one on the other.

80. Fig. 44 and Fig.

Fig. 40.

Fig. 41.

45 compare with Figs. 28 and 29 and correspond with different moments of the period of suspension (69).

81. Figs. 46 and 47 show the sixth and last type of runner and the one with which we are most familiar. It is identical with that of the Renaissance; and is the one generally adopted. The runner rests his weight on the leg in front, which has the knee bent: the other leg, sharply bent at the knee, is lifted high and backward. Comparison with Fig. 2 in Fig. 26 justifies the reconstruction of the ensemble.

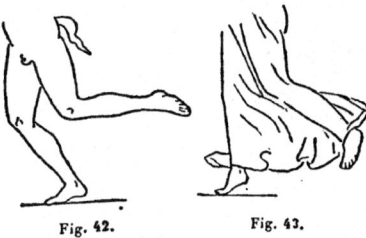

Fig. 42.   Fig. 43.

Both show how lightly the toe touches the ground. Artists use this

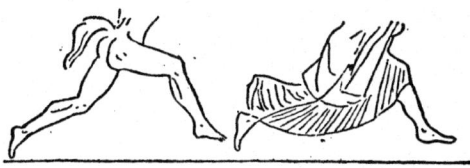

Fig. 44.

form more and more, though the Greeks rejected it for a long time because it was not strong looking.

82. On the whole, one can overlook the awkwardness and conventionality with which this ancient work is embarrassed for the sake of the underlying truth. Coexistent with the Greek ideal of exactness there is a singular contradiction, a spirit of routine which is distinguished by respect for tradition. Certain attitudes, certain movements, abandoned by the primitive artists, are taken up again by second-class artists and artisans, who regarded them as the last word in art.

Fig. 45.

Looking at the three persons (Figs. 48, 49, 50), it is hard to say whether they are walking or running. The bodies are presented full face, with the weight on the leg that is advanced, flexed at the knee and turned outward; the other leg, at the rear, has the heel raised, though this cannot be seen.

There are a great number of reliefs in the same posture. The west front of the temple of Athena at Ægina (14) furnishes prototypes: one of the warriors who brandishes a lance at Athena's side appears solidly set on both legs, the weight of the body carried on the left leg, which is bent at the knee and is in profile, though the other leg, stretched out, is full face. The attitude expresses great stability but not much movement: he could bend his body to deliver a blow to the enemy without losing his balance. The Lapithæ of the Parthenon, one of whom stands face to face with a centaur, presents the same aspect, and is visibly wrestling in place. This is likewise the case with one of the persons on the frieze discovered at Phigalia (15). Always the legs are spread wide to give greater play in wrestling.

Fig. 46. Fig. 47.

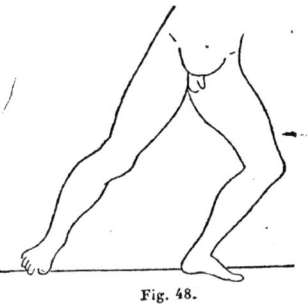

Fig. 48.

The statue of an athlete, called the Borghese Gladiator (Louvre), the work of Agasias of Ephesus (second century B. C.), excludes altogether the idea of forward movement; the athlete is "on guard" with very wide "base," ready to parry a blow. Such an attitude denotes momentary stability.

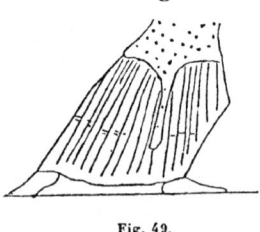

Fig. 49.

In the case of the high-reliefs, the "academic" pose has become banal—no trace of the walk or the run. There is no trace of the dance,—only of wrestling.

On the contrary, the painters of the vases used one unvarying form for the dance, the walk and the run (Fig. 494, A). Thus the type became conventionalized as it came into use in the industrial arts.

THE RUN

83. Hence it is easy to excuse some of the clumsiness that characterizes these vases. The legs of the running Hermes (Fig. 51) are somewhat stiff, but this is, evidently, an affectation. It is a deliberate return to the crude forms of primitive art. It is of the

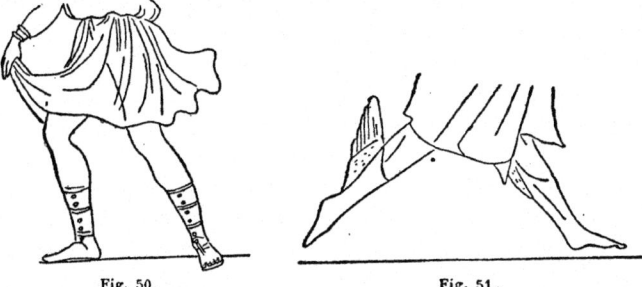

Fig. 50. Fig. 51.

first century B. C., an art that is retrospective, showing traces of all the periods of Greek work up to the time of Pericles.

84. The greater number of the preceding figures, that is to say, 15, 16, 17, 19, 20, 40, 42, 43, 45, 46, 47, 48, 49, 50,—are taken from scenes of the dance. The persons who walk or march or run are at the same time dancers who execute the natural movements of the walk, run and march, their dancing is not a movement confined to the feet alone. They dance with their arms, their heads, their torsos.

The *natural movements* of the walk and the run are, as has been stated, of many types, and, as they get farther and farther from the simple walk or run, tend toward the *artificial*, and take on the character of dance movements. Modified, transformed, often beyond recognition, they engender the dance-steps, which are of infinite variety.

In this study of the *artificial movements*—otherwise, the *dance*—the legs and the body will be considered in the following chapters.

TECHNIQUE OF THE DANCE
1—The Positions

NOTE. The modern French dance serves, in this study as the point of departure and the standard of comparison. It would not be possible to explain all of the mechanism in its multitudinous complexity; that task would need the combined labors of twenty ballet-masters. The author has omitted all movements of the modern dance which are not replicas of the Greek steps or related to them.

In order that dancers may the better judge this work, the technical expressions relating to the dance have been retained.

There are many books published on the dance, generally designed for the public which knows little or nothing of the subject, therefore the writer has endeavored to simplify terms and the groupings of subjects and sub-subjects so as to make their explanation more clear.

This is the reason why so much attention has been paid to *the five positions of the legs,* which are designated by the Roman numerals I, II, III, IV, V. The term Positions is also applied to the different aspects of the arms, head, and torso. It will be found advantageous to compare the formulas used with the pictures taken from the painted vases and the reliefs.

The attitudes called *The Attitude* and the *Arabesque* are treated together because they serve as the foundation of innumerable movements.

Following these there is a description of the movements of the arms, head, and torso in order to give them their proper place in the art of design.

The plan of study will correspond to actual lessons on the dance. There will be an analysis of the *tempos* and *steps* (205, 271). There are so many movements to consider that it has been found necessary to group them somewhat arbitrarily according to their gymnastic affinities, presenting the more simple ones first and ending with the more complex. Under one heading will be considered *tempo* in relation to equilibrium, in another category the *time,* the *leaping steps,* the *moment of elevation,* etc., proceeding by selecting and eliminating to get the proper terms of comparison with the Greek dance-steps.

I have called in geometry to my aid, but I must hasten to say that I do not intend to give the pupil the idea that the dance, which is an art, can be reduced to a geometrical formula. I shall speak of *symmetry,* of *contrast* (or *opposition*), of the *projection,* and the *direction* of movement, of the *vertical axis* and the *line of equilibrium.*

I shall not speak at length of the *chains of movements* as used in the modern classic dance, except to indicate the general conditions of their mechanism, coördinate and successive, the *superposition,* the *repetition,* the *alternation,* the *antimony* of the movements and their *determinism.*

I must insist upon the right to use the word *moment* in regard to positions at a certain instant, as, the *characteristic moment,* the *essential moment,* and the *secondary moment.*

All of these terms will be explained in their proper place.

In this manner I shall treat the subject, not in a complete fashion, indeed, but shall introduce, in the study of the classic dance, some ideas as to the sense of decoration of the movements.

This will really be a study of the elements of the dance as exhibited in the paintings and sculptures. The technical terms have been used in speaking of both the modern dance and the ancient.

Finally, like a philosopher, I reserve the right to borrow from science whatever words I need to make my meaning clear.

All that relates to the modern French dance is printed in italics, and all regarding the Greek dance in ordinary type, thus distinguishing between parallel explanations.

85. *Setting aside rhythm, the elements of the dance are the Positions and the Movements.*

86. *A Position is the point of departure or the end of a movement,—the preparation or the conclusion.*

Suppose, for example, a stop of greater or less duration, and which may be very brief. It is therefore opposed to a Movement that need not be defined.

87. *The Positions are distinguished thus:*
Positions of the legs.
Positions of the arms.
Positions of the torso.
Positions of the head.

88. *The only Positions of which the form and the number are regulated with absolute precision are those of the legs. Their rôle is of the greatest importance. They constitute the foundation of all dance-movements.*

POSITIONS OF THE LEGS

A.—Fundamental Positions on the Sole of the Foot.

89. *These are five in number. They are taken on the sole of the foot in such a manner that the weight of the body is carried on the whole sole. The hip and knee must be turned so that the entire leg and foot swing outward. The leg must be held stiff.*

The five Positions of the legs will be designated by the Roman numerals, I, II, III, *IV, V.*

POSITIONS OF THE LEGS

90. I

In the first Position *the heels touch one another* (Fig. 52).

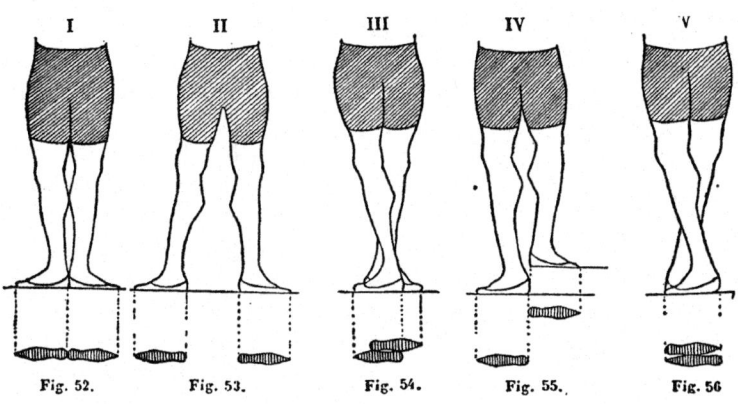

Fig. 52. Fig. 53. Fig. 54. Fig. 55. Fig. 56

91. II

In the second Position *the heels are carried apart the length of one of the feet* (Fig. 53).

92. III

In the third Position *the heel of one foot is set opposite to the instep of the other* (Fig. 54).

93. IV

In the fourth Position *the two feet are placed with the heels in line with each other, but with one foot placed forward of the other, both still turned sidewise, and separated by the length of one foot* (Fig. 55).

94. V

In the fifth Position *the feet are crossed so that the heel of one touches the toe of the other* (Fig. 56).

95. *In joining the five fundamental Positions two varieties of the IV produce the opening or the crossing of the legs.*

The IV open (Fig. 57).

The IV crossed (Fig. 58).

Seen from directly in front *it will be noted that they are different from IV* (Fig. 55).

96. *It goes without saying that* III, *the three* IV *and* V *are all double forms. Examples:*

III (*leg*) *right forward* (Fig. 54),
III (*leg*) *left forward.*

IV facing *right forward* (Fig. 55),
IV facing *left forward.*

97. *Holding the feet sidewise, which looks so strange, and which would be impossible to a person unaccustomed to holding his balance in that position, is one of the first rules of the modern dance. Notwithstanding its odd appearance, it gives to the dancer much stability and suppleness of the feet. It is graceful and always lends a sense of ease in movement, and, when the knees are bent it is possible to advance the foot while keeping the torso vertical, proving that it is a strong position.*

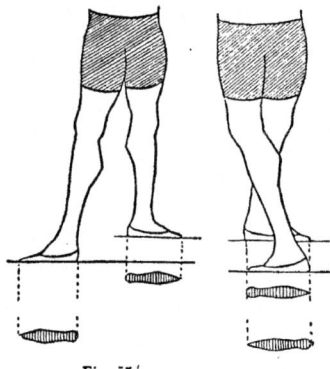

Fig. 57.   Fig. 58.

98. *These forms of fundamental Positions of the legs are the result of experience. The Positions enumerated above are, while simple, all that are needed by the dancer. They correspond to all the exigencies of movement; they fulfil the conditions required for stability; they serve as connections between the successive movements, when the eye of the spectator follows with difficulty the rapid evolutions of the dance; and they make it impossible for the dancer to lose the arrangement of the dance, and are guides to the more complex phases.*

B.—Principal Positions

99. *The* II *and* IV *show the beginning, by lifting one or the other of the legs, of the two Positions derived from them, which are called the* Principal Position of the II *and the* Principal Position of the IV.

POSITIONS OF THE LEGS 59

100.   PRINCIPLE II

Here the dancer, in II fundamental raises one leg laterally, holding the leg at right angle, by means of lifting the hip; this is the Principle Second (Fig. 59).

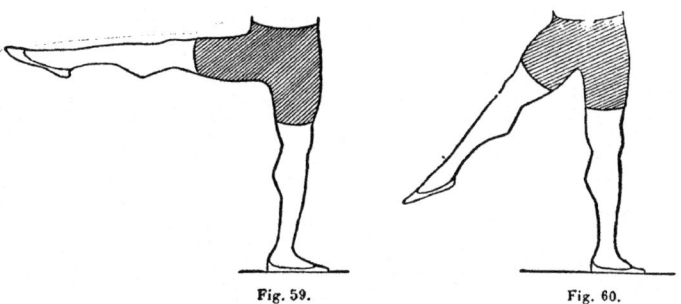

Fig. 59.   Fig. 60.

Here the leg is lifted just half as high as in the preceding, and this is called half-Second, or half-high, or half-Position (Fig. 60).

101.   PRINCIPLE IV

Fig. 61 shows the right leg of the dancer in Principle IV advanced, Fig. 62 shows the same leg in IV backward. The point of departure for both of the Principal Positions is fundamental Position IV: one of the legs being raised from the hip either forward or backward.

Here the leg is not lifted as high, and this is also called the half-Fourth.

C.—POSITIONS ON THE TOE AND ON THE HALE-TOE

102. The fundamental Positions, the Principal Positions, and the half-Positions are held on the sole of the foot, but are also taken on the ball or on the toe.

Throughout all of these modifications the form of the Position remains the same. For example:

Fig. 63: I, the left foot on the ground, the right foot on the half-toe.

Fig. 64: I, *both feet on the half-toe.*
Fig. 65: II, *left foot on the ground, right foot on the toe.*
Fig. 66: II, *both feet on the toe.*
Fig. 67: IV, *crossed on the toe.*
Fig. 68: V, *on the half-toe.*

103. *In carrying, the principal Positions, the half-Positions, the Positions on the half-toe, the Positions on the toe through all their variations, do not vary from the fundamental Positions where the whole sole of the foot is on the ground.*

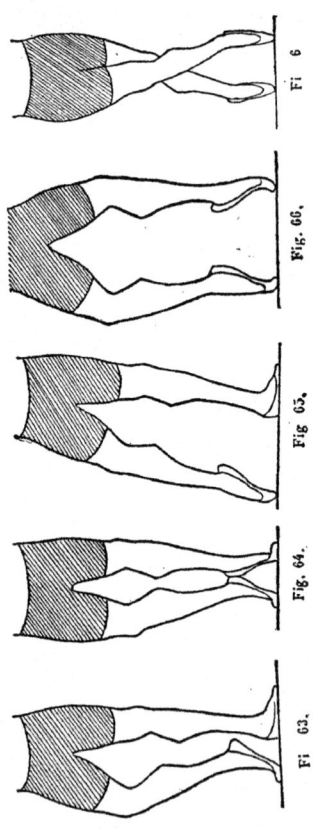

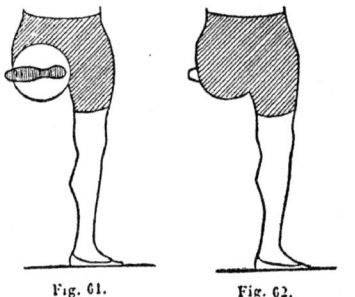

Fig. 61.   Fig. 62.

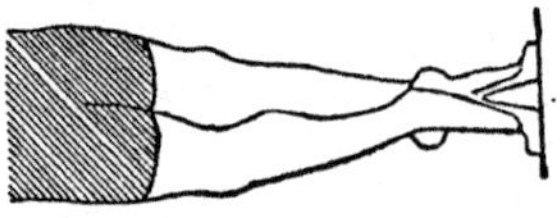

104. The rarest examples prove that the Greek dancers knew how to hold the hip and foot in the lateral position (Figs. 69, 70). But it was not an arbitrary rule imposed upon them (97). In searching the sculptures for equivalents of the modern Positions (86) it will be found that there are certain abstract rules governing the manner of holding the leg; these are both difficult to describe and ungraceful in practice. They present aspects that the primitive artists were opposed to, but which their successors adopted, only to discard at a still later period.

Painters and sculptors copied what they saw, in all its awkwardness and seeming unnaturalness, and the result has been accepted as the work of inexperienced men, who did not appreciate exactness.

105 FIRST POSITION = I

The three dancers (Figs. 72, 73, 74) turn by stamping on the feet (266); they are examples of the feet with heels close together, toes turned out. It is the fundamental form of the first Position, and the sole is on the ground.

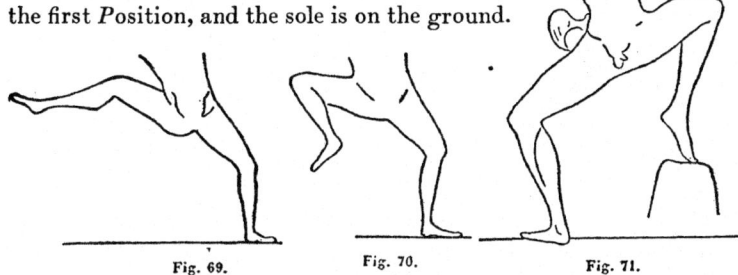

Fig. 69.   Fig. 70.   Fig. 71.

106. The contact of the heels is an essential point in the first Position, therefore a great number of examples have been taken from the sculptures and paintings. The modern dance excludes this pose, the Greek dance admitted it (Figs. 76, 77, 191).

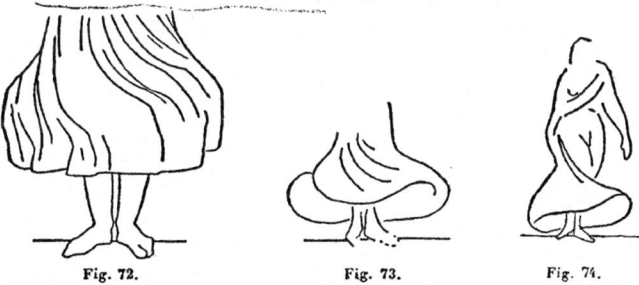

Fig. 72.   Fig. 73.   Fig. 74.

In the admirable archaic statues of women, discovered on the Acropolis in 1889, it is probable, judging from the positions of the legs, that the feet were separated in this manner. One of the figures, intact (Collignon, *Greek Sculpture* I, p. 179), wears red slippers. These women were not really dancers; yet taking the word "dance" in the Greek sense, it may be proper to apply it to these beautiful statues. All of them make the gesture of the tunic (44) with one hand while extending the other. This is not solely a decorative convention, though the legs advance in small steps, somewhat stiffly·

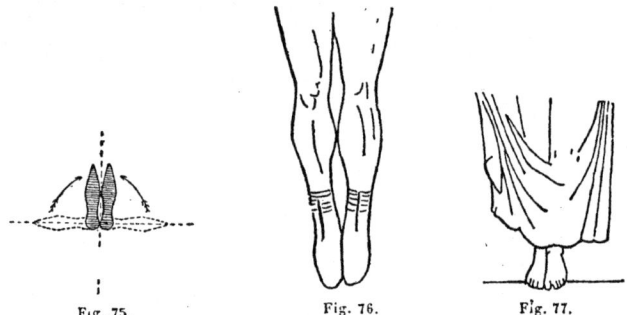

Fig. 75. Fig. 76. Fig. 77.

the attitude would seem to have a religious significance; there is an expression of adoration according to the ritualistic system of gesture. The feet may be held together only by accident.

107.   SECOND POSITION = II

Fig. 78 is a preparation for the II fundamental, which Fig. 79 expresses well, despite the long drapery.

Fig. 80 reproduces a turn on the half-toe, in II.

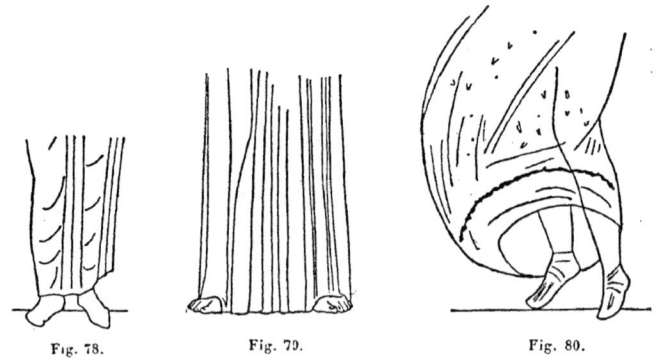

Fig. 78. Fig. 79. Fig. 80.

The Fig. 69 shows a remarkable type of dancer in Principle II (Fig. 59).

POSITIONS OF THE LEGS

108.   FOURTH POSITION = IV

The IV is represented on the vases in a great number of examples. The feet are usually separated, like those of our dancers, but in a variety of ways. It will be seen that Fig. 81, in IV, has the left leg placed with the sole of the foot on the ground, and the right on the half-toe.

Fig. 81.

Fig. 82.

Fig. 83.

The two figures 82 and 83 are in the IV on the half-toe.

109. *The IV crossed* is one of the favorite positions of the Greek

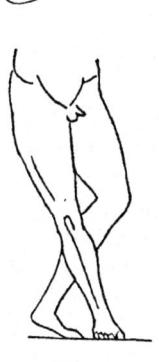
Fig. 84.

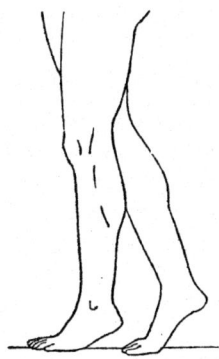
Fig. 85.

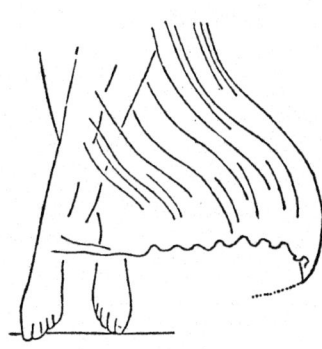
Fig. 86.

dancers, if one may judge by the vast number of representations of it. One may see (Par. 267) the excellence of the mechanism employed by the ancients in the use of the feet in turning by tripping.

Fig. 84: IV crossed, right forward on the sole—left at rear on the half-toe.

Fig. 85: IV crossed, on the half-toe.

Fig. 86: IV, crossed on the toe.

Fig. 87.

110. Perhaps the dancer in Fig. 87 is in the position of the *Principle IV forward* (Fig. 61), but it is not easy to be sure on account of the perspective which hindered the painter from striking out boldly to depict the Position of the Half-fourth (101). The style of design is mediocre but the dance represented is worse: the toe, instead of being held low, is lifted so that the sole of the foot is visible from the front, a most ungraceful pose and one never permitted in the better type of Greek dance any more than in ours (180).

111. Of the III and the V it is difficult to find precise examples. There is something resembling it in a dancer with a tambourine, from a Roman tomb, the figure being now in the School of Beaux-Arts; this dancer is on the toe in V. It is likely that, though executing the entrechat (cut), that figure 318 is in V Preparatory (86, 255).

POSITIONS OF THE ARMS

112. *The action of the arms in the dance differs essentially from that of the legs. The legs give the support, therefore they must conform to rules. The arms enjoy greater independence. The legs, by reason of their functions, must not stray outside the limits of equilibrium; the arms interpret the nuances and the expression of the dance, being plastic. The result is that the arms are carried in an infinite variety of poses. There are certain fundamental Positions of the arms as well as the legs.*

These, for brevity, are called Positions of the arms.

They are logically separated into two groups: 1, the symmetrical, *and* 2, the contrasting (or opposing) (114, 115).

113. *The arms are not always held stiffly; sometimes they hang*

POSITIONS OF THE ARMS

by their weight along the side of the body (Fig. 88). *From being lightly held at the side of the body, they are lifted, forming an arc, outward, from the shoulder to the finger-tips. It will be seen that the fingers, grouped around the palm of the hand, are themselves in opposition to the thumb. The wrist, much more than the elbow, is bent at an angle, by which means the dancer obtains a characteristic effect* (Fig. 93).

The hand, in most modern French dances, does not play any special rôle, though it cannot be said to remain inert. It has one

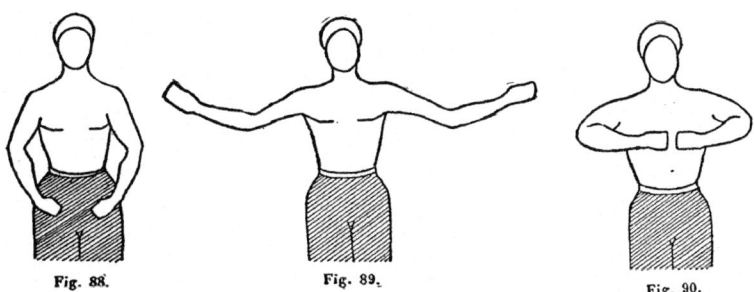

Fig. 88. Fig. 89. Fig. 90.

function,—to provide a finish for the arm. The fingers are always grouped in a manner worthy of praise.

One reason for the liberty allowed the dancer in the use of the arms is that holding them is one of the most difficult things connected with the dance.

The images reproduced above and on the next page represent the principal movements of the arms of our dancers.

114. Symmetrical Positions of the Arms.—*The two arms are held in these Positions with relation to the body.*

Fig. 88: Arms in repose, supported.
Fig. 89: Arms extended, without stiffness.
Fig. 90: Arms bent at elbow and held on the breast.
Fig. 91: Arms circled above the head.
Fig. 92: Arms high and outward.
Fig. 93: Arms in "lyre position."
Fig. 94: Arms at waist.

115. Contrasting Positions of the Arms.—*The two arms are held, in contrasting positions, in relation to the body.*

Each of these positions is, of course, double in form, as may be noted in Figs. 96, 97, 98, 99 and 101.

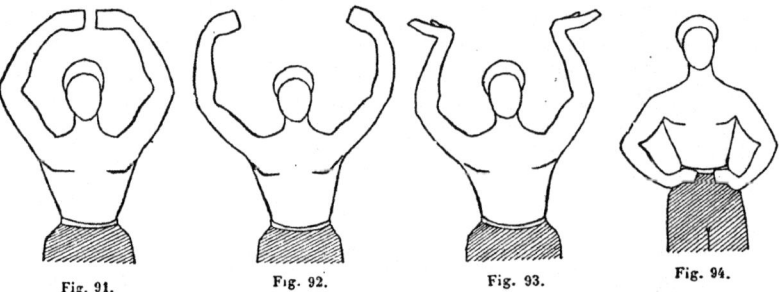

Fig. 91.   Fig. 92.   Fig. 93.   Fig. 94.

Fig. 95, A and B: one arm high, one arm extended.

Fig. 96: One arm curved over the breast, one arm held out horizontally.

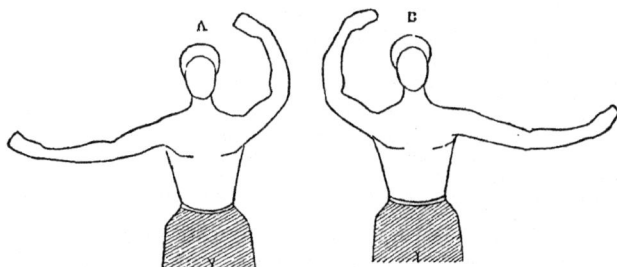

Fig. 95.

Fig. 97: One arm on the hip, the other held high.

Fig. 98: The two arms curved toward the same side.

Fig. 99: One arm curved high, the other low.

The Arabesque positions of the arms are positions in opposition, as seen on figures from the most remote times (170).

116. *Often the dancer plays with her skirts, which gives oppor-*

POSITIONS OF THE ARMS

tunity for many positions of the arms. Examples, Figs. 100 *and* 101: *the first is a symmetrical position; the second is a contrasting one. The position may be termed* restrained, *to distinguish it from free positions of the arms.*

117. Our dances called gymnastic are more imitative, there-

Fig. 96.

Fig. 97.

fore the arms move according to a system. The figures from 88 to 101 prove this.

The Greek dances, on the contrary, being both plastic and mimetic, use the arms so that they assist both the nuances of

Fig. 98.

Fig. 99.

gesture and add to the decoration. The dance, as has already been said, has a language of its own. It may be said, at this point, that, in study, we separate the postures that have a dramatic meaning from those that are purely decorative.

118. The Greek dancers did not, like ours, constantly move the arms in circles; they had no fear of rigidity, or of sharp angles. It is true, however, that in the noble dances the arms were moved in elegant curves; the statues tell us so, and it is not to be believed that the artists always sought their inspiration in themselves.

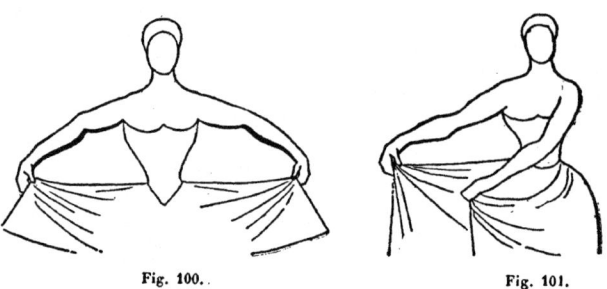

Fig. 100.   Fig. 101.

Consider the arms of the women on the Parthenon frieze; observe how Phidias clings to one rule (113). The arms of these Athenians never fall by their own weight along the side of the body,—they are lightly held up, grasping the folds of the tunics so that the garments fall in plaits like organ-pipes.

119. The hand of the Greek dancer is always active; it is not, like

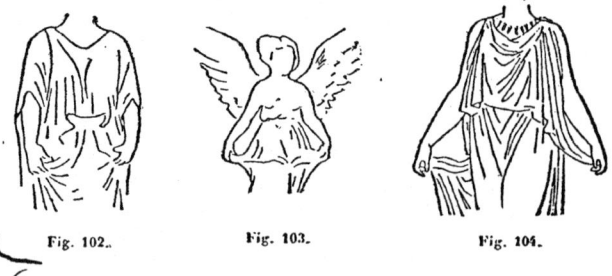

Fig. 102.   Fig. 103.   Fig. 104.

ours, content with a passive rôle (113); the principal interpreter of the mimetic language, it holds a sovereign importance in the dance of the Greeks.

120. Symmetrical Positions of the Hands.—The kinds of symmetrical positions have already been enumerated.

POSITIONS OF THE ARMS 69

Fig. 105

Fig. 106.

Fig. 107.

Fig. 102 corresponds to Fig. 88.
Fig. 107 corresponds to Fig. 100.

70 TECHNIQUE OF THE DANCE

Figs. 103, 104, 105, 106 are the intermediary Positions between Figs. 102 and 107.

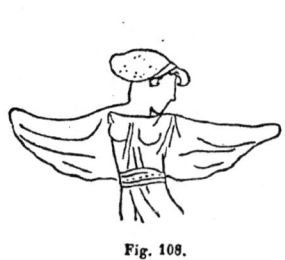

Fig. 108.

Fig. 109.

121. The Figs. 108 and 109 correspond to Fig. 89.

Fig. 110.

Fig. 111.

Fig. 112

Figs. 110, 111, 112 show the same Position, *rigid*.

POSITIONS OF THE ARMS 71

122. The dancers in Figs. 113 and 114 have the hand pressed

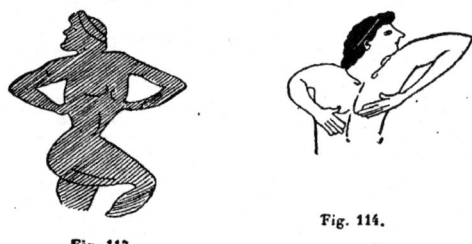

Fig. 113.   Fig. 114.

to the breast, but they resemble the figures with the hand crossed over the breast (Fig. 90).

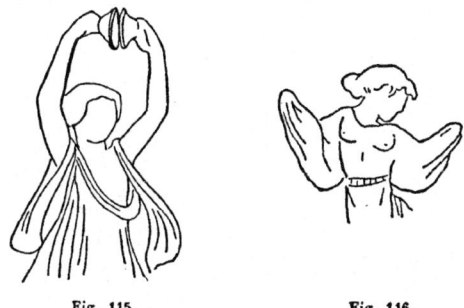

Fig. 115.   Fig. 116.

123. Fig. 115 corresponds to Fig. 91.

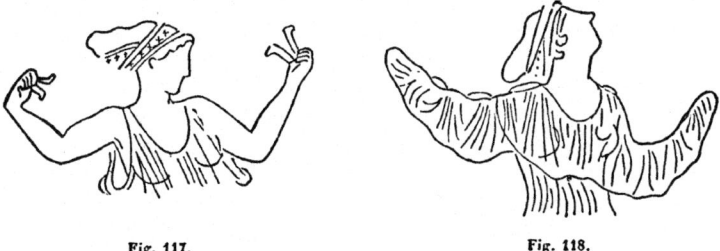

Fig. 117.   Fig. 118.

124. The Positions of Figs. 116, 117, 118 visibly tend toward that of Fig. 92.

Fig. 589 may be considered a transformation of the same pose as Fig. 92, and Fig. 119 is an exaggeration of the same form.

Fig. 119.   Fig. 120.

125. Fig. 120 corresponds to Fig. 93.

126. Figs. 121 and 122 correspond to Fig. 94.

Fig. 121.   Fig. 122.

127. These are some symmetrical Positions of the arms which belong to the Greek dance.

Fig. 123.   Fig. 124.

Arms extended outward (Figs. 123, 124).

POSITIONS OF THE ARMS 73

Arms extended forward, closer together (Figs. 125, 417).

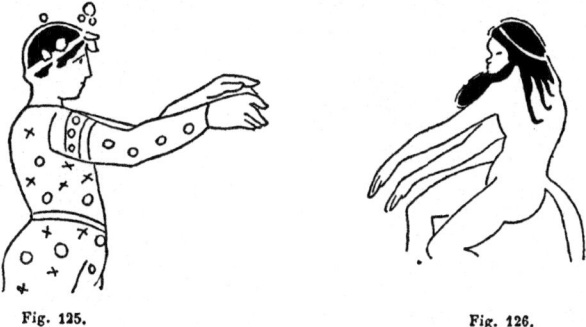

Fig. 125.   Fig. 126.

128. Arms extended downward, thumbs down (Figs. 126, 127 128, A).

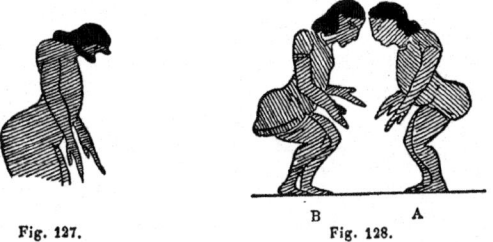

Fig. 127.   B   A
             Fig. 128.

Arms extended, thumb held high (Fig. 128, B).
129. Arms advanced, one open (Figs. 129, 130, 131).

Fig. 129.   Fig. 130.

130. Arms backward (Fig. 132).

131. Dancer who makes the gesture of Adoration (Fig. 133). An interpretation of perspective found again on Fig. 2.

Fig. 131.   Fig. 132.

132. Contrasting (or Opposing) Positions of the Arms.—Comparisons with the modern dance:

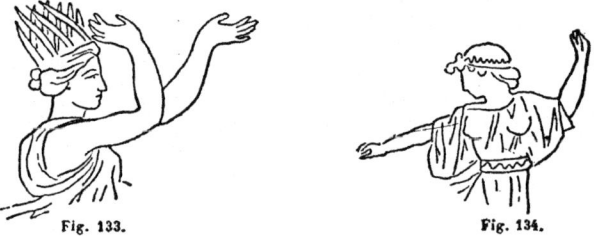

Fig. 133.   Fig. 134.

Fig. 134 corresponds to Fig. 95, A.
Fig. 482, by correcting the perspective, is seen to be of the same

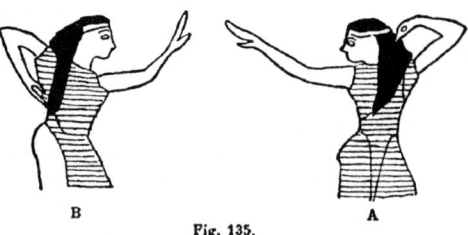

B   A
Fig. 135.

type. It is probable, despite the clumsy appearance, the position, turning with the castanets, is to be read in the same way.

There is only a remote resemblance between Fig. 286 and 95, B.

The Figs. 135, A, and 187 are transformations of the type of Fig. 95.

133. The Fig. 136 is something like Fig. 96.

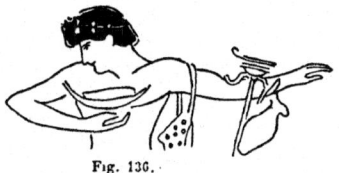
Fig. 136.

134. The hand on the hip is characteristic of the type of Fig. 97, as may be seen from Figs. 137, 138, 139, A and B.

Fig. 137.   Fig. 138.
C   B
Fig. 139.

When the arms are enveloped in the mantle they are generally back of the torso (Figs. 359, 447, A, 451).

76   TECHNIQUE OF THE DANCE

Sometimes the hand passes across the back (Figs. 140, 141).

Fig. 140.   Fig. 141.

Fig. 142.   Fig. 143.   Fig. 144.

135. Fig. 98 corresponds to Figs. 142, 143, 144 and 208.

Fig. 145.   Fig. 146.

136. Figs. 145, 146, 147, 148, 149, 150 belong to type of 99.

POSITIONS OF THE ARMS

Fig. 147. Fig. 148.
Fig. 149. Fig. 150.

137. Greek dancers who gesticulated with a veil (Figs. 458, 459), employed it much as our dancers do and presented the same aspect.

138. Contrasting (or opposed) positions proper to the Greek dance:

Fig. 151. Fig. 152. Fig. 153.

The gesture of the Pourer (52) is more or less transformed (Figs. 151, 152, 153, 584, 590). The latter represents a person playing with castanets.

139. The gesture with the veil (Figs 3, 447, B, 154).

Fig. 154

140. The gesture of the lifted arm is ritual and religious in principle (Figs. 155, 156, 157).

Fig. 155.   Fig. 156.   Fig. 157.

141. The gesture of the tunic is a dancing gesture: the Figs. 33, 50, 155, etc., show this gesture in its simple form. It is double in Figs. 102, 103, 104, 105 and 106, and is made with the two arms in symmetry.

POSITIONS OF THE ARMS

142. Gesture termed Bacchic because it is proper to Satyrs, Menades, and the companions of Komos, all of whom are called bacchants. Their characteristic aspect is sufficiently indicated by

Fig. 158.　　　　　Fig. 159.

Figs. 158, 159 and 160. It is a grotesque position, in which the hand is held back, the wrist often turned so that the palm is outward, and the thumb is held high (Fig. 160).

Fig. 160.

143. There are many differing types of positions, symmetrical and contrasting, to be found in the character-dances (Figs. 171, 178, 179, 180, 181, 460, 480, etc.)

144. The Chironomy.—The Greek dance is, essentially, dramatic, and the hand is, therefore, nearly always active. With our modern dancers it is simply an implement to move in pretty curves. The ancient dancers were more independent, and used their fingers to express the complicated meanings of the dance-language, to which the key is lost, but of which a great number of signs remain.

The word chironomy, as applied to pantomime, had, originally, a meaning that was perfectly clear. Plato and Xenophon use it to characterize the movements of the hand, and attribute a certain value to the expressions. The play of the hands is an element introduced into the dance from the earliest times, and developed until it outshone all other, except the foot-movements, in importance.

Fig. 161.

The study of the hand is not included in our dancing-lessons, because the modern classic dance excludes all of the mimetics. There are a few positions of the hand taught, but they are not considered as of dramatic value, and are entirely separated from dramatic expression.

145. Observe that, when the hand of the Greek dancer assumes a rôle that is simply passive and decorative, it takes on much the same attitude as the hands of our modern dancers: the fingers are grouped without touching, the middle finger is opposed to the thumb (Figs. 155, 161). The beautiful bronze dancers, discovered at Herculaneum, show this detail worked out with absolute precision. Few of the sculptured figures furnish as good an example of the plastic rôle of the hand and fingers. Fig. 138 shows the left hand speaking, the hand is in process of being transformed from a passive to an active rôle.

Fig. 162.

146. One of the types which is the most ancient is the flat hand, with the palm turned out (Figs. 129, 162, 163, 164). Flat hand, horizontal (Fig. 165).

147. *The index finger separated from the others* dates from the fourth century B. C. and is one of the motifs used in *dactylology* (Figs. 166, 167, 168, 169). It is interesting to see how similar the pose of the fingers is in the charming painted figure (Fig. 170)

POSITIONS OF THE ARMS 81

Fig. 163.

and the bronze of the Roman period (171), which is, quite evidently, a caricature.

Fig. 164.   Fig. 165.

Fig. 166.   Fig. 167.

148. *Body bent to the side.* To the left (Figs. 187, 188, 441, a gesture used principally by bacchants, and is of the fifth and

82   TECHNIQUE OF THE DANCE

Fig. 168.   Fig. 169.

Fig. 170.   Fig. 171.

fourth centuries B. C. It is rarely found (Fig. 172). Fig. 173 may be called a later type of the same form. The Figs. 174 and

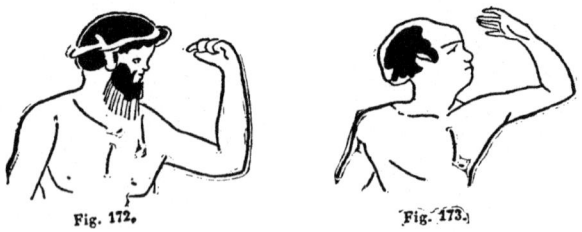

Fig. 172.   Fig. 173.

175 are worthy of notice in the manner in which the hand is lifted, the index finger being detached from the others (147). It is the

POSITIONS OF THE ARMS 83

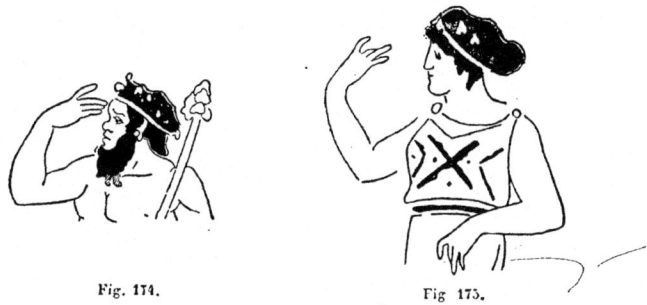

Fig. 174.   Fig. 175.

same as Fig. 176, which represents a hierodule of the Hellenistic period, and shows the diffusion and the transformation of the gesture.

Fig. 176.   Fig. 177.

Fig 178   Fig. 179.

149. Figs. 178, 179, 180, 181 reproduce exceptional positions of the hand and fingers, applied to character dances. The gesture executed with the right hand by the four men in Fig. 277, and by

Fig. 180.   Fig. 181.

the right hand of the dancer represented in Fig. 278 are purely grotesque.

POSITIONS OF THE BODY

150. *Positions of the body, where the legs do not move, are five in number. Between two of these are some that are double.*

I. Body erect (Fig. 182). *This Position, which is one of repose, in which the dancer stands straight and firmly, without stiffness, with the chest well forward.*

II. Here the body is bent to the side (Fig. 183). *This Position is double, that is, it can be taken with the Body bent either to the right or the left.*

III. Body turning at the shoulder (Fig. 184). *The Shoulders turn so that the torso is facing in the direction in which the legs appear in profile. The rotation is about one-eighth of a circle. It may be made toward either side.*

IV. Body bending forward (Fig. 185).

V. Body bending backward (Fig. 186).

151. The Positions of the Body, being determined by the structure of the body, are the same among the dancers of all times. But by incessant use, the two extremes,—*the torso bent forward* and the opposite position, the *torso bent backward*, have become the predominant characteristics of the Greek dance.

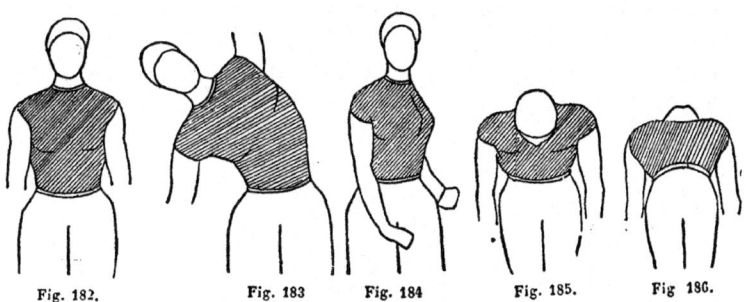

Fig. 182.   Fig. 183.   Fig. 184.   Fig. 185.   Fig 186.

152. *The body of the dancer erect.* This position is one of repose, and is represented by the dancers of Herculaneum (Figs. 138, 155, 161) who perfectly illustrate the rule.

Fig. 187.   Fig. 188.

153. *Body bent to the side.* To the left (Figs. 187, 188, 441, 472). To the right (Figs. 189, 190, 286, 470).

154. *Body bending at shoulder.* To the right (Figs. 438, 439).

To the left (Figs. 177, 538). In these two figures the **Body bends** both sidewise at the shoulder and to the right.

155. B*ody bending forward* (Figs. 411, 413, 417, 418, 427, B, 469).

156. B*ody bending back* (Figs. 191, 193, 154, 171, 369, 494, B). The dancer (Fig. 193),

Fig. 189.

Fig. 190.

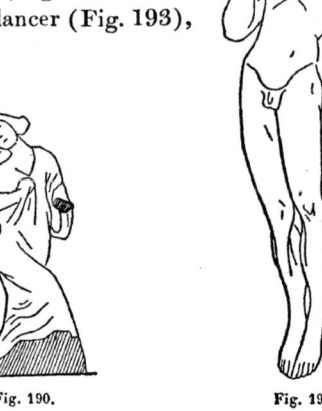

Fig. 191.

who twists her body so strangely, is one of the bacchic dancers who

Fig. 192.

were so given over to the orgiastic frenzy that it was really a matter for pathologists, had such a science existed then. Dr. Meige has not hesitated to assert that

Fig. 193.

this representation and others very much like it indicate a nervous crisis.

157. *The body bending forward and the body bending back*, are, without any reservations, then, exclusively the positions of the bacchic dancers, who play an important rôle in the Dionysian dance.

POSITIONS OF THE HEAD

158. *Adice, author of "The Gymnastics of the Dramatic dance," says that there are five Positions of the Head, corresponding exactly to the positions of the Body.*

I. Head facing (Fig. 194).
II. Head bent to the side (Fig. 195).
III. Head turned (Fig. 196). *Both of the last two Positions are double. This Position is taken by first turning the Head facing, then moving it to the side one-fourth of a circle to the left or right.*

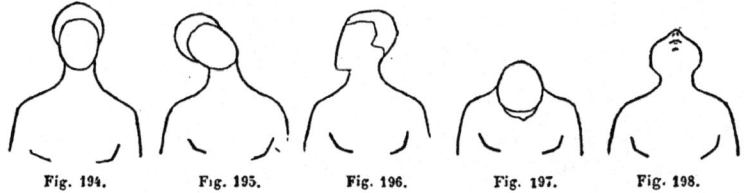

Fig. 194.   Fig. 195.   Fig. 196.   Fig. 197.   Fig. 198.

It is difficult to turn it more than that, owing to the tension of the muscles of the neck. In general, it cannot be turned more than one-eighth of a circle.

IV. Head bent forward (Fig. 197).
V. Head bent back (Fig. 198).

159. The Positions of the Head, like those of the Torso, are determined by physiology which does not change greatly with the passing of centuries. The last two mentioned, the H*ead bending forward or back*, while common in the Greek dance are seldom seen in our own.

160. *Head bent to the side* (Figs. 450, 457), right or left.

161. *Head turning* to right or left (Figs. 468, 498, B, 521). The head turned completely, as in Fig. 485, is a comical exaggeration, but, of course, quite impossible.

162. *Head bending forward* (Figs. 451, 461, 476, 483, 575, 577).

163. *Head bending back* (Figs. 352, 449, 505).

164. An admirable vase in the Louvre, of which Fig. 199 shows a fragment, furnishes a valuable example of the study of the *P*ositions of the head which are characteristic: *Head bent forward and Head bent back*. The three dancers are Nymphs. The one in the center makes the dancing gesture of the tunic (44), presenting the head

Fig. 199.

bent backward and in profile, while the body is in full face. It is a convention of design that needs but one explanation, the facility with which it may be carried out. This ceramist has substituted for the displeasing drawing a charming silhouette (Fig. 198).

165. An examination of innumerable examples of dances shows the favorite formula to have been:

Position IV crossed, for the legs (109).

Body bent forward or back (155,156).

Head bent forward or back (162, 163).

The bending backward of the Torso and Head is exaggerated in the bacchic dances.

166. Combination of the Positions.—The manner of treatment of the different Positions of the Body, Arms, Head and Legs has up to this place been as though each were independent of the others. They are now to be considered as parts of a whole, combined to give a great number of variations.

The following list gives the principal ones:

Fundamental positions of the legs, soles of feet on the ground..............................	13
Principal positions of legs with half-positions..	8
Positions on the half-toe.....................	13
Positions on the toe........................	13
	47
Positions of the arms, symmetrical...........	10
Positions of arms, contrasting...............	20
	30
Positions of the body......................	7
Positions of the head......................	7

The sum of these typical positions, reduced to a minimum is $47 + 30 + 7 + 7 = 91$.

Divide these into four groups, the positions of the legs being represented by M: the positions of the arms by N: the positions of the body and the head by P and Q. Every one of the positions of groups M, N, P, and Q may be combined with the positions of the other three groups, and each of these may be combined with the remaining groups.

MN + MP + MP + NP + PQ
 + NMP + NMQ + MPQ + NPQ
 + MNPQ.

Replacing these letters with the figure which they represent, we get:

$47 \times 30 + 47 \times 7 + 47 \times 7 + 30 \times 7 + 30 \times 7 + 7 + 7 + 47 \times 30 \times 7 + 47 \times 30 \times 7 + 47 \times 7 \times 7 + 30 \times 7 \times 7 + 47 \times 30 \times 7 \times 7 = 95140$ possible combinations.

Not all of these combinations would be good, and a great number of them are purely gymnastic and of no use to the dancer.

167. *Paragraphs 63-70 indicate the rôle played by the opposition in the Run and the Walk, and some of the contrasts so produced between the legs and the arms. These oppositions are instinctively produced in order to maintain the equilibrium. The dancer thus escapes being thrown out of balance, a thing that the artificial conditions of the ballet render extremely likely to happen. Opposition between the different parts of the body may be called a constant readjustment of weight among the members, and was so used by Noverre, who revived the dance in the last century, and by whom the principle was considered essential to the stability as well as to the effect. In a word, the oppositions advised by Noverre are those dictated by nature.*

It is clear that Opposition does not reduce the dance to a purely mechanical movement, like the walk and the run. The principle is the same: the application is very different. The Opposition, as used in the dance, becomes a special technique of esthetics.

168. *Of the different ways in which the Body, Head, Legs and Arms may be combined, some are good and some are not: how is the student to know? To answer this question would take many pages of figures, and, even then, the answer would be incomplete. The art of the dance escapes dead formulas. Its special grammar can be learned only by using it in practice. It is possible to note only a few of the more important combinations.*

Among these are:

The Attitude and the Arabesque.

169. The Attitude.—*This word, in the technical language of dancers, has a signification which is traditional and precise. It designates a Position on one leg, usually on the half-toe. The other leg, bent at the knee, is raised from the hip. The vertical line of equilibrium passes through the shoulder* (298).

The two principal forms of the Attitude are:

The Attitude outward, *in which the body is facing the spectator.*

The Attitude crossed, *in which the body is presented with the shoulder facing the spectator* (Fig. 201). *This produces in per-*

spective the appearance of crossed legs. In both cases the legs are in the same position.

170. **The Arabesque.**—Derived from the Attitude, the Arabesque is a special combination of positions of the legs, the Arms and the Torso, quite different from those already noted. It is characterized by a tension of the members which gives length, while preserving the same outward arc, and holding the body in equilibrium. The body of the dancer is held, as in the Attitude, on one leg, with the other lightly lifted so that it describes a long curve in relation to the body.

Fig. 200.,   Fig. 201.

Fig. 202 shows the pose in the outward form, and 203 in the crossed form.

171. The grace of the dancer is intimately connected with the conditions of equilibrium, which are latent. When a pose looks

Fig. 202.,   Fig. 203.

uneasy, it ceases to be pleasing. The secret of grace consists in knowing how to apply constantly the laws of stability. The Greeks had this knowledge, and used it just as our dancers do.

Observe the manner in which the masters of the modern French dance, Noverre and Blasis, take advantage of the law of opposition. Then note how the Greeks used it.

Fig. 204.

There is a graceful and beautiful answer to that question in the charming child of Tanagra, an Eros dancer (Fig. 204).

The left leg and the right arm are advanced to the same degree.

The body is lightly bent backward, the head lightly bent forward.

The head is turned to the right, the side on which the leg is at the rear.

The directions show a diagonal line through Arms and Legs, and through Legs and Head; the direction of the Head and Torso are in opposition. The little Eros uses the code of Noverre and Blasis, like an accomplished dancer.

172. An example of the rope-dancing Satyr of Pompeii (Fig. 205) shows no application of the same principle. He advances the arm and leg on the same side at the same time: this is not the way a true dancer holds himself. It is an expression of the joyous companion of Bacchus who gambols dangerously along under the effect of copious libations: the effect is correctly interpreted.

This may be proved by looking at a vase painted with red figures (Fig. 600), in which the dancers seem to have adopted a cult of unequilibrium. There is a strong resemblance in position, between the Satyr of Pompeii and the more pleasing types who play on the vases. The painting exhibits a good citizen, who is somewhat awkward, who dances because he likes to do so, and is untroubled by the fine dis-

Fig. 205.

tinctions of the art. Here there is the same tendency to put the same side forward, and the head following them: the figure, therefore, lacks stability.

This kind of representation is rare. More often (leaving the archaic work out of consideration), the law of Opposition is instinctively applied by the Greek dancers. Noverre and Blasis did not copy the figures on the vases and reliefs: they held that the best form of design resulted from the *crossing in equilibrium* which results in stability as well as grace.

173. It has been remarked that, in the earlier centuries of Greek art, the painting was in advance of the sculpture. The dry-point and the pencil of the ceramic artists, who copied the great painters, had already created masterpieces, while the statues still retained the stiffness of the archaic period. The joyous dancers of Komos, the Satyrs and the Menades, marvelously supple, give themselves up to the eccentricities of delirious dances at an epoch when the sculptors had not yet learned to separate the arms and legs of their figures from the body (10, 11, 14, 15). They do not present the poses of the more elegant dance. When their statues walk, the arm falls heavily along the side of the body, in a see-saw motion opposed to the legs. Though ignorant of the law of Opposition, they applied it in the matter of arms and legs, as a necessary concomitant of equilibrium, and this is at the same time one of the secrets of the dance.

It is only in the fifth century B. C. that suppleness which makes for eurhythmy begins to find its way into statuary. The Nike of Pæonios, though much mutilated, shows the application of the principles of elegance which the ballet-masters, without the aid of instantaneous photography, discovered from nature.

The name Athenian is given justly to all the masterpieces of Greek sculpture. "The ancient statues are the monuments of the antique dance." . . . The sculptors sought to render the most beautiful movements freely and with elegance, in bronze and marble.

174. Throughout all periods of the Greek dance the Positions, as a whole, are analogous to the Attitude (169). These three examples, taken respectively from the first half of the fifth century

94   TECHNIQUE OF THE DANCE

B. C., the Hellenistic period, and the Roman period, show three varieties of the same form.

Fig. 206: *Attitude, crossed.*
Fig. 207: *Attitude, crossed,* bent back.
Fig. 208: *Attitude,* body bent back and sidewise.

Fig. 206.   Fig. 207.   Fig. 208.

Compare with Figs. 200 and 201 and note the difference in perspective.

(These figures are not the best examples of the Arabesque; the modern type has not been surpassed by any antique figures so far discovered.)

TECHNIQUE OF THE DANCE
II. Preparatory Exercises

175. *So far the dancer has been considered motionless. Separate notice has been taken of each pose, but nothing has been said about the means by which the transition from one to the other is effected.*

The Positions and the tempos create their own limitation, like a pendulum, they are limited to the two extremes of space between which they may move.

176. *The dancer is now familiar with the Positions which will be spoken of as the statics of the art: next comes the study of motion, in which it will be necessary to move according to certain formulas, and, by degrees, acquire the suppleness and the force needed in the*

Fig. 209.

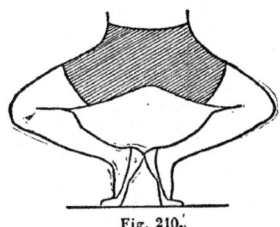
Fig. 210.

articulations. These special gymnastics may be compared to those of the pianist, who must practice many hours each day to make the fingers agile and strong.

The first exercises for the dancer are called the Preparatory for the legs, *and are:* Bending, Separating, Striking, *and the* Circles with the Legs.

177. Bending and Holding.—*The pupil bends in each of the five Positions, on both feet and on one foot. Examples:*

Bending in I on the sole. (Fig. 209.)
Bending in I on the half-toe. (Fig. 210.)
Bending in II on the sole. (Fig. 211.)
Bending in Principle II on the supporting leg. (Fig. 212.)
Bending in Principle IV on the supporting leg (Fig. 213.)

Bending in V on the sole. (Fig. 214.)

Immediately after bending, rise to the same Position and repeat the exercise, each time bending lower and lower.

178. The exercises to make the knees supple are the same simple

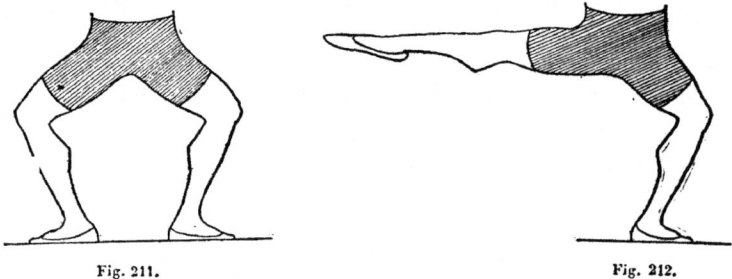

Fig. 211.   Fig. 212.

and natural ones that were used in ancient Greece, as may be seen from the figure of a grotesque dancer taken from a Corinthian bowl. (Fig. 215.) He bends in Principle II, with legs widely separated, in

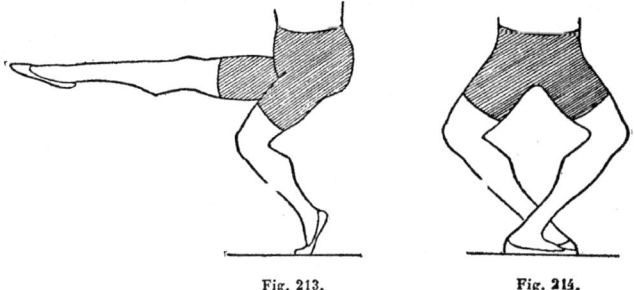

Fig. 213.   Fig. 214.

a burlesque attitude of defence, with both feet planted on the ground, as our modern dancers stand. (Fig. 211.)

179. Separating.—*The active leg is separated from the supporting leg, of which the toe rests on the ground, the rest of the foot being somewhat lifted. The movement may be made forward, at the side, or the back.*

Suppose the dancer stands in one or the other of the Positions III or V, right leg forward; he carries the right leg in IV advanced on the toe, or the left leg in IV to the rear on the toe, or one or the other of the legs in II on the toe, he executes thus the Separation on the ground.

Example of the Separation in II on the ground (Figs. 217, 1, 2):

Assume that the dancer, standing in III or V, carries one leg to half II *(Fig. 60), or to Principle* II *(Fig. 69), or to half IV, or to Principle IV (Figs. 61, 62), he executes thus the Separation in half* II, *or in Principle* II, *etc.*

Fig. 215.

The rule for the Separation is, as may be seen from the preceding, easy to state. The rule following is particularly applicable.

180. **Toe Low.**—When the dancer lifts one leg, he holds the toe down and stiff, the movement beginning in the hip, which lifts the upper leg: the movement extends to the knee, which, in turn, lifts the foot, heel first, the toe being the last to leave the ground. This succession of movements is logical: it is a transmission of movement from high to low. The photographs, 8, 9, 10, 11, 12, of Plate II, show the application of the mechanism used by the dancer during the Separation of V, right advanced, to principle IV outward (186).

Fig. 216.

181. Fig. 81 shows the right leg of a Satyr *separated on the ground* in IV advanced.

Fig. 279 gives an example of the *Separation in half IV*.

Fig. 69 is a *separation of the right leg in Principle* II.

182. The Greek dancers, as well as the modern, had a horror of the lifted toe. When the separation is held for any length of time, the *toe is held downward*. When the leg is lifted, the movement is transmitted from high to low, as with our dancers. (Figs. 69, 70.)

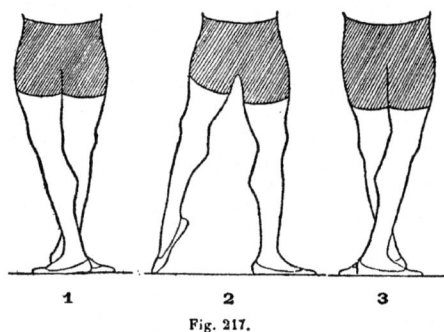

Fig. 217.

It is rarely that the rule of the *toe low* is not observed. The exceptions (Figs. 87, 216, 469) are explained by the intention to caricature, or a mistake in the drawing. The scene from which the Satyr (Fig. 216) is taken represents the triumph of a grotesque Hercules. The hero, flanked by Victory, is mounted on a chariot drawn by four Centaurs. The Satyr is frisking along ahead, wearing a mask, and brandishing two torches, and caring nothing at all for rhythm.

Fig. 218.

The painter who reproduces his ridiculous antics shows the whole sole of his foot, a thing that no dancer would dream of doing. Fig. 87 is taken from a vase of the degenerate period, and is in poor style. In regard to Fig. 489, it is in flat contradiction to all the other images of the same series, which uniformly present the foot with the toe down.

These three exceptions only serve to prove the rule.

183. The Strike (Battement).—*To execute the* Battement, *quickly move the active leg away from the supporting leg, and then bring them together again.*

The three principal types of Battement *are: The* Battement *on the ground, the* Battement *held, and the Grand* Battement.

184. Striking the Ground.—*The leg in the* III *or* V, *is advanced or put back* (96), *separates to* II *on the toe, and returns to its original position* (Fig. 217) *in this order:* $\overline{-1, 2}$—$\overline{1, 2,}$—$\overline{1, 2}$. *The leg that commences forward finishes in the rear* (Fig. 217), *recommences at the rear, and finishes forward* (*in the order*, 1, 2, 3), *the second part of the movement being* 3, 2, 1. *The successive movements are* $\overline{1, 2, 3, 2,}$ $\overline{1, 2, 3, 2,}$ $\overline{1, 2, 3, 2, 1}$. . . . . . .

185. Battement Held.—*This differed from the preceding in that the upper part of the leg is held, continuously, in a lateral position; the foot that strikes does not touch the ground, and it crosses the supporting leg, toe high, drooping from the instep. The upper leg rests motionless, only the lower leg being moved. Taking the images in their order,* 1, 2, 3, 2, 1, *gives an exact idea of* striking *on the instep, alternated* over *and* over. (*Note back and forward.*) *Chains, in series like this, higher each time,*

$$\overline{1, 2, 3, 2,} \ \overline{1, 2, 3, 2,} \ \overline{1, 2, 3, 2, 1.}$$

186. Grand Battement.—*Often serves as the finish of* Principle II *or Principle* IV, *and is called* Battement *in* II *or* Baitement *in* IV

Plate II *is a photographic analysis of the* Grand Battement *in fourth outward, on the ground.* (*Duration of the movement*, 4/5 *of a second.*)

Image I *shows the extreme limit of the Position. The leg is wholly held in Principle IV outward.*

Image 2: *The toe is inflected, the leg lowered, carrying the knee.*

Image 3: *The leg is lowered more and more: the toe is pointed toward the ground; the upper leg is held so that it produces an angle with the knee.*

Image 4: *The toe touches the ground.*

Image 5: *The angle formed by the knee is straightened.*
Image 6: *The heel is posed in V right forward.*
Image 7: *The leg is held.*
Image 8: *Pause between the two Battements, corresponding to the V fundamental.*
Image 9: *The upper leg is lightly lifted, followed by the lower leg, and, lastly, by the heel. The toe rests on the ground.*
Image 10: *The foot quits the ground at the toe.*
Image 11: *The upper leg is elevated more and more: the toe is low: the lower leg is held back so that an angle is produced at the knee.*
Image 12: *The angle is effaced. The leg comes back to the same position that is presented in Image 1.*

The pupil should read the series in the following order: 8, 9, 10, 11, 12, 1, 2, 3, 4, 5, 6, 7. The images 8, 9, 10, 11, 12 I correspond to the Separation of the right leg in Principle IV outward and the images 2, 3, 4, 5, 6, 7 a high and low movement which brings the leg back to V advanced, held on the ground.

187. This analysis shows the rule applied to the mechanism of the Separation (180). So in Separation the movement is made from high to low, with the leg and with the toe, inasmuch as the upper leg is lifted first, and the last member to leave the ground is the toe. The movement is then made in an inverted form, the motion transmitted from the toe to the hip, the toe being flexed first, with the leg low, then the rest of the leg follows.

188. The preceding should give a good idea of the Grand Battement, or Strike. The leg is stiff on the ground, in the III or the V, forward or back, carried in Principle II or in Principle IV, facing, outward, crossed, in advance, or to the rear, and returns to its initial Position. The second plate proves that the leg that executes the Battement is held in two extreme positions, and that in the interval it is more or less bent.

189. The illustrations of the Battement indicate the *essential moments*, which are: the initial Position, the extreme Position, and the final Position, which are indicated by the three figures (284) Figs. 217 and 218. The sculptures give little assistance in the matter of successions, nor do we demand it of them. It suffices, in order to

reconstruct the Battement, to find the two essential moments; they correspond to the two extremes noted in regard to the modern dance (285).

Fig. 219 justifies us in supposing that the dancer's leg, raised outward, in Principle II, will re-approach the supporting leg, thus executing the Grand Battement. Comparisons between Fig. 219 and Fig. 12 of the second plate show a close analogy.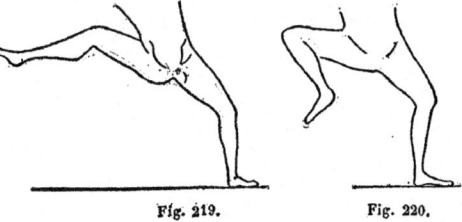

Fig. 219.   Fig. 220.

The conviction becomes stronger upon comparing Figs. 3 and 11 of the same plate with Fig. 220, taken from the same vase as Fig. 219. Thus we obtain the moments of the series 2, 3, 4, 5, 6, 7, 8, 9, 10, 11, 12 (plate II), 3, 11, and 12. The rest must be interpolated in order to reconstruct the movement in its entirety. To be exact, it should be noted that the Greek dancer does not execute the Grand Battement in IV outward, but rather, a Grand Battement in II. The mechanism of the movements is much alike.

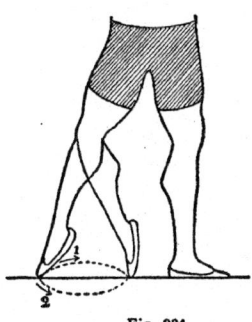

Fig. 221.

190. The vase from which Figs. 219 and 220 are taken is a psytere in the Louvre, and was used to cool wine, being surrounded with ice (plate I). The figures are in red on a black ground, and is incised, a process usually ascribed to a later date than the beginning of the fifth century B. C. It is a moment of transition, just before the return to the more ancient technique, as spoken of in detail in paragraph 9.

Fig. 219 represents the legs of the dancer 5 in plate I: Fig. 220, those of the dancer 2. By an artifice most simple and not unnatural, the dancers are shown in the copy in such arrangement that they are opposite one another.

191. Circles with the Legs.—*These are related to the Battement. They differ in the form of the figure defined on the ground or in* space. *In the Circle of the Leg, the figure is a circle more or less regular.*

Following the direction of the rotation, the Circle is outward *or* inward. *To fix this in the pupil's mind, assume that the active leg is in the II on the toe* (Fig. 221, 1).

The circle is made by commencing the rotation by advancing (Fig. 221, 2).

Like the Battements, *the Circles of the Leg are in three forms,— on the ground, held, and Grand Circle.*

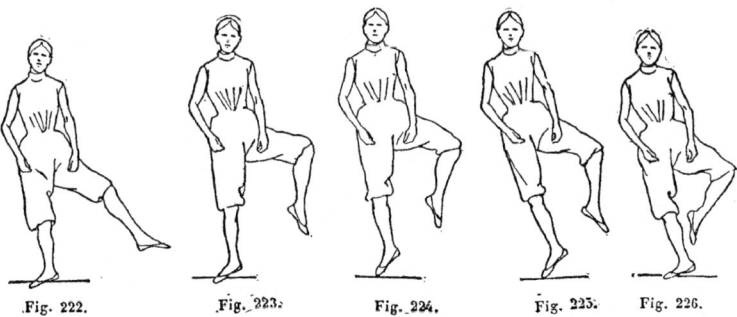

Fig. 222.   Fig. 223.   Fig. 224.   Fig. 225.   Fig. 226.

Fig. 227.   Fig. 228.

192. Circles on the Ground.— *The toe describes a circle on the ground, either outward or inward. The lower leg only moves: the upper leg is motionless.*

193. Circle of the Leg, Held.— *The leg,—that is, the upper leg, is tense and motionless while the lower leg, moving only at the knee, describes a circle in space.*

An analysis of the circle, inward, *is presented in the photographic reproductions of the actual movement in Figs.* 222, 223, 224, 225, 226, 227, 228, *from which it is seen that, during the time the movement is being executed with the active leg, the supporting leg is elevated on the toe, returning to the sole of the foot at the end of the circle.*

The inclination of the body to the right, which reaches its maxi-

mum in Fig. 226, is an instinctive reaction opposing the movement of the leg in the other direction.

194. The Grand Circle of the Leg.—*This is made from the hip, executed with the leg stiff, in either the outward or the inward form* (Fig. 191).

Assume that the dancer stands on the right foot in Principle II and is about to execute the Grand Circle of the leg outward. From the Principle II he passes to Principle IV at the rear (Fig. 62) *by a horizontal movement: from the Principle IV, to the Principle IV advanced* (Fig. 61 *and* 229) *and, by a half-circle of the plane determined: finish Principle IV forward to Principle II by a horizontal movement.*

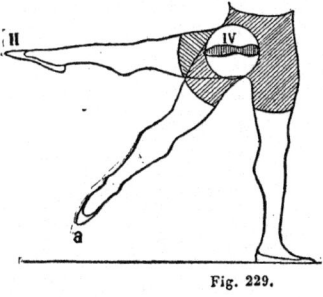

Fig. 229.

(*Geometrically, the toe describes two half-circles, one horizontal, between the two IVs, and passing to II, the other inclines at an angle of* 44°, *to a horizontal plane, between the two IVs, passing by Position A.*)

195. The form and extent of the movements of the different Circles of the Leg cannot be represented by one illustration.

Fig. 230.

Compare Fig. 220 with the dancer 472. The identity of the moment is apparent (282). It is, therefore, possible that the little dancer is executing the Circle of the Leg, left leg, following this with a Circle of the right leg, sustained: (321 and Fig. 473).

Comparing the series of photographs, Figs. 222 to 228, with Fig. 230, which presents a true series, one is struck by the analogy existing between the legs of these grotesques and those of the dancer. Allowing for the difference of perspective, the likeness is even greater. The five images of Fig. 230 represent the five moments of the Circle of the Leg.

196. The preceding exercises, Bending, Separating, Striking (Battement), and Circles of the Leg, are essentially simple and instinctive. They do not appear to be even exaggerations of natural movements. Anatomical conditions have not changed with the centuries. To make the joints supple, to permit the legs to deflect in any direction, to hold them, or to dart them at will, the Greek dancers, like ours, had recourse to exercises which are enumerated. It is enough to prove that their primary studies were not different from ours.

197. Movements of the Arms.—*The play of the arms is a part of the dancer requiring the greatest delicacy, and is one of the most difficult things to acquire. The dancer's talent may be judged by the way she uses her hands, and this is even more true of hands in repose than in movement.*

The arm follows the same rule of movement as the leg.

The arm consists of the shoulder, the upper arm, the lower arm, and the hand; the movement which begins at the shoulder flows down to the hand: inversely, the movement begins in the hand, working up along the arm, and ends at the shoulder, taking its direction from the point toward which the hand is inflected, vertical or horizontal. (Figs. 331 to 334.)

The same directions apply to the inferior members as to the superior ones. (187.)

198. *The dancer holds the arms in the separation which, as it develops, passes to the Position of repose* (Fig. 88), *to all the others* (*Fig. 89 and those following*) *which are a chain, or series, of different Positions.*

The movements of the arms, unimpeded by the necessity of keeping the equilibrium which limits the movements of the legs, are capable of an infinite variety of poses. They are also important in that they control the mimetics of the dance, which may be even more important than the gymnastics. It is difficult to make rules, because each dancer decides the hand-movements for herself.

The only general observation to be made regarding the arms as they are used in our modern dance is that they must get their dramatic expression by means of their curving motions.

There is also the question of the part they play in holding the whole body in balance. There is no doubt that motions sometimes begin in the arms and spread to the whole body (260). But while their action is mechanical, they must always add grace to the dance, or, as the Greeks expressed it, eurhythmy.

199. The essential differences between the Greek dance and ours, while the arm-movements of the French classic dance are limited to certain conventional forms, which have little intellectual expression in them, the Greeks, who were more dramatic than we are, gave greater mimetic value to arm and hand movements, making them not only more varied, but also less artificial.

In our dance, the arms may circle above the head, with the torso animated, to produce a graceful equilibrium, which is supposed to give enough variety, and about all that is proper for a dancer to indulge; a few conventional gestures of this kind form part of the education of every dancer.

In the Greek dance, on the contrary, the hands *spoke:* being at perfect liberty, they sang in lovely curves; though, if occasion called for it, they could be brusque, angular, sharp. The Greek dancer cared less to exhibit beautiful curves than to be expressive. He or she must be able to make all of the gestures that possibly could be used in the dance (144 to 149), all of the traditional gestures, which were understood and translated by the spectator. There was a liturgy of gesture and movement.

Enough of their work has been preserved to show that these movements of the Greek dance cannot be reduced to a set of formulas.

200. **Movements of the Torso and the Head.**—*The movements of the body and the head, are, both in the matter of their radius and their direction, strictly limited by anatomical conditions. The positions mentioned* (150, *Figs.* 182 *to* 188; 158, *Figs.* 194 *to* 198) *mark the extremes between which the head and torso can act. It is not easy to reconstruct in thought the mechanism and the forms of the natural movements. In the movement of the head and the body, the liberty of the dancer is curtailed. The difficulty is not in them-*

selves, but in their harmonious combination in connection with the leg movements.

201. The positions of the head and the torso are, because of anatomical conditions, the same in all ages (151, 159). The same thing may be said of their movements; their mechanism cannot change.

Particularly in the Greek dance it is well to lay stress upon the use of the movements which join positions 5 and 4 of the torso and the head (150, 155, 156, 158, 162, 163). The Greek dancers who carry the head or the torso forward, who sweep the body about, or throw back the head, are numerous, through all periods of Hellenistic art, adding more life and more brilliancy to the dance. Were these things originated in the Dionysian cult? Did they express the excesses and the disgraces of that insane orgy? It must be taken into consideration that not all of these dances were the exclusive property of the companions of the bacchic thiase (Figs. 199, 450, 469, 474, 476).

202. **Combinations of Movements.**—*The combination of Movements of the Legs, Arms, Body and Head remains to be practiced. Only experience enables the dancer to learn their proper correlations, which are simultaneous, which successive, which contrasting.*

In the Walk and the normal Run the Opposition is produced by instinct (63, 70), between the legs and arms. The dancer obeys an instinctive reaction produced not only between the superior and inferior members, but also between the members and the Torso, between the members, the Torso and the Head. The rule is modified to suit the occasion, but it always conforms to the natural laws which are the foundation of all grace and equilibrium.

203. The Greek dancers obeyed the same laws and the same customs. The *eurhythmy* of the walk may not be perfectly embodied in the crossed movements which modern science has enabled us to photograph (Figs. 14, 26, and following). But the eurhythmy of the dance, if one may judge by the great number of representations of the dance, was due in part to Opposition (171, 173). The rhythm *seen* corresponded to the rhythm *heard:* the same Greek word expressed both kinds of rhythm. The Greeks understood the conditions of *equilibrium in movement,* and applied it in most exquisite nuances.

204. There is one kind of Greek dance that quite excludes eurhythmy: the orgiastic dances (400), even when not positively repulsive, are most bizarre and are lacking in harmony. Here every movement goes beyond the bounds of mimetics: the dancer expresses by the contortions of the body and obscene gestures, certain symbolic ideas. The cult of Rhea and the cult of Dionysos added one permanent contribution to the Greek dance,—the *arrhythmic dance*.

THE TECHNIQUE OF THE DANCE
III.—Tempos and Steps

205. *Our dancers do not move over a wide space: they even stand in one place, with the legs in the same pose, neither advancing, retreating, nor turning; one would suppose them incapable of taking a Step.*

But they do step, always in one of two directions indicated in Fig. 231, a, b, c, d.

In advance (a), to the rear (b), laterally (c), obliquely (d). The dancer is supposed to face (a). The space traveled by the dancer is represented by a line to the right, by a broken line or a curved line, the pattern traced by the feet on the ground being often somewhat complex.

The dancer is, therefore, moving in place, like the soldier, who, commanded to "mark time," marches without advancing.

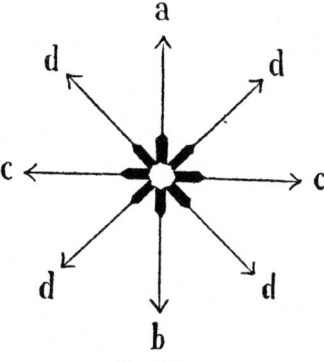

Fig. 231.

206. *Whether the dancer walks or runs, leaps or whirls, these motions are spoken of as Steps, a word which also designates the every-day walk. Thus, the word has but one meaning, but a wide one; it applies to a large number of elementary movements which are as simple as the walk, and which are combined to form certain figures on the ground or in the air.*

These movements are called the Step, or the Tempos of the Step.

207. *When we speak of the Minuet Step, or the Bourrée Step, or the Basque Step, or the Valse Step, we thereby designate a group of these elementary movements which are combined, and, in combination, are spoken of as a Step. The Valse-Step, for instance, is a combination of six Tempos, and consists of six elementary movements.*

It must be borne in mind that the word Tempo, *as applied to the dance, is to be considered as synonymous with movement. A* Tempo

114 TECHNIQUE OF THE DANCE

Battu *is an abbreviated term meaning a more or less complicated movement of the legs in the* Battement.

208. *The* Tempo *on the ground and the* Tempo *in the air must not be confused; the first is a movement executed by the dancer without leaving the ground; the second supposes the dancer to dart through the air with a movement more or less high, by means of a leap, the feet being, both of them, off the ground.*

209. *A great number of movements are executed in double form, on the ground and in the air.*

210. *It is usual to study* Tempo *before step, because it is the* Tempo *that controls the step. We shall not proceed in this logical order, but will compare the Tempos and the steps to those of the Greeks, presenting a number of simple examples, without trying to grade them.*

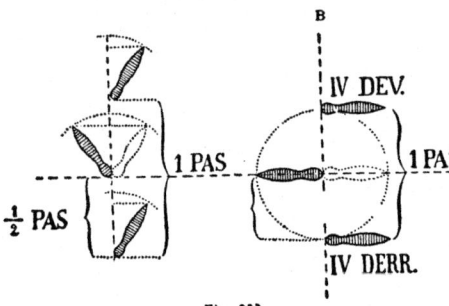

Fig. 232.

The practical study of the dance demands rigorous application. This book will present no such plan of study, but, in its incomplete way, will outline a course of study (326) with certain advice. (See page 55.)

211. The Step and the Position of the Feet.—*The dance Step, like the walk, is made by changing the weight from one leg to the other, leaving one free.*

When considered separately, the parts of the Step appear quite simple, differing from the normal walk in that the feet are turned (97) sidewise, and that the length of the Step never exceeds the length of one of the feet.

Figure 232 shows (a) the position of the feet in the normal walk; in (b) is shown the position of the feet in the dance-walk. Explanation is not necessary. The relative shortness of the step in the dance-walk is clearly indicated. One foot is separated from the other by its own length. An entire Step is the distance which separates the two IVs on the same foot (IV in advance and IV to the rear). A demi-Step is one-half as long (Fig. 232, B).

212. The Step changes through three positions of the feet (102).

The position of the feet on the sole.
The position of the feet on the half-toe.
The position of the feet on the toe.

213. *Our dancers do not wear heels. They are, at best, an imitation of the exquisites of the Directoire, and they should never return to favor. The high heels of the seventeenth and the eighteenth centuries throw back the instep and depress the toe, giving an affected sort of elegance, without having the true elegance which every dancer should endeavor to acquire* (180, 182); *the dancer who wears high heels may find the toe position easy, but many others must be given up on account of the artificial pose into which the feet are thrown, so that the whole gymnastic of the dance must be changed to accommodate the fashion.*

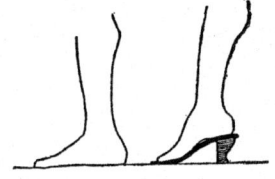

Fig. 233.

The ancient Step allowed movements more rapid and of greater freedom, and the muscles of the feet were correspondingly more active and more resistant.

By suppressing the heels, at the commencement of the present century (nineteenth), the feet of our dancers were enabled to resume their natural position, thus regaining the stability of the Greek dancers (217).

214. The three forms of pose of the feet (on the sole, on the half-toe, and on the toe) are shown on the figures of dancers taken from the paintings and sculptures.

It must be noted that the vases and reliefs of the archaic period are not always to be taken as authoritative, because the primitive technique of the early artists made it impossible for them to depict complex positions of the feet of dancers in the many forms of walking and running (64, 66,—76 to 84). The result is confusion in all work prior to the end of the sixth century B. C.

There are two other postures of the feet to consider.

215. Pose of the Foot on the Half-toe.—Figs. 234, 235, 236, 237 are much like Figs. 82, 83, 85, 585, 589, 590, etc., and are examples.

It is remarkable that the greater number of the "archaisant" figures representing Satyrs, hours, Bacchants, as well as the superior divinities, walk on the half-toe. This is their special manner of dancing. On one of the more ancient monuments, the frieze from the temple at Samothrace, built in the fourth century B. C., there is found a particular instance (Louvre, XII salon). The long file of dancers, who hold each other's hands, and Step to the rhythm of the tambourine, advance on the half-toe. The sculptor has chosen to present these figures stiff and sheathed in tightly-wrapped tunics; certainly an imitation of an earlier temple. He has indubitably copied the postures of the feet from primitive work. The archaic sculptors show, neither in high nor in low relief, the same walk on the half-toe. But the vases of the sixth century B. C. show that the artists of that date occasionally had recourse to a similar formula (Figs. 234, 235). At the end of the fifth century B. C. it is employed on some bas-reliefs of Trysa (Figs. 490, 491), and applied to figures that whirl about the doors of the temple. It is more than likely that the restorer of the temple at Samothrace took an earlier temple for his model, and that this is the reason that his dancers walk on the half-toe.

Fig. 234.

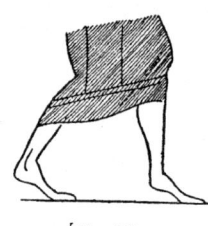
Fig. 235.

Fig. 236.

Fig. 237.

Whatever the origin of the art,—and it is of very ancient date,—

as depicted on the sculptures, the dance-walk on the half-toe appears at nearly all periods, from the archaic to the Roman, but, in the later work, became an affectation by which the figures can be accurately placed.

216. **Position of the Foot on the Toe.**—The Step on the toe is more rarely found on the sculptured figures than the Step on the half-toe, but it was, without doubt, used by the Greeks.

A few terra-cotta figurines of the Hellenistic period (17) represent persons with wings, who seem to be posed on the toe; but this is only an illusion. The figurines, intended to be suspended, were not placed in the toe position in order to make them appear to be walking (383, 384).

217. The feet of the dancers on the sculptured figures are generally bare: this is another convention, and, in a number of cases, presupposes shoes. It is likely that the sandals were omitted in order to show the flexions of the feet more perfectly than could be done if shoes were worn.

Examples of the heavy and rigid soles are very rare (Fig. 453).

Thus, it is easy to see that the Greek dancers rested their feet on the ground in the same manner as do the modern French dancers: whatever shoe was worn was perfectly flexible.

DESCRIPTION OF SOME OF THE TEMPOS AND STEPS

218. **The Slide.**—*The toe of the foot skims over the ground. This is one of the most wonderful of all the movements on the ground. The slide may be made in any direction* (205).

219. **The Chassé** (*Fig. 238*).—*Suppose that the right foot of the dancer is ready to slide in IV advanced. Then, in place of carrying forward the left foot, it is moved up to the other in III, with an abrupt movement, the whole constituting a* Chassé *forward.*

In the Chassé to the rear the movement is inverted.

Example of a Chassé *to the side: the dancer is in II fundamental. To Chassé to the right, carry left in III back of the right foot,— otherwise speaking, set the left foot back of the right foot—and it immediately leaves the right in II.*

The Chassé to the left is made by reversing the process.

To learn the simple Chassé, re-commence on the same leg, then Chassé with both legs alternately, then successively. (The movement executed by infantry at the command "change the step" is related to the Chassé.)

220. The Coupé.—*The Coupé is the movement of the leg which, in coming down, Chassés the other. It differs from the Chassé in that the leg which Chassés the other touches it in the air instead of on the ground and that the supporting leg is lifted more or less high on the toe or half-toe.*

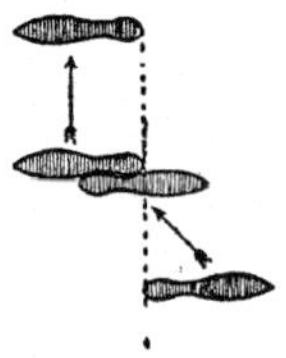

Fig. 238.

Figs. 239 to 243 give a photographic analysis of a Coupé of the left leg.

Fig. 239: *The left leg is lifted at the rear.*

Fig. 240: *The left leg descends: the right leg is lifted on the toe.*

Fig. 241: *The left leg joins over the right leg making the Chassé, and at once separates* (179).

Figs. 242 and 243: *The right leg separates in demi IV outward.*

Figs. 244 to 247 *are an analysis of the* Coupé forward with the left leg.

Fig. 244: *The left leg is separated in demi IV outward.*

Fig. 245: *The left leg descends: the right heel is lifted.*

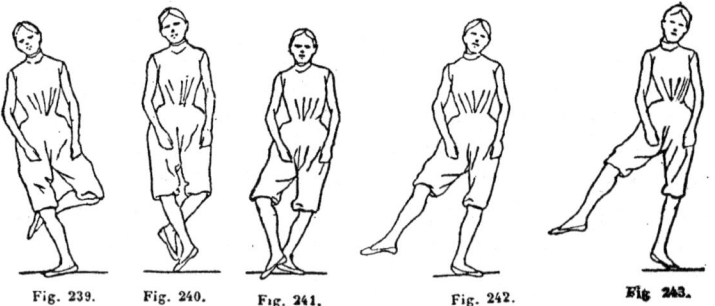

Fig. 239.   Fig. 240.   Fig. 241.   Fig. 242.   Fig. 243.

Fig. 246: *The left leg is posed forward of the right leg, which is lifted on the toe.*

2

8

Plate II.

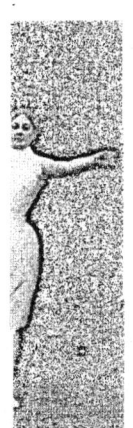  

5   6

11   12

DESCRIPTION OF SOME OF THE TEMPOS AND STEPS   119

Fig. 247: *The right leg is lifted and back.*

221. Fouetté.—*Fouetté is the action of the leg which, without touching the ground, makes a rapid, whip-like movement*

An analysis of this movement is given in Figs. 248 to 251.

Fig. 248: *The left leg is separated in demi IV advanced.*

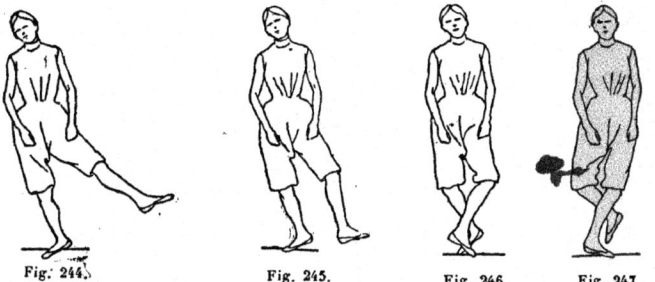

Fig. 244.   Fig. 245.   Fig. 246.   Fig. 247.

Figs. 248 and 250: *The Fouetté is produced by a movement of only the lower leg, the upper leg remains motionless.*

Fig. 251: *Finish of the Fouetté.*

There is, of course, the Fouetté forward: *in it, the active leg is in front of the supporting leg.*

The Fouetté takes different forms. Example: What is called the

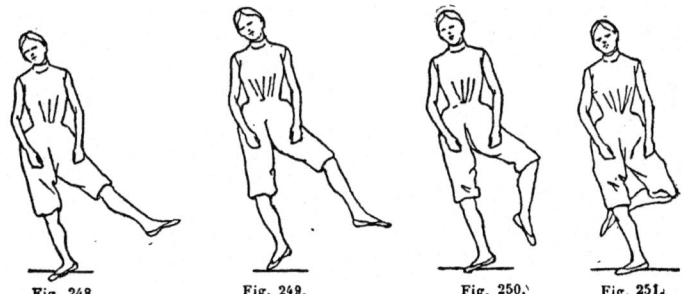

Fig. 248.   Fig. 249.   Fig. 250.   Fig. 251.

Fouetté to the side is made thus: the leg leaves the V forward and separates successively through the three principal positions of the IV advanced, of the II and the Arabesque, at which it stops. The movement is rapid and unrestrained.

The Fouetté may be made once or repeated as a series.

222. Jeté (the Throw).—*The Jeté is related to the leap which is part of the run (69). It consists of a leap which throws the weight of the body on the leg which is about to touch the ground, the other leg being more or less lifted, and bent back at the knee.*

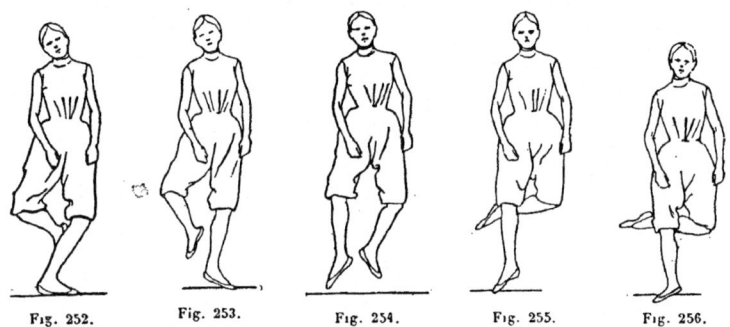

Fig. 252.   Fig. 253.   Fig. 254.   Fig. 255.   Fig. 256.

When the leg is thrust forward, it is called Jeté over.

The Figs. 252 to 256 are photographs of the Jeté at different stages.

Fig. 252: *The right leg is raised at the rear; the left leg rests on the ground, and is bent for the first part of the leap.*

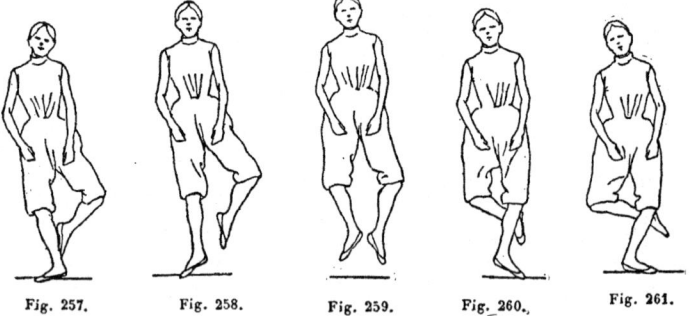

Fig. 257.   Fig. 258.   Fig. 259.   Fig. 260.   Fig. 261.

Fig. 253 *The right leg, knee bent, is carried in advance to make the Jeté over; the heel of the supporting leg is lifted to continue the movement to the position which precedes the leap.*

Fig. 254: *(Essential moment). Leap, or moment of suspension*

DESCRIPTION OF SOME OF THE TEMPOS AND STEPS 121

(69). *The dancer is descending on the right leg and lifting the left at the rear.*

Fig. 255: *The right leg descends on the toe: the left leg is lifted at the rear.*

Fig. 256: *The heel of the right leg is lowered; the left leg is lifted as high as it is intended to lift.*

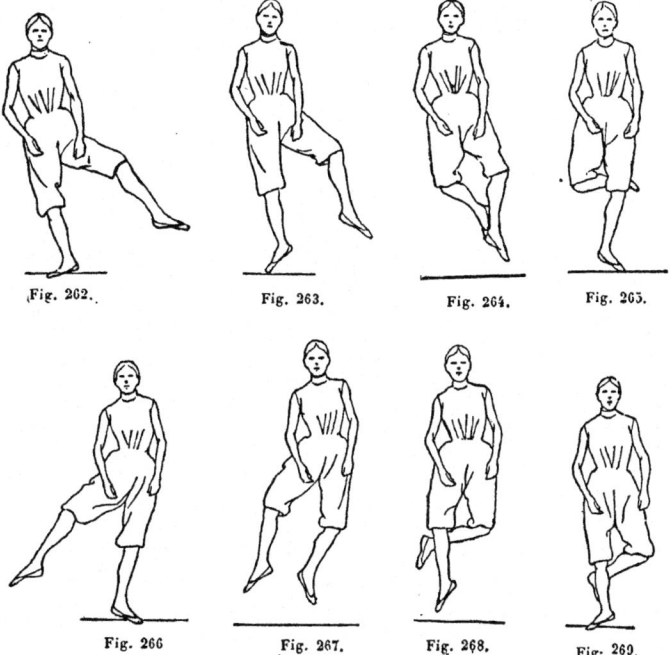

Fig. 262.   Fig. 263.   Fig. 264.   Fig. 265.

Fig. 266   Fig. 267.   Fig. 268.   Fig. 269.

The Figs. 257 to 261 are an analysis of the Jeté over, with the left leg, and their moments correspond with those of the figures just analysed.

Jeté is called the under Jeté when the descending leg is the one at the rear: in that case, the other leg is lifted in front. The Jeté over is executed backward.

223. *The Jeté may be made, not only forward or back, but laterally, by a leap to the side.*

Figs. 262 to 269 analyse a Jeté over, to the left.
The Figs. 266 to 269 analyse a Jeté over, to the right.
The two series explain themselves.

224. *The Slide, the Chassé and the Coupé are movements on the ground; the Jeté is a movement in the air; the Fouetté is executed on the ground or in the air, depending upon whether the Step is on the ground or a leap.*

225. In the analysis of the modern dance, by means of photo-

Fig. 270.   Fig. 271.   Fig. 272.

graphs, the figures are all made to face the spectator. In the case of the figures taken from the paintings and sculptures of ancient Greece, this is manifestly impossible. Their resemblance to the modern dance is chiefly in the leg-movements. In comparing them with the modern photographs, the perspective is entirely different.

The representations in sculpture are seldom arranged in a series (269). Often a movement is indicated in its characteristic moment, —a moment when there would be no possibility of confounding the movement with any other.

It is impossible to show, in one picture, either the Chassé or the Coupé. They are dependent upon the most simple movements, but they have no *climacteric moment* (283). Of these there is no trace found upon the paintings or reliefs.

226. The *Slide* (218) is easy to follow from one picture. The

DESCRIPTION OF SOME OF THE TEMPOS AND STEPS 123

Satyr (Fig. 270) carries his right foot forward in IV, touching the ground lightly with his toe,—there is no doubt about this repre-

Fig. 273. Fig. 274.

senting a Slide. Fig. 271, which is small and dainty, expresses the same thing. The interpretation of Fig. 272 is facilitated by the

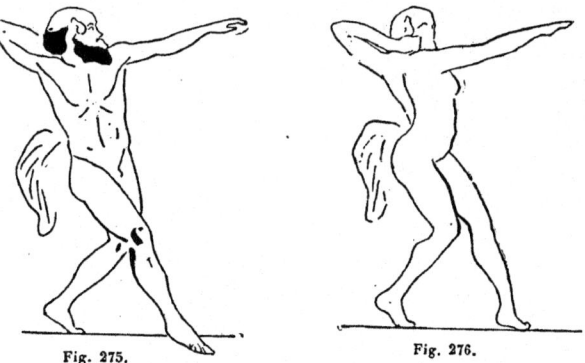

Fig. 275. Fig. 276.

inclination of the body in just the pose needed for the Slide, as though he were about to spring.

Of the Slide made simultaneously with the two feet the Step is best explained by Figs. 273, 274, 275, 276, 199, A, 399 and 400.

The change of pose is represented by Fig. 273 to much the same pose in Fig. 274, the dancer, whose body is inclined backward, slides on the half-toe on both feet at the same time; the left leg, which is in IV forward in Fig. 273, passes in IV backward in Fig. 274; the

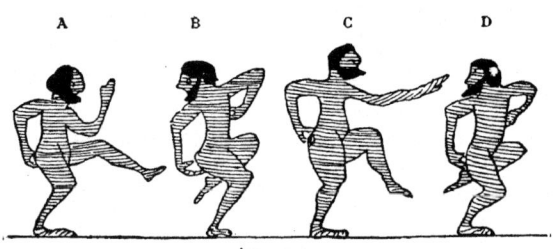

Fig. 277.

movement of the right leg, simultaneously, is inverted. The Satyr (Figs. 275, 276) executes exactly the same movement.

227. As said in another paragraph, it is seldom that a series of figures in successive movements is found in Greek art; one of the few examples is shown in Fig. 277.

This is a grotesque dance-game, played by four clowns, each of whom is, in turn, the victim and the actor: it looks as though the point of the game were "step on your neighbour." It is a dance, though but one remove from an absurd bit of mimicry.

Fig. 278.

The two extremes of action are indicated in A-C, for one part, and in B-D for the other. These are variable "instantaneous" pictures, analogous to the modern photographs, and are made at four moments,—in pairs,—a unique thing (289).

The movement is a *Fouetté*, to *the rear, with the left leg* (221). Compare with the series of dancers 248 to 251, and follow the difference: the dancer in the photographs makes the *Fouetté oblique*, IV outward (Fig. 248), in the Position marked by Fig. 251; the four men Fouetté right, principle IV forward (Fig. 277, A and C), in the position B-D of the same figure.

228. The dancer represented by Fig. 278 belongs to the same group as the preceding; the Position of the legs is identical with

the *Position* B-D of the Fig. 277. This shows that he, too, must be executing a Fouetté to the rear, but on the right leg.

229. The mechanism of the Jeté is reduced to a leap terminating on the same leg (222), the other leg being lifted and curved backward from the knee. The different moments of the Jeté were quite

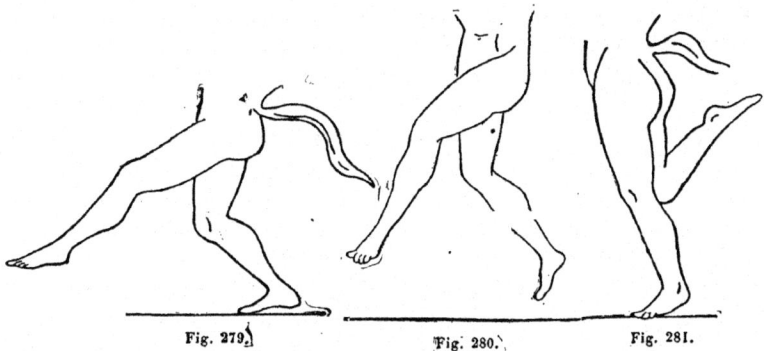

Fig. 279. Fig. 280. Fig. 281.

perceptible to the eye, and the Greek artists copied them with wonderful fidelity.

Figs. 279, 280 and 281 correspond to the three essential moments (284) of an *over Jeté on the left leg.*

Fig. 279: The flexion of the leg prepares for the leap; the leap begins by raising the heel.

Fig. 280: Period of suspension.

Fig. 281: The dancer comes down on left leg; the right leg is lifted and bent back at the knee.

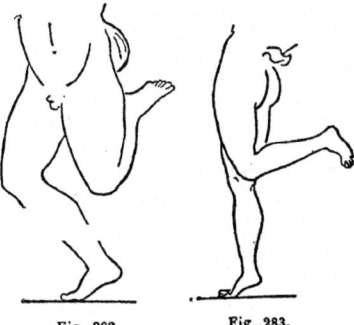

Fig. 282. Fig. 283.

230. The artists were pleased to exaggerate the movement of the leg which has the knee bent back at the end of the Jeté (Fig. 282). A charming cameo (Fig. 579) shows the exact measure of the movement. Fig. 283 is likewise a good type of moderate action.

231. **Tempo Increasing (Ballonnes).**—*One leg increases movement when advanced in the pose on the toe, describing an arc in the air,*

in which the leg seems to pass over a ball. The Tempo-Ballon is applied to a variety of steps. Example, Jeté-Ballonné.

232. *This movement cannot be represented by a single image, but if the paintings and reliefs give no information, the texts lend themselves to plausible comparisons between the movements depicted and the Tempo-Ballon of our dancers.*

233. **Balance Steps.**—*This division comprises steps of various forms, of which the Torso, Head and Arms provide, by their curving movements, a rhythmic accompaniment to the movements of the feet.*

The oscillation may be toward either side of the vertical line of equilibrium, their two extreme moments being in opposition. At one of these moments the right arm is lowered and the left arm raised. So, too, the Torso maintains its equilibrium by bending to the one side or the other (277, 280).

Sometimes the arms alone or the Torso alone gives the Balance: sometimes they are combined. Then the head begins to take part in the opposition (167). All of the oppositions must be made in the same Tempo as the leg movements.

234. Examples of the Balance Steps are numerous: Figs. 284, 285 suffice to fix the idea.

The moment (282) of Fig. 284 is furnished by the antique statue called the Faun of Pompeii. Fig. 285 shows a reconstruction of the same statue in the opposing pose.

The following analysis of the two figures may be of assistance:

(1) Fig. 284
- right leg advanced:
- body inclined to the right:
- right arm low:
- left arm high.

(2) Fig. 285
- right leg at rear:
- body inclined to the left:
- right arm high:
- left arm low.

The Step of the dance is executed by successive Balances, right and left, combined in a rhythmic walk on the half-toe.

235. The advance to the play of the castanets (Fig. 286) is re-

lated to that of the preceding dancer, except in the matter of some secondary details, such as the play of the hands and the Position of the head.

It is easy to follow the analogy between these dancers (Figs. 284, 285) and Figs. 111, 137, 177, 188, 189, 190, etc., representing one and the same moment. The imagination can supply the moment

Fig. 284.

Fig. 285.

of opposition in every one of the figures, and the form of the movement which unites the two extreme moments.

236. Tempos and Steps on the Toe.—*The Positions and the movements on the toes cannot be practiced by the dancer except after long and painful preparatory exercises, without danger of dislocation.*

The terminal phalange of the toe must acquire strength before it can be used to support, not only the foot, but the whole weight of the body.

Rise on the toe and stand firmly in all of the Positions; pass from one Position to another; pass from a Position on the sole to a Position on the toe, and return to the first, etc. The two series of photographs give an analysis of the exercises on the toes.

Fig. 286.

237. Leaving II, on the Toes.

Fig. 287: *The Preparation: the Position is here the V, left advanced.*

Fig. 288: *The two heels are raised at the same time.*

Fig. 289: *The two legs separate and slide on the toes: the heels are lifted more and more.*

Fig. 290: *The two legs are in II, on the toes.*

Fig. 291: *The two legs reapproach, and slide on the toes: heels low.*

Fig. 292: *The legs cross: the heels are lowered more and more.*

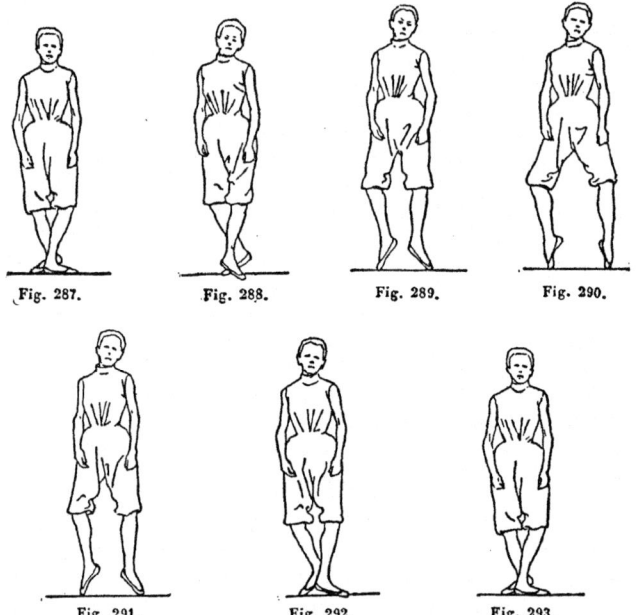

Fig. 293: *Held steadily, left advanced, returning to Position.*

238. Rising on the Toes.

Fig. 294: *Preparation: left forward: Position bent.*

Fig. 295: *The two heels are lifted; legs separate.*

Fig. 296: *The dancer rises on the right leg: the left upper leg is lifted; the left lower leg is bent back.*

Fig. 297: *The right leg remains raised on the toe: the left leg is bent backward, with the toe higher than the knee.*

DESCRIPTION OF SOME OF THE TEMPOS AND STEPS 129

Fig. 298: *The upper leg and the lower leg (left) descend.*
Fig. 299: *The left leg passes to the rear.*
Fig. 300: *The left foot posed at the rear in IV.*
Fig. 301: *The dancer bends in V to recommence on the other foot.*
Fig. 302: *Beginning of the Lifting the toe of the left foot.*

239. Steps on the Toes.—*They are generally short steps, on ac-*

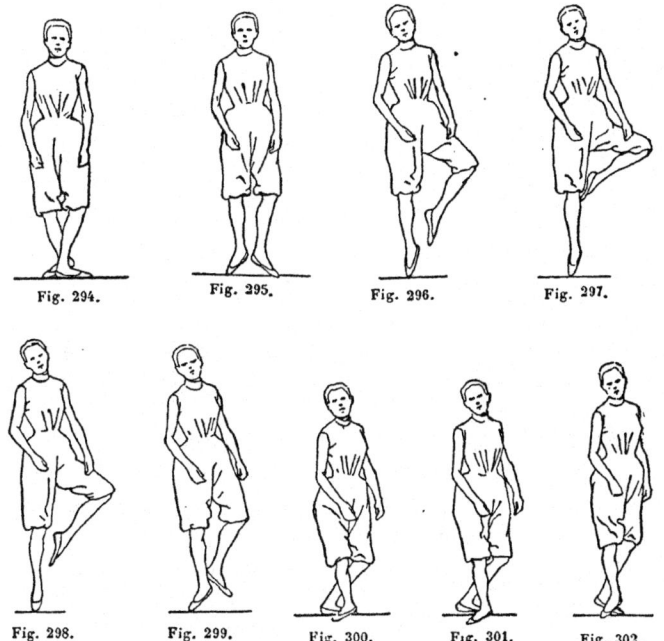

Fig. 294. Fig. 295. Fig. 296. Fig. 297.

Fig. 298. Fig. 299. Fig. 300. Fig. 301. Fig. 302.

count of the position of the feet. Whether used in walking, running, or turning, they hold to their own characteristics. Figs. 306 to 309 give an analysis of the step used in walking on the toes: they are executed by a dancer in Greek tunic, and serve to interpret Figs. 303 and 304.

240. The Greek dancers practiced the *Tempos on the toes.* Therefore, they must have used exercises much like those of the

Escape on the toes and the Rising on the toes of our dancers. Fig. 305 shows a sort of lift on the toes, on the left leg.

241. Fig. 303 represents one of the hierodules, or daughters of Zeus, wearing the kalathos, which belongs to a series of early date: she advances with *small Steps on the toes*, head bent forward, as though she were watching her steps. Figs. 306, 307, 308 and 309

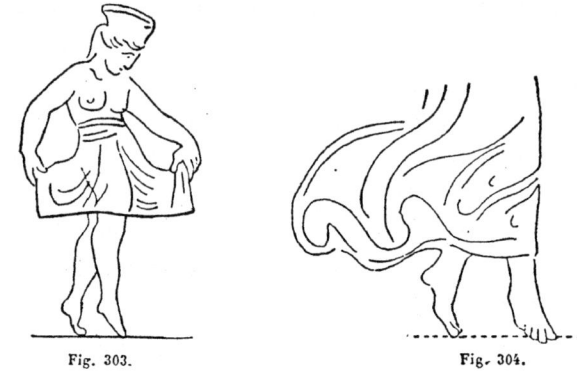

Fig. 303.   Fig. 304.

are a reconstruction, by means of photography, of the different moments of the same Step, and show how the feet were held in all movements of this nature.

Fig. 306: Initial Position: III or V on the toes.

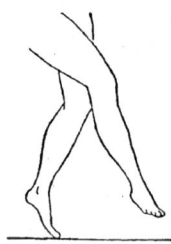

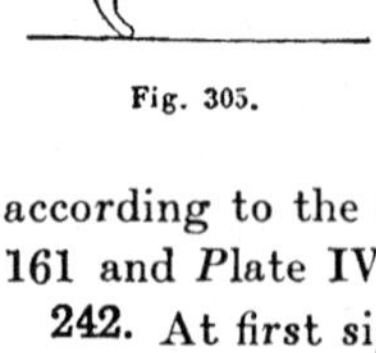

Fig. 305.

Fig. 307: First step: right leg advanced.
Fig. 308: Second step: left leg advanced.
Fig. 309: Third step: right leg advanced.

Fig. 303 corresponds in *moment* to Fig. 307, the same as Fig. 304. A different aspect is presented by the modern dancer from this daughter of Zeus, through turning the feet sidewise, according to a rule already stated (97). The difference in costume explains a part of the unlikeness. The long tunic of this dancer is draped according to the fashion of the fifth century B. C. (Figs. 138, 155, 161 and Plate IV).

242. At first sight the Figs. 310 and 311 would seem to be walking on the toes. The first is walking, the second makes the *running*

DESCRIPTION OF SOME OF THE TEMPOS AND STEPS 131

Step on the toes. The dancer Jetés on the right foot (222) like the Satyr (Fig. 279), except that he makes the Jeté on the left foot.

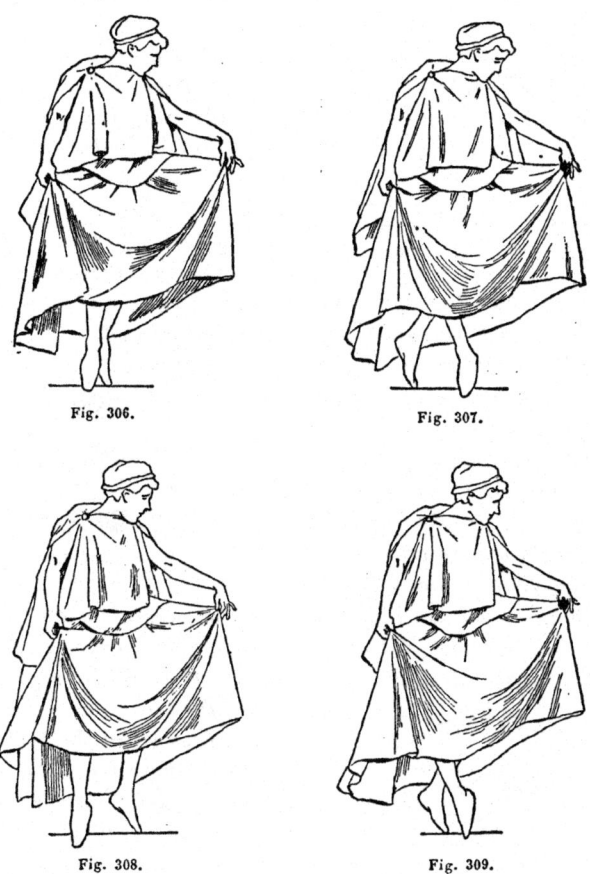

Fig. 306.   Fig. 307.

Fig. 308.   Fig. 309.

The turning movement shows that the toes are turning the body toward the back.

243. The Assemblé (Fig. 312).—*This figure is both a plane and a horizontal projection of the two Assemblés in succession: the first of the left foot, the second of the right foot. The direction of the* arrows indicates altitude. The dots represent the horizontal projection of the feet in the air, at the moment corresponding to the

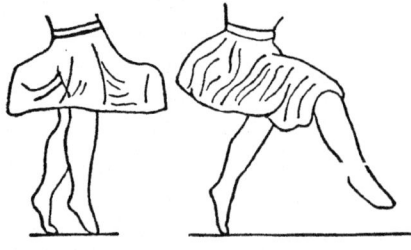

Fig. 310. Fig. 311.

extreme Position of the leg which separates in demi II, moving as seen.

The mechanism of the Assemblé is explained by an exercise called the Assemblé Exercise.

Preparation (237): Left advanced: the left leg separates in demi II (179. Fig. 60), during which the right bends to leap (73): the two feet descend in V, left forward: this makes the Assemblé over (185). Continue on the other foot. There is an advance on the ground.

244. To make the Assemblé under, the same exercise is made backward. By changing the direction of the arrows in Fig. 312, from high to low, the movement will be clearly understood.

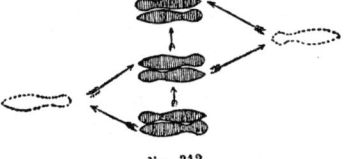

Fig. 312.

245. **Mutation of the feet** (*Fig. 313*).—*This figure is composed, like the preceding, of plane and horizontal projections, with dots corresponding to the extreme Positions of the legs, which are separated for the leap, and represent the feet in the air.*

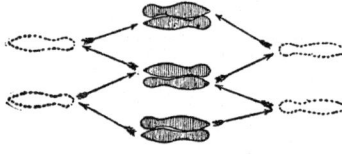

Fig. 313.

The exercise of the Mutation of the feet *differs from the assemblé in this; in the Assemblé only one leg separates; in the Mutation, both are separated.*

Preparation: V, right advanced. Then the two knees are bent and the dancer leaps. While in the air the legs Change position, turning aside from each other in a double separation, crossing in descent, so that the rear leg comes forward: they meet in V, left advanced; the second Mutation descends in V, right advanced.

246. *This exercise is also done with a rear movement; to understand how it is accomplished, reverse the arrows in Fig. 313, and read it downwards.*

247. **Beating Steps (Battus).**—*In these, as in the Battement* (188), *the active leg is set widely apart from the supporting leg, and moves rapidly. The Battus is made in the air, and implies action with both legs, which, during the leap, are crossed. The Battement is made on the ground.* When the legs beat the air, one or the other separating without being crossed, the movement is called the Cabrioles. *In what is known* as the Cut (Entrechat), *the feet cross during the leap.*

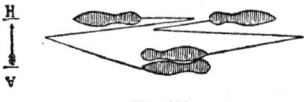

Fig. 314.

The Cabriole, which was very popular with our ancestors, flourished in the sixteenth century. The Cut (Entrechat), which is derived from it, is of more recent date (1730 or about that time).

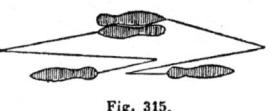

Fig. 315.

248. **The Cut (Entrechat).**—*This leaping movement, during which the legs cross, is preceded by a bend, which prepares for the leap* (73). *It terminates in the descent, toe down, on one foot or on both. In the former case, the lifted leg is in the* Attitude (169).

249. *The Entrechat is counted by the number of segments of broken lines which are described by the two feet during the leap.* They are called Three Cuts, Four Cuts, etc. *Figs. 314, 315, 316 and 317, which show between the tracings of the feet the horizontal projections of their movements in the air, give the reason for these names.*

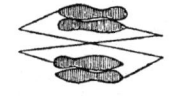

Fig. 316.

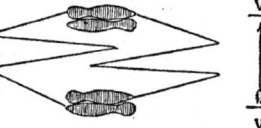

Fig. 317.

Two Cuts are not used,—nothing less than Three Cuts, but the Mutation of the feet may be considered like the point of departure of the Cut, so we may speak of Cut Two (Fig. 313). *It is composed of two segments of broken lines, the feet crossing as they return to the ground.*

250. **Three Cuts,** *presented in three forms.*

First form is that in which the legs pass from the V to the II. The V is the Preparation (237). (*The figures in dots are not used here, being unnecessary. The arrow placed at the side indicates direction of movement.*)

Second form: as in Fig. 315, the legs pass from the II to the V, the II being the Preparation.

Third form, like Fig. 316. *In this the legs are in V, the Preparation, and return to a V reversed. That is to say, the first Position is the V, right advanced, the end is the V, left advanced.*

251. Four Cuts, *of which Fig. 317 shows a plan. Another illustration which will assist the pupil being Plate III, which gives an analysis of the different phases of the movement.*

No. 1: *Preparation: V left forward, Bending both knees for the leap.*

No. 2: *The knees straighten: the dancer is posed on the toes, about to leave the ground.*

Nos. 3 and 4: *Two moments of the period of the leap, or suspension, corresponding to the crossing of the legs which constitutes the Cut.*

No. 5: *During suspension. The crossed legs separate as they descend.*

No. 6: *The dancer descends on the toes, in V, left advanced, which is the initial Position.*

No. 7: *The heels are lowered: the two knees bend to make the new leap.* No. 7 *reproduces* No. 1, *and makes the first of a new series of figures in which the moments correspond to the moments of the preceding series.* No. 1 = No. 7, No. 8 = No. 2, *etc.*

In the same way, No. 13 *corresponds to* No. 1 *and begins a third series.*

In each of the three series, the Preparation is given in one figure; the rising on the toes, one figure; the period of suspension occupies the next three figures of *which the first two show the two moments* of *the Battu; the descent on the toes, which is the end, is expressed by the sixth figure.*

By placing them all on one page, the pupil is enabled to compare them closely, thus noting differences of movement that would otherwise escape the eye.

252. *Regarding the question of rhythm in the dance, though it is outside the scope of this chapter, the following generalisations are given: the isochronism of the movements follows the successive uniform movements in time, resulting in monotony: we should have the slower movements of the Greek dance to give variety.*

253. *There are movements known as Five Cuts, Six Cuts, Seven— the number is limited only by the skill of the dancer.*

254. *The Assemblé (243) and the mutation of the feet (245) have no characteristic moment, therefore they cannot be represented by a single illustration, nor can they be adequately described.*

255. A vase of mediocre style, made in Etruria in the third century B. C., of poor quality of clay, coarsely painted, is, notwithstanding all of these defects, highly interesting to the student of the dance. It is a unique example, because it proves conclusively that the Greeks practiced the *Battu step*, which is much like our Entrechat (Cut). A comparison of Fig. 318 with No. 10 of *Plate* III decides that question and permits a reconstruction of all of the phases of the movement. The whole series of photographs on *Plate* III should be considered as one in an analysis of the Entrechat Four of the modern dance: they constitute a restoration of the Greek Step, of which the painting on the vase shows a characteristic moment.

Fig. 318.

256. Turning Movements.—*A great number of Tempos and Steps are executed while turning, without which the whole mechanism would be altered. A short list of these follows:*

The Slide, turning.
The Chassé, turning.
The Fouetté, turning.
The Jeté, turning.
The Rise on the Toes, turning.
The Step on the Toes, turning.
The Battus (Entrechats), turning.

The turn may be on the ground or in the air, depending on the nature of the movement. The modern French dancer uses all of these forms.

257. *The whirling steps are turns made very rapidly, usually on the toes or the half-toes of both feet, continuing in a series, depending on the ability of the dancer, and advancing on the ground in any desired direction.*

258. * **The Pirouette.**—*Among the turning movements practiced by our dancers, the Pirouette has an important place. It consists in turning one or more times on the toe or the half-toe of one foot, the other leg being raised and motionless, knee bent. The impulsion necessary for the rotation of the body on its unique pivot is principally the arm, which, here, plays the rôle of motor.*

259. *There are numerous varieties of the Pirouette: nearly all of the Positions taken by the free leg may be used here, while the active leg executes the movement.*

The greater number of the Pirouettes are in double form: according to the direction of the rotation, they are Pirouettes inward or outward.

The Pirouette outward, which is most used, is a turn to the side on which the leg is in the air (Fig. 220).

The Pirouette inward is when the turn is toward the side of the supporting leg (Fig. 321).

260. The Preparation for the Pirouette.—*The foot which is to execute the Pirouette is the pivot. The rotation of the body on the supporting leg is determined by the action of the arms and the swing of the torso. The spring is accomplished by the abrupt lateral movement of the arm which crosses in front of the chest* (Fig. 319), *and which impels the body toward that side* (Figs. 336, 337, 338). *The legs are in* II *or* IV.

Pirouette outward:

The dancer turns to the right, crossing the right arm and turning on the half-toe or the toe of the left foot (Figs. 319 and 320).

Or, the dancer turns to the left, crossing the left arm and turning on the toe or the half-toe of the right foot.

---

* Translator's note: The Pirouette belongs to the steps classed as "natural" in that it is a movement that seems to be instinctive among children. All children pirouette in their play.

Pirouette inward:

Here the dancer turns to the right, crossing the right arm and turning on the toe or the half-toe of the right foot (Figs. 319 and 321).

Or, the dancer turns to the left, crossing the left arm and turning on the left foot.

In other words:

If the Pirouette is outward the dancer turns on the foot opposed to the arm which crosses in front.

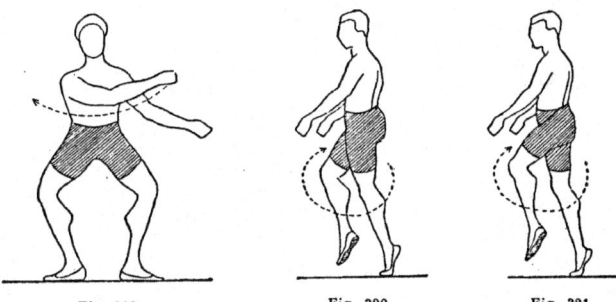

Fig. 319.   Fig. 320.   Fig. 321.

If the Pirouette is inward, the turn is made on the foot which is on the same side as the crossed arm.

261. Execution of the Pirouette.—*When the rotation begins, the foot which is not the pivot is lifted, and, according to the kind of Pirouette to be made, the leg in the air is separated, being higher or lower, and held motionless during the step, or it may execute certain movements* (263). *The first spring of the arms and torso is made with vigor, enabling the dancer to spin around four or five times before the heel of the supporting leg touches the ground. Zorn cites one dancer who pirouetted on her instep seven times without losing the initial spring, but this is exceptional.*

262. *Reviewing the photographic analysis of the Pirouette, it is seen to be a simple example: the Pirouette on the instep (Figs. 322 to 345). It is here preceded by a Coupé (220) which serves as the Preparation for the Pirouette, the right leg chassés in II, during the time the arm crosses.*

138   TECHNIQUE OF THE DANCE

Fig. 322: End of the foregoing Pirouette on the instep, in which the left leg serves as the pivot. The right leg, posed in V forward, as in Fig. 344.

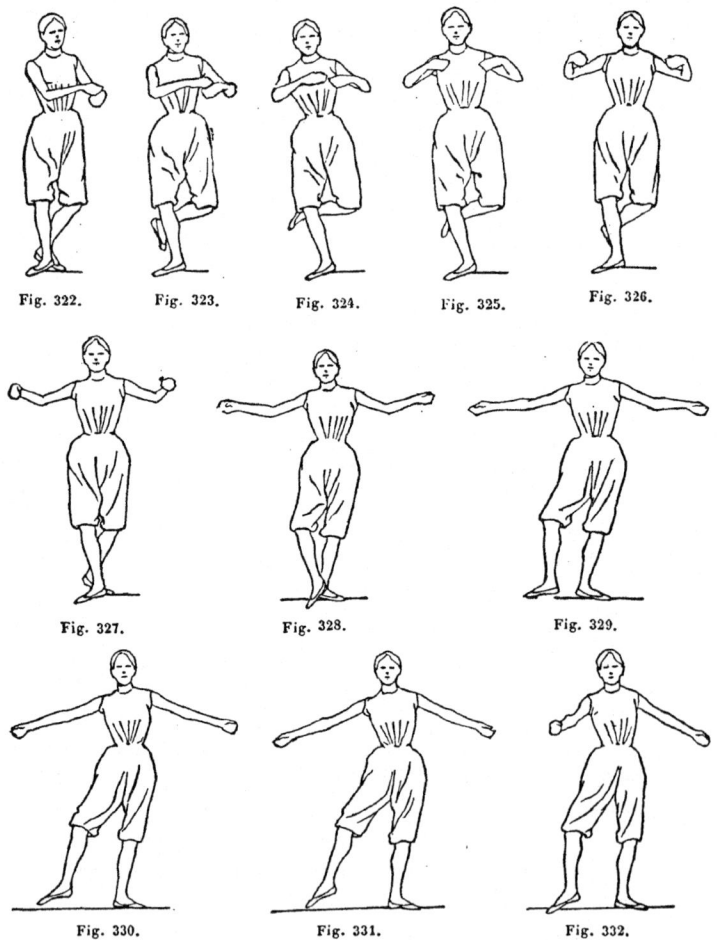

Figs. 323 and 324: The left leg is lifted and bent backward at the knee; the upper leg is motionless.

Figs. 325, 326 and 327, the left leg is lowered in order to cross at

DESCRIPTION OF SOME OF THE TEMPOS AND STEPS 139

the rear; the two arms move at the same time to develop the Step (179).

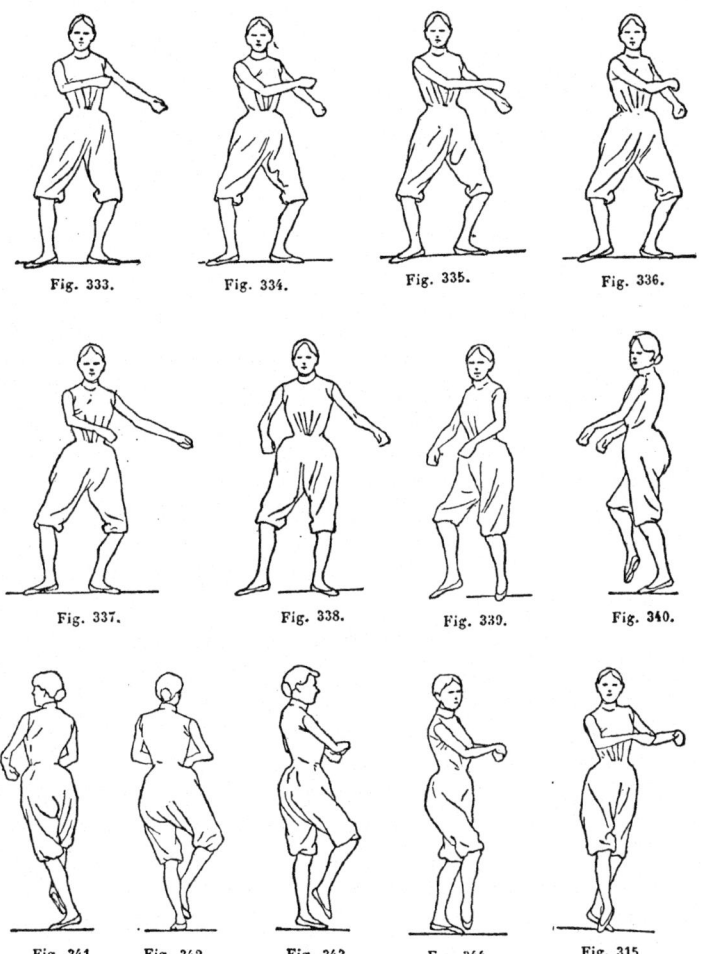

Fig. 333. Fig. 334. Fig. 335. Fig. 336.

Fig. 337. Fig. 338. Fig. 339. Fig. 340.

Fig. 341. Fig. 342. Fig. 343. Fig. 344. Fig. 345.

Fig. 328: The left leg makes the Coupé, and chassés the right leg, of which the heel is raised: the arms reach the climax of their movement.

Figs. 329, 330 and 331: The right leg Separates in II and the toe touches the ground.

Figs. 332 and 333, the right heel is lowered, the dancer is now in II: the right arm is firmly crossed, in obedience to the rule (197).

Figs. 334, 335 and 336: the right arm crosses more and more, carrying the body lightly with it toward the left.

Fig. 337: The right arm makes an abrupt movement from left to right, and by this impulsion the motive power and the balance are obtained.

Fig. 338: The rotation begins. The body turns to the right, the right leg being lifted.

Figs. 339 to 345: The rotation is made. It is produced by carrying the right foot, lifted (Fig. 339), and drawing nearer to the supporting leg (Figs. 340, 341), keeping the toe as high as the instep of the other foot. The arms, which have finished their work, are posed high before the chest.

Fig. 345: End of the Pirouette. The moment of this figure corresponds very nearly to that of Fig. 306.

Thus, by the aid of photography, tempo can be shown, without the aid of music.

263. Varieties of the Pirouette.—Pirouette on the instep (*Figs. 322 to 345*).

Pirouette in II, *in which the free leg separates in Principle II (100) during the rotation made by the toe of the other foot.*

Pirouette in II, finishing on the instep.

Pirouette in the Attitude, *in which the free leg is lifted in the Attitude (Fig. 200).* The Pirouette in Attitude begins with two turns in II and terminates with four turns in the Attitude, executed with a very rapid movement in the first two turns; the good effect of the Pirouette depends, according to Bournonville, on the second part of it being doubled in speed and in the number of turns.

Pirouette in Arabesque, *in which the free leg is extended in the Arabesque.*

Pirouette in Arabesque, finishing in the Attitude. *In which the leg passes from the Arabesque to the Attitude.*

Pirouette in II finishing in the Attitude. *During the rotation the free leg passes from the II to the Attitude.*

DESCRIPTION OF SOME OF THE TEMPOS AND STEPS   141

Pirouette with small Battements on the instep. *During the rotation, the free leg executes several small strikes on the instep (Fig. 185).*

Pirouette with small Circles with the Leg. *During the rotation, the free leg executes many small circles (193).*

Pirouette backward. *Always executed inward, and is characterized by backward bending movements. It takes on a great number of forms.*

These are a few of the variations on the theme of the Pirouette.

264. *In the language of dancers, the word Pirouette always carries the idea that one leg supports the body on the toe or the half-*

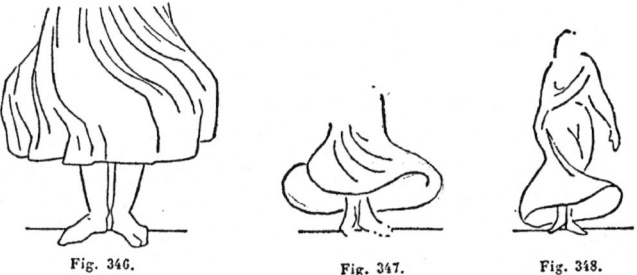

Fig. 346.   Fig. 347.   Fig. 348.

toe, and makes the rotation. While this rotation is being made, that is, while the dancer is in the air, it is called the turn in the air.

The dancer, having made the turn in the air, descends to a simple position, or to the Attitude, or the Arabesque, etc.

265. The turning movements, though highly valued by the Greeks, were fewer in number of kinds than ours (256, 263). Their mechanism is simple: it is usually a stamping of the feet on the sole or the half-toe, resulting in a whirling movement which is very rapid, if one may judge by the movement of their draperies. These forms of stamping are of few types, many times repeated, their physiognomy always the same.

It is definitely settled that the Greek dancers of the fifth to the second century B. C. practiced the Pirouette, and that the mechanism was the same as that of modern dancers.

266. **Turning by Stamping.**—The constant employment of this movement proves that they were ignorant of the more scientific

method used by French dancers. It is a charming motion, more because of the foot-action than on account of the turn itself. The form is as simple as it is good. *The turn by stamping on the soles*

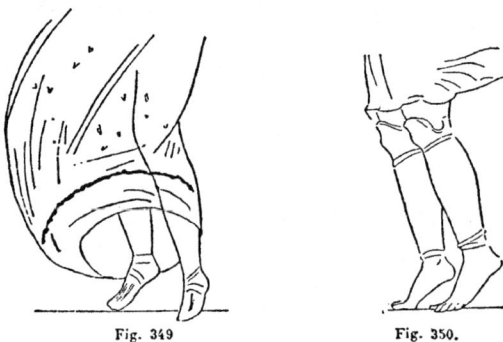

Fig. 349   Fig. 350.

of the feet (Figs. 346, 347, 348) *or on the half-toe* (Figs. 349, 350, 351, 352) is seen in Greek sculpture of the Hellenistic period. It is always held in high esteem. It is sometimes accompanied by a

Fig. 350A

strange backward bend (Figs. 352, 199, C) or by the flexion of the knees (Fig. 353).

267. **Turning by Stamping in IV Crossed.**—One of the *Positions* favored by the Greek dancers, who turned by stamping, was the IV crossed (95) on the half-toe or on the toe. It is one of the most

DESCRIPTION OF SOME OF THE TEMPOS AND STEPS   143

striking features of the ancient dance. Often the stamping is slight, owing to the close crossing.

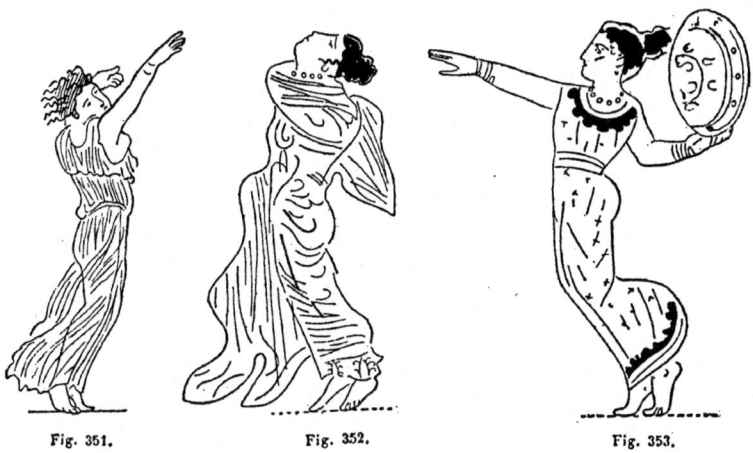

Fig. 351.   Fig. 352.   Fig. 353.

Our dancers do not practice this kind of rotation: they are even opposed to executing a IV crossed while turning rapidly, the position

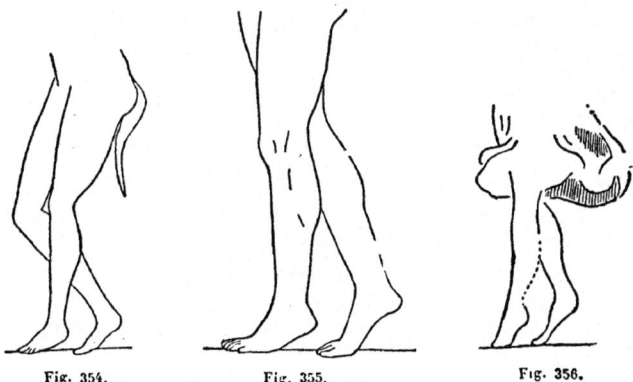

Fig. 354.   Fig. 355.   Fig. 356.

being a serious obstacle to quick movement. The Greek dancers, however, turned while in this pose, and moved rapidly, using a mechanism strange to us.

It is all a question of the celerity of the motion. Figs. 84, 355 and

354, in which the feet are crossed, support the body heavily and do not express rapidity of movement. By reason of the oscillation of the torso, the dancer represented in Fig. 189 does not appear to be turning rapidly. The turn is accelerated in Fig. 356 which is executed with a light movement on the half toe; the same remark applies

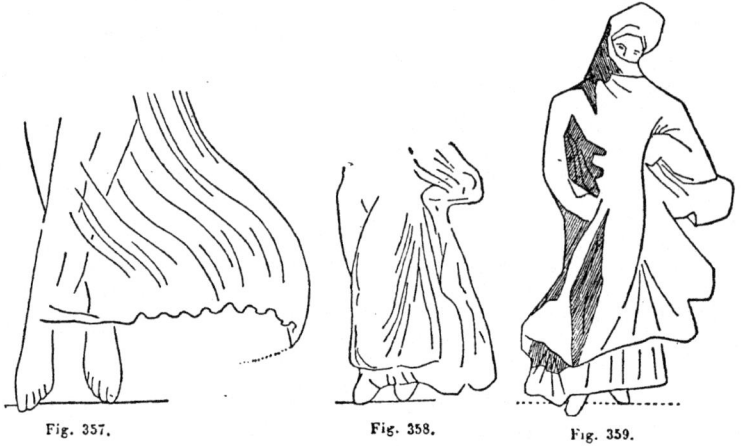

Fig. 357.   Fig. 358.   Fig. 359.

to Fig. 357. The veil dancers, 358 and 359, turn more slowly, on the half-toe or on the toe.

268. In what direction do these figures rotate? Is it possible to discover this?

It is certainly difficult to determine this point from an examination of the legs alone. But the movement of the torso many times furnishes a clue. For instance, the Borghese Faun, of which the feet are shown in Fig. 355, and of which the *Torso* turned to the left, is certainly turning to the left, the side on which the leg is crossed in front. It is the same with Fig. 490. Fig. 491 also turns toward the side on which the leg is crossed in front; in this case the left leg is free and lifted.

When the dancer is not nude, the direction of the motion can be discovered from the swirl of the draperies. *Painters and sculptors expressed the lightness of a dancer's whirling movement by the billowing and twisting of the garments.* When the drapery swings from right to left, the rotation is to the right (Figs. 346, 347, 348,

DESCRIPTION OF SOME OF THE TEMPOS AND STEPS   145

357, 476, A): if the swing is from left to right, the dancer is turning from right to left (Figs. 349, 476, B). This becomes a convention (316).

Although the draperies usually indicate the direction of the movement, there are cases where it is impossible to determine the matter in this way.

269. The *Pirouette* was certainly practiced by the Greek dancers. It is not a little surprising to find that the mechanism of the ancient dance was the same as our own. To turn on the foot when the heel

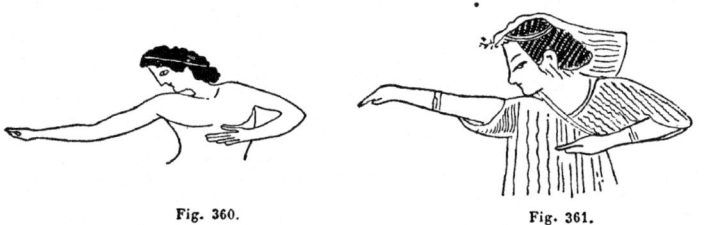

Fig. 360.   Fig. 361.

is not on the ground it is necessary to make the spring with the arms or the torso, and it imposes upon the dancer a certain tempo.

The Figs. 360, 361, 362, 363, 364 and 365 are the *Preparation*

Fig. 362.   Fig. 363.   Fig. 364.

for the Pirouette. The rotation must be made toward the side to which the arm crosses (260), it being the left for the dancers represented in Figs. 360 and 361, and the right for the others. It is easy, notwithstanding the bad defects, to discover from these six figures and the two following the equivalent of the movement of the arms analysed in the photographs in Figs. 331 to 365. The two legs of the dancers, Figs. 361 to 365, are on the ground: this makes the Pirouette ineffective, as the preparation was not good. Looking

Fig. 365.

at Figs. 362 and 363 there will be seen a light inclination of the torso to the left, much like that of Fig. 336, and which immediately precedes the reversed pose (262).

270. The joyous citizen who celebrates Komos (Fig. 366) is executing a *Pirouette outward* (259), turning to the right on the half-toe (Fig. 320). One of his companions (Fig. 367), who does not raise his heel, Pirouettes somewhat heavily, also outward, and to the left. The professional dancer (Fig. 368) poses on the half-toe, and turns to the right, making a *Pirouette inward* (259 and Fig. 321).

The three figures (366, 367, 368) are, in one respect, remarkable; the Preparation for the Pirouette by the arms and its Execution by the legs being made at the *same time*. This is an artifice of the

Fig. 366.   Fig. 367.

painter and the sculptor who are the authors of these two representations of the dance: each has superposed one moment of the dance upon another. Compare with the preceding series of photographs: the moment of the arms of Fig. 333 and the moment of the

DESCRIPTION OF SOME OF THE TEMPOS AND STEPS 147

legs of Fig. 340, really widely separated from each other, are combined in the Figs. 366, 367 and 368; this impossible combination is, of course, wholly conventional.

271. The charming little dancer in Fig. 369 who executes *a Pirouette outward on the instep* (259, 262) is posed on the toe, and, if one may judge from

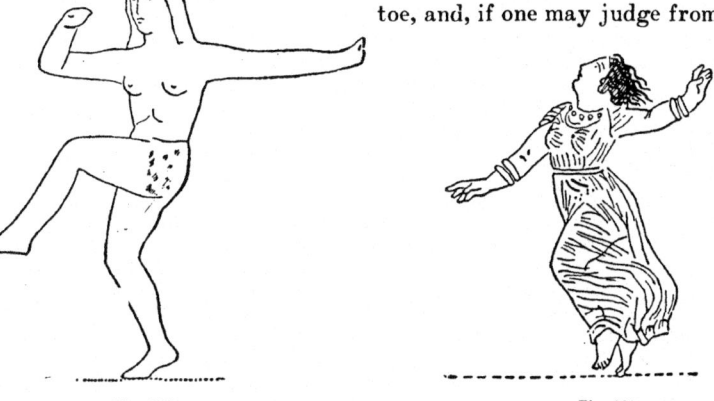

Fig. 368.   Fig. 369.

the direction of the torso, is turning to the left. She accompanies the *P*irouette with movements of the Arms, Head, and *T*orso which render her aspect quite different from that of our dancers. Nevertheless, the likeness between this and Fig. 340 is decisive.

RECONSTRUCTION OF TEMPOS AND STEPS

from the antique figures

COORDINATION OF MOVEMENTS

272. Superposition of Movements.—The Movements, *T*empo and Step, may, under certain conditions, be superposed, amalgamated, forming by their union new Movements the composing elements of which are easy to recognize. For example, the *P*irouettes with Battements, or the *P*irouettes with Circles of the Legs, etc.

By analogy it can be seen how the Jeté-Battu, *J*eté with Circles of the Legs, may be combined.

The many combinations made by fusing must not be confounded with Movements made in a series.

273. Successions of Movements.—*T*hose series of Movements in which certain *T*empos and Steps succeed one another without interruption are called *Enchainments,* or Chains of movements.

*T*here are good and bad Chains, that is, series in good style and in bad. It may make the matter of *T*empo clearer to say that the *T*empo corresponds to the syllables, the Step to the word, and the Chain to phrases of the dance. Therefore, the study of the Chain is the climax of the dancer's education: he must understand the bond between the isolated movements, must execute the phrases,—compose the words.

Example of a very simple Chain:

Coupé over (220) with the left leg. Fouetté to the rear (221) with the right leg (Figs. 370 and 375). Which is the same as saying the Fouetté commences as the Coupé ends.

The photographic analysis presented in Figs. 322 to 345 is a Chain composed of *Coupé over + Preparation and Execution of the Pirouette* (260, 261).

274. Repeated Movements.—*T*his statement of the rules governing the Chain may seem empirical, but there are reasons for the apparently complex and arbitrary requirements. Only the principal modes of succession will be noted here.

The formula of succession is simple where it is a *repetition of identical Movements.*

Examples: a series of Battements on the ground (Fig. 217), or of

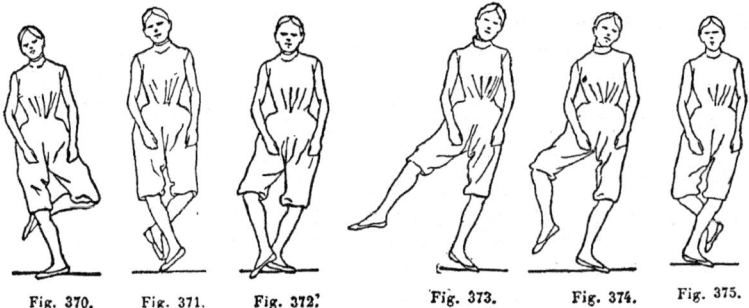

Fig. 370.   Fig. 371.   Fig. 372.   Fig. 373.   Fig. 374.   Fig. 375.

sustained Battements (Fig. 218), or the Grand Battement (Plate II), or the Circles with the Legs (Fig. 221), etc., executed in the same direction and with the same leg;—a succession of many Four Cuts (Entrechats) (Plate III), etc.

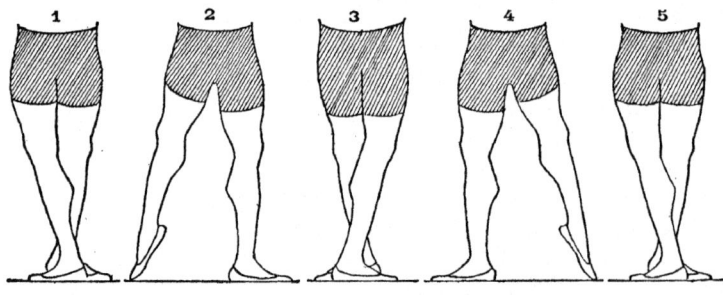

Fig. 376.

The repetition of the same Movement does not, properly speaking, constitute a Chain.

275. Alternating Movements.—In these the dancer, having executed a movement with the left arm or the left leg, at once repeats it with the right arm or the right leg, thus making one pair of *alternating Movements.* Example:

Battements on the ground, alternated (184, Fig. 376) No. 1: legs in III right advanced;—No. 2: right leg separates in II on the ground, raised on the toe;—No. 3: the right leg joins in II, rear;—No. 4: left leg separates in II on the ground with the toe;—No. 5: left leg joins in III at the rear.

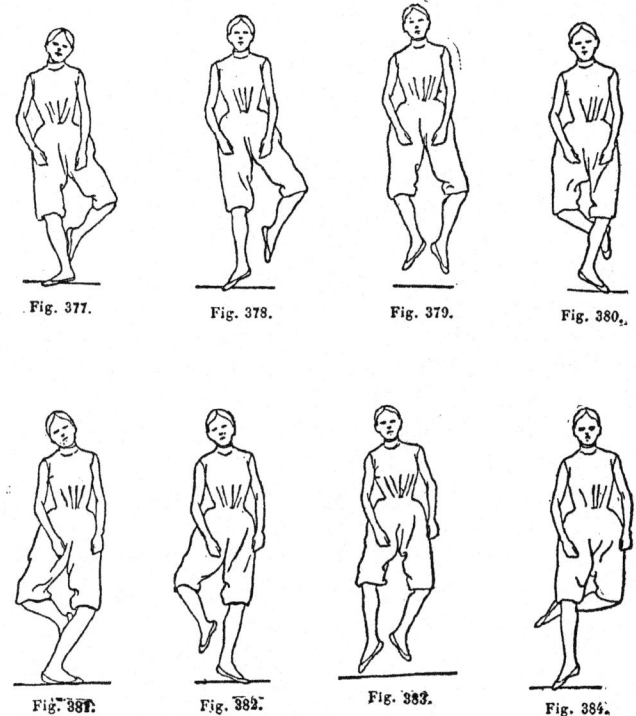

Fig. 377. Fig. 378. Fig. 379. Fig. 380.

Fig. 381. Fig. 382. Fig. 383. Fig. 384.

Jeté over, alternating, to the left and to the right (223 and Figs. 377 to 384).

These two examples enable the student to comprehend the meaning of expressions like the following: Slides alternating, Chassés alternating, etc.

276. The Chains themselves may be made in alternation. Those

represented in Figs. 370 to 375 are made in this manner, and according to the formula (273).

$+\begin{cases}\text{Coupé over with the left leg,} \\ \text{Fouetté to the rear with the right leg,}\end{cases}$

followed by this Chain:

$+\begin{cases}\text{Coupé under with the right leg,} \\ \text{Fouetté to the rear with the left leg.}\end{cases}$

The whole Chain is thus seen to be composed of two alternating Chains.

277. Movements in Opposition.—These are best described as movements in which two members are posed or moved in opposite directions.

The movement opposed to a movement beginning at the rear and advancing would be one where the motion commenced at the front and moved toward the back.

A movement opposed to one from low to high would be that which would be from high to low.

The movement opposed to that from right to left would be that which was from left to right.

278. When the arms or legs are active, the opposition may be simple or double.

It is simple when the two opposing movements are executed by the same member. Examples:

Simple Opposition $\begin{cases}\text{right leg is lifted in } Principle \text{ IV } forward; \\ \text{followed by lifting the same leg in } Principle \text{ IV} \\ \quad backward.\end{cases}$

The Opposition is double when the movement is made by two members. Examples:

Double Opposition $\begin{cases}\text{the } right \text{ leg is lifted in } Principle \text{ IV } forward; \\ \text{the } left \text{ leg is immediately raised in } Principle \text{ IV} \\ \quad to\ the\ rear.\end{cases}$

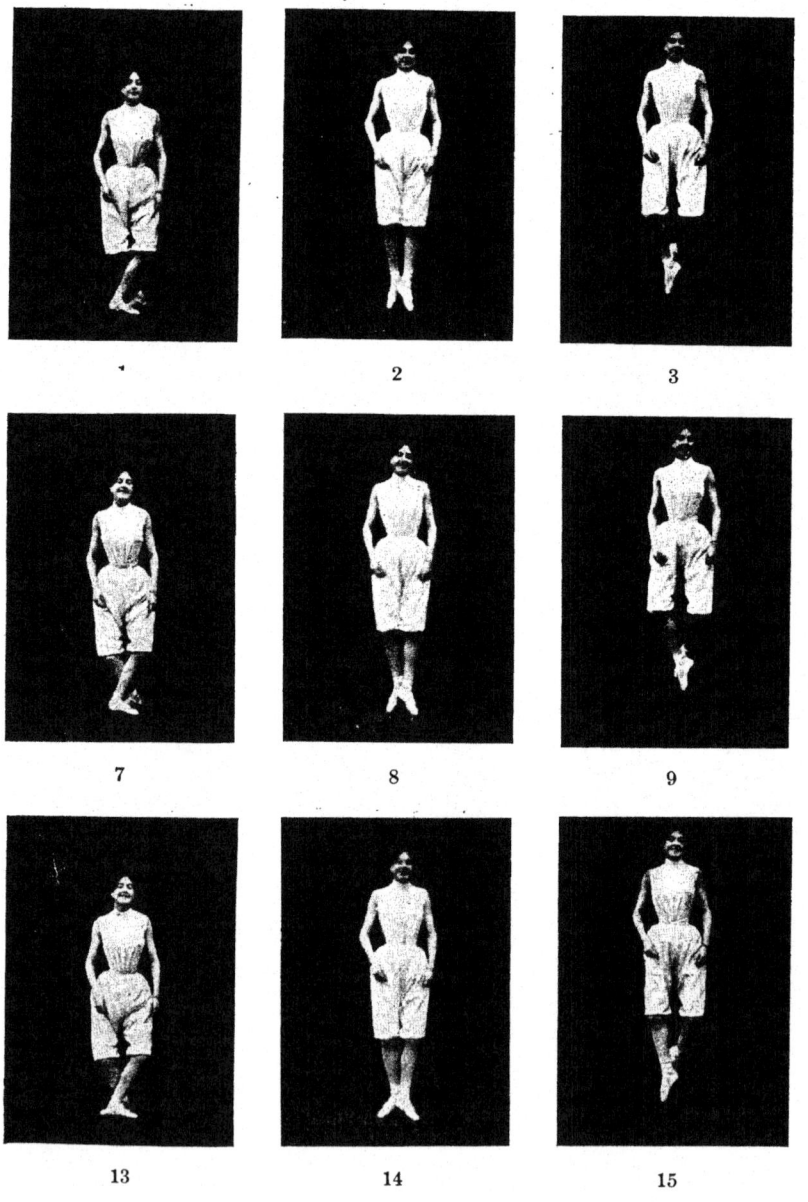

Plate III.

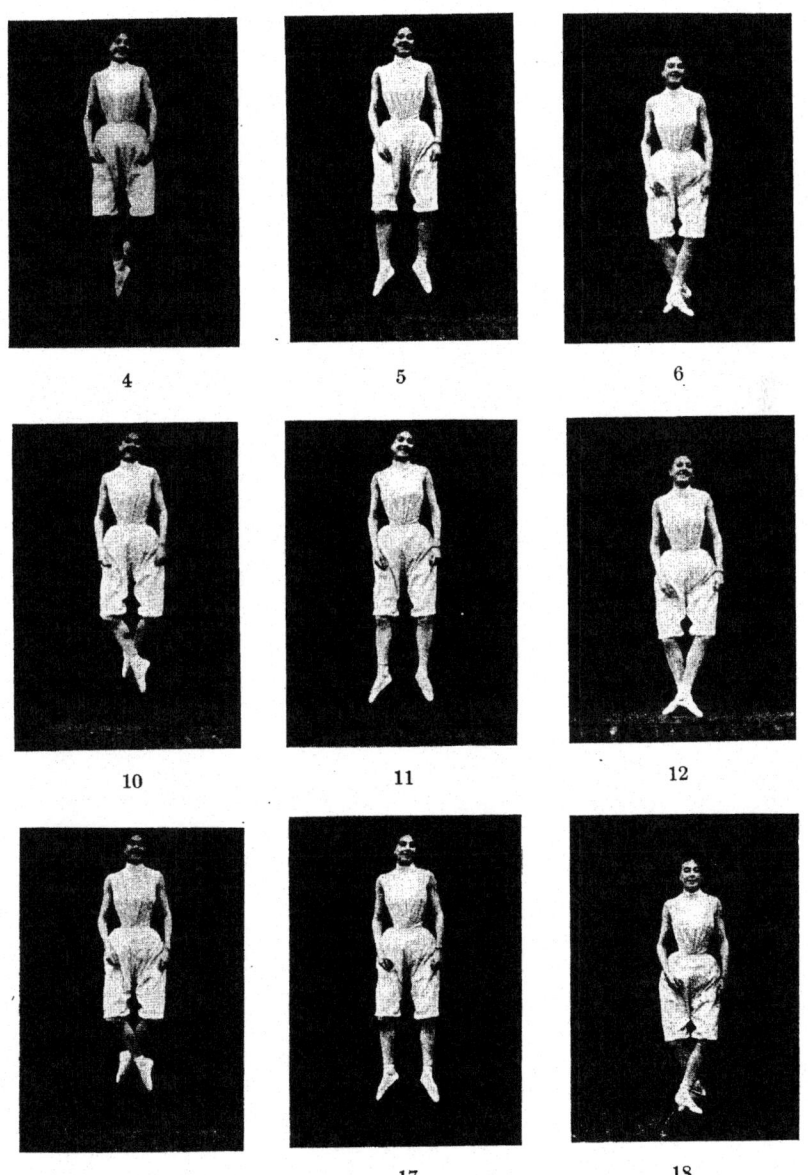

COORDINATION OF MOVEMENTS 155

The movements executed in opposition are numberless. The generalities given above are only the beginning.

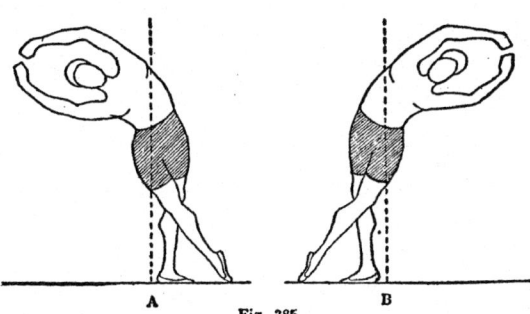

Fig. 385.

279. The opposing movements possible between the torso and head are, for anatomical reasons, limited. Below is a complete list.

Oppositions { bending the body to the right (Fig. 385, A);
bending the body to the left (Fig. 385, B).[1]

Opposition { right shoulder turned front (Fig. 184);
left shoulder turned front (Fig. 538).

Opposition { bending the torso forward (Fig. 285);
bending the torso backward (Fig. 186).

Opposition { bending the head forward (Fig. 197);
bending the head backward (Fig. 198).

Opposition { bending the head to the right (Fig. 195);
bending the head to the left.

Opposition { turning the head to the right (Fig. 196);
turning the head to the left.

280. Between the opposed movements executed by the members (arms and legs), but above all, between the two terms of the six Oppositions noted (body and head), there exists a relation most useful to the dancer who desires to pass from one to the other. This relation exists by reason of the latent conditions of equilibrium, by

[1] The vertical line of equilibrium is traced in dots.

which the movements are made from right to left, advancin
retreating from the vertical line of equilibrium (298).

The dancer thus obeys instinct in choosing these forms of mo
and the opposed action results in opposed reaction.

281. In review. The succession of movement may be:

I. By simple repetition.

II. By alternation.

III. By opposition.

IV. By free forms of which the limits are independent from other.

IDENTIFICATION OF THE MOVEMENTS BY MEANS OF THE SCULPTURES AND PAINTINGS

282. The Moments of the Movements.—The photographic analysis shows the movements at successive *moments*. Every one of the figures composing the series is an analysis of that *moment*.

By analogy it may be said that every figure taken from antique pictures represents a *moment* of the dance. In this way one of the phases of the movement is fixed by the artist's pencil, just as his alert eye saw it.

283. Characteristic Moments.—Among the movements of a step there is always one known as the *characteristic moment*, sufficiently defined for the student to determine which it is.

For example, take the Entrechat (Cut),—the characteristic moment is the period of suspension, corresponding to the crossing of the feet in the air, during the leap (*Plate III, Figs. 3 and 4, 9 and 10, 15 and 16*). The other moments are of no great value in determining the movement of which they are a part. In a word, if the student looks at a picture, he should have no difficulty in recognizing the movement depicted, provided it represents a characteristic moment.

As has already been stated, there are movements that have no characteristic moment.

284. Essential Moments.—All movements have two essential moments, some of them more. The definition of *essential moment* of movement is—*that which corresponds to the Positions which limit the movement, and between which it is effected.*

Example of movement in which *the essential moments are two in number:* Separate on the ground from the III right advanced to II on the toe (Fig. 217, 1 and 2). These are the *limiting Positions*, the first being III right advanced, the last being the II on the toe. It is enough to know the *limiting Position* to determine the entire movement by which the leg passes from one to the other. Because the two Positions correspond to the two essential moments, they are called the *extreme moments*, and give a correct idea of the scope of the movement.

Another example: symmetric oscillation of the Torso from either side to the vertical and past it to a similar pose on the other side, by a succession of two movements of Posing the Body to the left or to the right (Fig. 385). The two figures, A and B, mark the limits of the movement, and are sufficient to determine its scope.

Example of a movement in which *the essential moments are three in number:* Battement on the ground (184). The three limit positions between which the movement is effected are (Fig. 217, 1, 2, 3): the III advanced, the II on the toe, the III to the rear. The three figures are all that are necessary to make it clear to the student that the three movements are the essential moments.

Example of a movement having *five essential moments:* the Grand Circle with the Legs, made high (194), and in which (Fig. 229) the leg moves successively through the positions of—Principle II, Principle IV to the rear, position Principle IV forward, returning to Principle II. The passage from the Principle II to the Principle IV rear makes a quarter-circle horizontally. The Principle IV rear to Principle IV forward describes a half-circle inclined from the horizontal. From the Position marked *A* one sees one-quarter of the circle. From the Principle IV advanced the leg returns to Principle II, which is both the initial and the final Position, the circle being complete. Give these five Positions, the movements between them *can* be reconstructed.

285. From these examples it may be seen that one movement may not be enough to *determine* the step, making it in some cases necessary to have two, three, five, or as many pictures as there are essential moments.

Then, there is the question as to what *is* the essential moment, which is repeated (274), alternated (275) or combined in chains (276). If the movement is repeated twice, three times, four times, five times, etc., or alternated, or made one of a series, the smallest number of illustrations which will make it clear must be equal to the number of essential moments of the series.

Conclusion: A single figure, which is not the expression of a characteristic moment (283) is useless in determining the character of the movement. The characteristic moment must be determined by some other indication, and, if the precise limits cannot be set, there will be some doubt as to its nature.

But if the movement does not conform with the characteristic moment, whether there be one or several, the matter is not to be determined by fewer figures than there are essential moments (284).

The reader may prove this for himself by referring to the series of instantaneous photographs, finding the essential moments, and from them deducing the characteristic moment. He will also find that the photographs separate the movement, so that they show all of the *secondary movements* as well as the essential ones, keeping each in proper sequence. Thus, in Plate II, images 1 and 8 may be considered the same as the essential moments in the Battement analysis; all of the others are intermediate moments.

On Plate III is shown the characteristic moment of the Entrechat, which is the crossing of the feet in the air, as in the two figures 3 and 4, and 9 and 10, and 15 and 16. However rapid the motion, it is caught and fixed by the photographer.

On the contrary, a minimum of photographic images, corresponding to the essential moments of the movement, are deduced from figures 217-218, 273-274, 275-276, 284-285, etc.

286. These considerations permit us to formulate the conditions under which the dancing figures of sculpture were intended to be considered, and serve as a solid basis for the reconstruction of the movements of the dance.

(1) A single figure is sufficient to determine a movement when it presents a characteristic moment:

(2) Lacking a figure showing a characteristic moment, the movement cannot be reconstituted without several figures, their number being at least equal to the number of the essential moments of the movement.

RECONSTRUCTION OF THE TEMPO

287. The case is simple when the figure shown in the painting or statue expresses a characteristic moment of the movement (283).

Fig. 281 is an interpretation of the end of the Jeté. One figure is enough to reconstruct the movement. This is the order of succession:

1., bending the right leg,

2, leaping on the right leg,

3, descending on the left leg and withdrawing the right leg from the knee: *characteristic moment.*

In the same way, Fig. 318 is the characteristic moment of the Entrechat, from which the whole movement can be reconstructed in these three phases:

1, bending both legs,

2, leaping—*characteristic moment.*

3, descent.

288. The Pirouette has two characteristic moments, which are successive: one corresponds to the Preparation (Fig. 319), the other being the Execution of the movement (Figs. 320 and 321). The first is made with the arm crossed over the chest in the direction in which the rotation is to be made (260); the second is made during the time consumed by the rotation on the toe or the half-toe.

These two moments are represented in great numbers in Greek art, sometimes singly, sometimes superposed (270). It is possible, by taking a number of them together, to reconstruct the Pirouette.

289. Figures in Series.—By assembling these vases and reliefs, there is every opportunity to trace from the figures the essential moments of the movement (286). Although the paintings and sculptures do not exhibit anything that may properly be called a *series* of instantaneous and successive movements, they do show many dancers grouped on the same vase in the same movement, and represented at different moments of that movement.

The next point to be considered is, how to take a single figure, and, from it, make a true analysis of the whole step. The following example is remarkable on this account.

290. The three Satyrs with goat's feet (Fig. 386) are taken from the same vase. Notwithstanding the monstrous feet, there is the

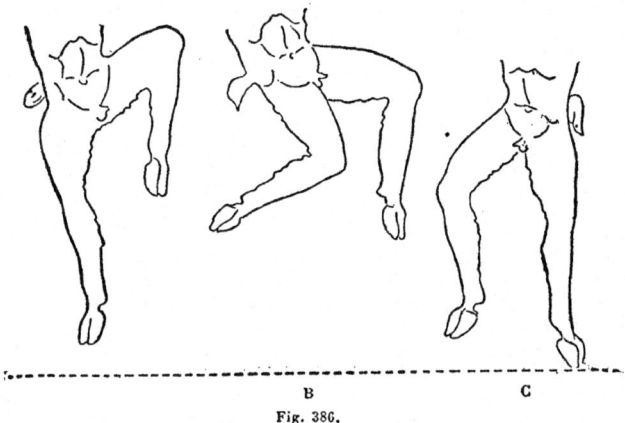
Fig. 386.

same ease of movement as in the photographs that begin with Fig. 387 and end with Fig. 398.

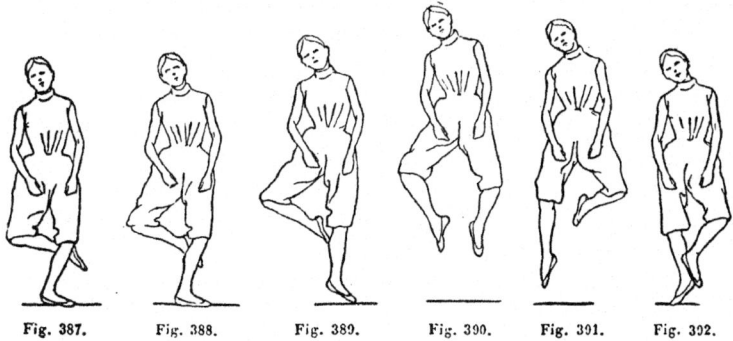

Fig. 387. Fig. 388. Fig. 389. Fig. 390. Fig. 391. Fig. 392.

This series is an analysis of one of the numerous forms of the leap used in our modern dance: the *Cat-leap*, executed laterally from left to right (Fig. 387 to Fig. 392); and from right to left in Figs. 393 to 398.

162   RECONSTRUCTION OF TEMPOS AND STEPS

The feet of A (Fig. 396) are shown at the same moment as Fig. 395. Figs. 390 and 396 are, no doubt, the same as figure B (Fig. 386).

The feet of C, like those of Fig. 397, express the end of the leap and the descent on the toe of the left foot. The three images of Fig. 386 are an analysis of the Cat-Leap from right to left. The essential moments of this are the period of suspension and the instant when the foot comes down on the toe.

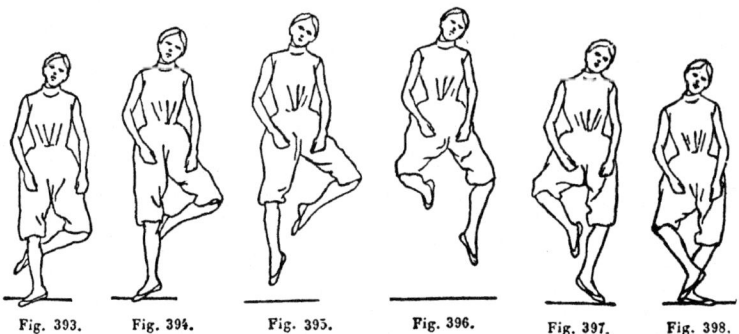

Fig. 393.   Fig. 394.   Fig. 395.   Fig. 396.   Fig. 397.   Fig. 398.

291. Another simple interpretation is possible in the case of Fig. 404 which marks the two extreme moments; the reconstruction of a character step may be made from the two Figs. 417 and 418 (307).

The analytic series presented by Fig. 405 is more than complete; the intermediate moments as well as the essential ones are pictured. The nature of the movement will be indicated later (301).

292. On the other hand, there are figures that give no hint of the essential moment; with these it is necessary to make up the deficiency by comparison. For example:

Figs. 219 and 220 are,—the first, an essential moment, the second, a secondary moment of the Grand Battement (Strike). It lacks the other essential moment,—that is to say, a moment corresponding to No. 8, Plate III. Still, by comparing these with the photographic series, the reconstruction becomes possible, by *interpolating* a number of figures (189).

293. It is not only the groups of dancers on the same vase or the same relief (289) which constitute an analytic series; often the information is gained from independent images from different sculptures or vases. Thus, the left arm of the beautiful statue part of which is reproduced in Fig. 155 shows the climax of the movement which begins with the arm of another statue (Fig. 161). In the same way, the three figures, 279, 280 and 281, which show three essential moments of the Jeté, are taken from three different vases. The series shows the movement of which Fig. 281 is the characteristic moment (283).

294. To recapitulate; it is possible to reconstruct a movement from one figure which gives the characteristic moment, or from a series containing one or more essential moments, it being possible to fill in the missing moments with photographs from living models.

RECONSTRUCTION OF THE STEPS

295. The sculptured and painted figures offer all the necessary elements for the reconstruction of the Steps of the antique Greek dance.

As with our own dance, the Step is composed of movements repeated (274), alternated (275, 276), opposed (277), in chains (273), simultaneous (226), superposed (272), etc.

These dancers of a long-passed age also understood the importance of movements of the Head, Torso, and Arms. This may be said of the antique dance much more truly than of the modern.

296. A number of these Steps have already been described; the Steps on the half-toe (215), the short Steps used in walking on the toes (214), the running Steps on the toes (242), the sliding Steps (226), the Jeté Steps (229), the balance Steps (234), the battu Steps (255), the Steps where the turn is made by stamping (266) the whirling Steps (267). (The Fouettés, Pirouettes, etc., are not here considered as Steps, but as Tempos.)

The elements of reconstruction, then, are: figures which present the characteristic moment of the Step: those that show the essential moments: and those which, by the blowing of their draperies, show which way the dancers are turning.

297. It is proper to employ Figs. 274, 276, 285 to reconstruct a Step already described (226, 234).

Fig. 274 and Fig. 276 placed next to Figs. 273 and 275 give the restoration of the essential moments at the two extremes (284) which are opposed to the moments of Figs. 273 and 275, and complete the plan of the two Steps. The reconstruction of these two restored figures is founded upon the following considerations:

To note the manner of holding the arms and their direction, etc., and, by this process, recognize the identity of the oppositions of the moments shown in Figs. 273 and 275, which are taken from two vases. Fig. 273 is according to this formula:

RECONSTRUCTION OF THE STEPS 165

(I)
- Left leg held on the ground in IV forward.
- Right leg backward and bent.
- Left arm held high and back of the vertical line of equilibrium.
- Right arm extended forward the same distance from the central line.
- Left shoulder turned front.

Fig. 275 shows the following opposition:

(II)
- Right leg held in IV forward.
- Left leg held back and bent.
- Right arm high and somewhat back of the vertical line of equilibrium.
- Left arm extended in front the same distance that the other is backward.
- Torso turns with left shoulder front.

These two figures mark the two extreme moments of the same Step.

Fig. 274 is in opposition to Fig. 273 and Fig. 276 is in opposition to Fig. 275.

The same extreme moments are found on Figs. 399 and 400, and determine the Step.

The Step, of which the fundamental mechanism has been fully explained (226) is characterized by the movements of the Legs, made by simultaneous Slides,—the torso being all the time inclined backward, though not as far as in some of the ritualistic dances of Dionysos,—and by the Opposition of the movements of the Legs and Arms.

298. Vertical Axis, Line of Equilibrium.—Fig. 285 expresses the extreme moment, which is opposed to the moment shown in Fig. 284. It is an inversion, made from a bronze statue (Figs. 180 and 237).

Fig. 401 shows a dancer in equilibrium, with the vertical axis passing through his head and the point of contact of the two hands.

The intersection of the *vertical axis* with the horizontal line of the shoulders determines the vertical line which is the *line of equilibrium.*

Fig. 402 expresses the relation of the moment represented in Fig. 284 to this line. By it, it is seen how far the right leg is in advance and how far the left leg is posed to the rear, that the head inclines back of the same line, and how far it bends toward the shoulder.

Fig. 399.   Fig. 400.

By imagining these two lines the distance of any part of the body from the center can be computed.

Fig. 401.

By constructing a figure analogous to the preceding, and like Fig. 285 in moment, Fig. 403 is obtained. This shows how the dancer establishes the compensation of the preceding rupture of equilibrium, it being in opposition to Fig. 402 in every way. In other words, *Opposition* by reaction.

It is the search for compensation that impels the dancer to oscillate between two opposing positions, repeating an effect produced on the right side with the left. The object is not merely to please the eye of the spectator, but to secure equality of muscular movement by exercising, successively, the muscles on each side of the body.

Fig. 285 is the moment of the Step that is opposed in the most simple manner to Fig. 284. This is not merely a hypothesis, it is the attitude that the body would assume by instinct.

RECONSTRUCTION OF THE STEPS 167

299. These explanations of the mechanism of the Steps, taken from the Greek paintings and reliefs, sufficiently indicate the likeness of their Steps to ours.

The Greek dancers were more often contented with a rudimentary dance which consisted of *marking time* in place, and withdrawing the leg by bending the knee or lifting the hip. The movements were most simple, and were, without exception, exaggerations of the walk or the run. These are the primitive dances the world over.

Fig. 402.

Fig. 403.

The alternating movement shown in Fig. 404 is a leap from one leg to the other, of which these two figures show the essential moments.

Fig. 404.

300. **Knees Flexed: From Antique Vases.**—There is one general remark to be made concerning Figs. 128, 404, 405, 406, 407, 408, 409, etc., which is also applicable to a great number of these dancing figures.

The ceramic painters, down to the end of the sixth century B. C. seldom represented the dancer at the moment when, by a leap, he was suspended above the ground (69, 72); always one foot, sometimes both feet are on the ground: this is because of the artist's inability, or because he was timid about breaking through tradition, so he had recourse to a subterfuge to express a leap. Unable to draw a dancer in the air, the artist presented his dancers before or after the leap, with knees bent, as though he had just descended to the ground. Even these early painters saw that there could be no leap without bending.

The knees are bent on the most ancient vases and on those of the sixth century B. C., as the *symbol* of the *moment in the air* which is understood. It is, no doubt, a mistake to always interpret

Fig. 405.

as a leap the postures of the legs which were favored by the early painters.

Fig. 406.

But, the moment the painter ceases to pose the dancer on the ground and makes him dart through the air, he stops using the symbol: he has learned to express the movement by more direct means.

Between the two moments of Fig. 404 must be interposed the moment of suspension during which the dancer leaps from the right leg to the left.

301. Fig. 405, in which the raising and lowering, progressively, of the dancer's legs is shown, is a remarkable example of a complete analytic series (291). The knee of the supporting leg is bent and it is evident that the dancer is leaping from the left leg to the right: he lifts the upper left leg as well as the upper right leg. He executes, in place, a series of leaps from one leg to the other, the hip-action being exaggerated.

Fig. 406 is one of the best types of the lifted hip.

Fig. 407.

302. While lifting the hip as high as he can, the joyful dancer in Fig. 407, a dancer of Komos (415), passes his hand under his knee, the hand holding a horn of wine. The left leg, bent at the knee, indicates a leap (300), which here seems to be reduced to a leap on the same foot.

303. Fig. 408 shows two Komos dancers, who, standing face to

RECONSTRUCTION OF THE STEPS 169

face, execute a Step for Two (334). Dancer A executes a small Jeté in place. Dancer B lifts the upper legs alternately (301). The gesticulation and the wild play of the arms is strange enough.

304. Figs. 409 and 410 present the same movements of the legs alternated (299, 301). One can imagine the movements of the legs from those of the arms. The backward inclination of the body is not awkwardness of design, it is a part of the dance.

305. Figs. 411 and 412 are the two moments of a gross Bacchic dance. Fig.

Fig. 408.

412 is a reconstruction, made to get the opposition (277). The dancer, whose body bends forward, leaps from one leg to the other with an exaggerated motion of the hip (301). He descends upon the half-toe.

The gambols of the Satyr (Fig. 413) are of the same nature. But the motionless arms are held in a strange Position, and the leap is *in place*. The face of this dancer

Fig. 409.   Fig. 410.

Fig. 411.

Fig. 412.

of Dionysos is stupid and drunken. The dance is a comic allegory.

306. The Satyr, painted on a little skyphos in the Louvre (Fig.

414), expresses equally a joyous surprise at finding a great vase of wine. By a *lateral kick*, resembling one of our movements, he manifests his contentment. The right leg is extended sidewise, while the left leg, which makes the leap, is in the air. He descends upon the right leg to continue the lateral kick on the left side.

307. In the Russian dance the crouching pose is used, as it was by the Greeks at all periods of their dance-history. Figs. 415, 416, 417 and 418 are proof of this. Fig. 415 is of the sixth century B. C., Fig. 416 of the fifth century B. C. Figs. 417 and 418 are taken from a Pompeiian painting. Figs. 417 and 418 mark the two essential moments of the Step, which is a leaping movement, and between which would

Fig. 413.

Fig. 414.

come the moment of suspension. While in the air the position of the legs is changed, the dancer crouching (Fig. 418) and, by a violent effort, leaping high enough so that he has time, while in the air, to extend one leg backward, bending it, and at the same time, to put the other forward.

Fig. 419 reproduces an instantaneous photograph taken during the moment of suspension. The change of leg-position has already

Fig. 415.   Fig. 416.

been made and the dancer is returning to the crouching Position.

308. Dances with the Body Bent Backward.—Of these there are

Fig. 417.   Fig. 418.

many (157, 165). This pose is used in the Greek dance in all kinds of Steps. With each century that passed it became more exaggerated. In the Alexandrian bas-reliefs, the Greco-Roman work, the plaques of terra-cotta, and the cameos of the imperial period, the type is more and more accented. It must have originated, like most of the exaggerated movements, in the Bacchic dances, although, before the third century B. C. it was not a part of the Dionysian dances.

The backward bend of the torso is often accompanied by backward bending Head. Sometimes, to get the contrast, the Head is posed forward (158) with a backward bending Torso (Fig. 199, C).

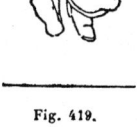

Fig. 419.

In some of the dances the backward bend is used at intervals, and in some it is maintained all through the dance.

309. Backward Bending Maintained.—Two examples are given (266). The dancers represented in Figs. 199, C, and 352 turn by stamping on the half-toe, holding the body backward, but not to the point of exaggeration: unless kept within well-defined limits, it presents an obstacle to the working out of the movement.

If taking small steps, the dancer may walk or run with the torso bent to a slight degree, but not more.

Fig. 420.

310. Intermittent Bending.—If the curve to the rear is used with large and rapid movements of the legs it must be intermittent, the dancer being obliged to stand erect in order to take the Step.

This is the case with the dancer in Fig. 420, who is shown at a characteristic moment of the Step. The Jeté, bending back, must, by reason of its mechanism, be preceded and followed by movements that demand an erect pose. The photographic series which is given below is a reconstruction of the whole Step.

The dancer advances rapidly, with short Steps—or leaps—on the half-toe. After three or four steps (Figs. 421, 422, 423) she lightly bends on the right leg, and, with a vigorous spring, Jetés with the left leg, forcibly pushing the right leg backward, while the body bends very far back, the feet and the back approach each other (Figs. 424, 425, 426). In the next figure the right leg descends and the backward bend is hidden by the readjustment of the position of the torso. The dancer will next recommence the series of small Steps which will end in another Jeté.

The Jeté of this figure (425) is the same as that pictured in Fig. 420, except that one is on the right foot and the other on the left.

Between the Figs. 424 and 425 there comes the period of suspension (222).

The charming dancer in Fig. 579 uses the same mechanism. Here the backward bend of the torso is accompanied by a backward drooping Head; Fig. 427, A shows the length to which the pose was sometimes carried at the climax of the Bacchic dances,

311. Body Alternately Bending Backward and Forward.—The extreme limit of the pose is attained by the dancer in Fig. 427 who advances with short steps on the half-toe. If this dancer is not one

Fig. 421. Fig. 422. Fig. 423.

Fig. 424. Fig. 425. Fig. 426.

of those mad with hysteria, she certainly holds the pose indefinitely. Many of these dances can be explained only on pathological grounds.

The pose is an integral part of a Step which is composed of backward inflections of the body alternated with an equal swing forward. The torso oscillates from one side of the vertical line to the other by opposition (279), by instinct (280, 298), swaying both head and body backward or forward.

The dancer (Fig. 427) passes from Position A to that of B, which is held by her companion. These are the essential moments of the same movement.

312. The Backward Bend Made as a Part of the Step.—To ob-

Fig. 427.

tain an average between the types of Attitude furnished by Figs. 207 and 208, take Fig. 428. This figure is, without doubt, an expression of one of the extreme moments in a character-Step. The application of the same principles already stated (280, 298) enable one to reconstruct the other moment.

An analysis of the whole Position of Fig. 428 is given.

(I) Members
- Left leg supporting.
- Right leg bent back at the knee.
- Left arm circled above the head.
- Right arm extended laterally.

(II) Body, head
- Body bent backward and to the right.
- Head inclined to the right.

By proceeding according to the rule, we get the opposite pose:

(III) Members
{
Right leg supporting.
Left leg bent back at the knee.
Right arm circled above the head.
Left arm extended laterally.
}

(IV) Body, head
{
Body bent forward and to the left.
Head inclined to the left.
}

Fig. 429 shows a new ensemble: this is the natural opposition to the moment of Fig. 428 (298).

313. In order to fix the *intermediate moments,* instantaneous photographs were made, commencing with the first moment, and ending with the last (Figs. 428, 429), to determine, in other words, the secondary movements between these essential moments.

Fig. 428.

Fig. 429.

This series is the one ranging from Fig. 430 to 437. One image (Fig. 428) is enough to enable us to reconstruct the entire movement.

The dancer, having arrived at the Position reproduced by Fig. 428, passes to the contrasting Position. This means oscillating between the limit-Positions (Fig. 430 + 434 + 437); the intermediate moments will come naturally.

Fig. 430 = Fig. 428: essential moment (284).
Fig. 431: intermediate moment.
Fig. 432: intermediate moment.

Fig. 430. Fig. 431. Fig. 432.

Fig. 433. Fig. 434.

Fig. 433: intermediate moment.

Fig. 434 = Fig. 429: essential moment, the opposite of the first.

Fig. 435: intermediate moment.

Fig. 436: intermediate moment.

Fig. 437 = Fig. 430, returning to the point of departure: essential moment.

314. Body Bent Forward all Through the Step.—In contrast to the positions of the body held backward are those where it is posed

Fig. 438.   Fig. 439.

forward all through the Step or dance. Figs. 438 and 439 show the essential moments of which 3 and 4 on Plate IV show the execution.

On a fragment, painted in red, dating from the first half of the fifth century B. C., is pictured a dance of the Bacchantes, which expresses all of the disorder that characterized these rituals. There are eleven of the figures, one of them playing on the double flute. An idol of the god, in form a column surmounted by a head, presides over the evolutions of the chorus; it is impossible to say why the latter are grouped as they are. Four of the women brandish the thyrsus. The others gesticulate in the manner common to this type of dances. Some have empty hands, others shake their tambourines or carry vases, all combine their movements much like Spanish dancers. With head bent, their eyes seem to follow the movements of their feet. They repeat over and over the Separation (Fig. 438), Pose (Fig. 439), Separate (Fig. 438), Pose (Fig. 439), etc.

It is easy to see that No. 3 of Plate IV corresponds to Fig. 438 and that No. 4 of the same plate is, except for the hands, like Fig. 439.

315. Dancers Who Crouch or Kneel.—The being represented in Fig. 440 walks in a crouching position, turning his body from right to left alternately.

Fig. 440.

The other (Fig. 441) descends on the right knee. He springs, leaps and descends upon the left knee (Fig. 442), to recommence upon the right, etc. The inflections of the Body are to the left when the dancer descends on the right knee, and on the right when he comes down on the left. Fig. 442 shows the opposition, and is a minor moment of the Step.

The two Satyrs, A and B (Figs. 444–5), turn, the first, to the left, the second, to the right, using the knee as a pivot. They appear to be trying to throw their right legs over the vase without touching it. B shows the manner in which it is accomplished. His companion

Fig. 441.   Fig. 442.

makes a half rotation. This odd exercise is not merely a game, it is a dance.

The Satyr who is represented in Fig. 446 is one of a grotesque band. Each of the dancers who compose it supports himself on the knee and hand that are on the same side, alternating the knee and hand as he progresses,—not a brilliant feat, considered from the point of view of Eurhythmy; it is the buffoonery of a Satyr dance-drama.

The kneeling posture of the two Satyrs at the ends of the picture (Fig. 578) is not especially remarkable as a gymnastic: but it is certainly a dance, of an obscure sort, and not a posture of adoration.

316. Dances with the Mantle.—The supple mantle worn by the women of Greece was utilized by the dancers. Being ample in size, it allowed the arms to move freely, or, it could be wound as tightly as a sheath. In shape it was a large rectangle of wool cloth. At one moment it might envelop the whole body,—the next, it would be flung about the shoulders as a simple cape, or might take on a score of other forms.

Fig. 443.

The gestures which would naturally be made by the wearers of the garment were used by the dancers also; the gesture with the veil

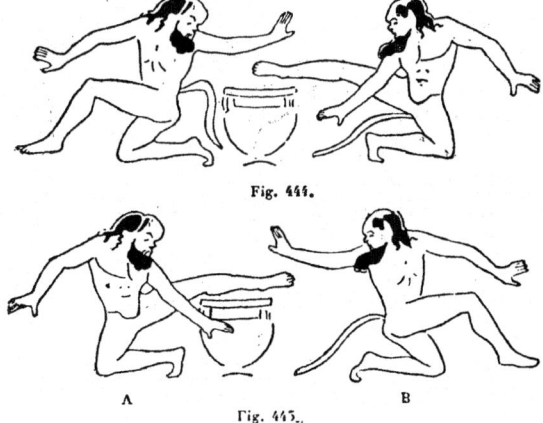

Fig. 444.

Fig. 445.

(43), the hands hidden in the mantle (45), the hand on the hip, causing the drapery to ripple,—all of these were introduced into the dance, partly as an imitation, partly for the sake of their decorative effect.

The dancer did not play with the mantle at will, the gestures with it were all determined by the mechanism of the Step.

Fig. 447: compare with image B of Figs. 3 and 4 (43).

Fig. 199, A: the dancer is entirely enveloped in a mantle which is supple and transparent. The Step has been described (226).

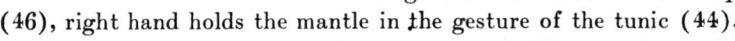

Fig. 446.

Fig. 448: compare (129).

Fig. 352: arms covered; right hand lifted to left shoulder. Description of Step (266, 309).

Figs. 449 and 450: the mantle is held over the breast by one hand which is kept covered (160, 163).

Fig. 451: left hand on the hip (46), right hand holds the mantle in the gesture of the tunic (44).

Fig. 452: the dancer turns, by stamping, in IV crossed, on the half-toe (267). The likeness existing between this terra-cotta figurine and the preceding illustration leads to the conclusion that the movements are the same. The right foot of Fig. 452 is flat on the ground, otherwise the posture is the same as that of the right foot of Fig. 451. The dancer turns in the same manner, at a moderate rate of movement. Comparing the two, it is difficult to say what is the direction of the rotation.

Figs. 1, 2, 3, 4, 5, 6, 7 of Plate V are a photographic analysis of a turn continued by crossing, by stamping, left toe on the ground. The

B   Fig. 447.   A

antique model is of the type of Figs. 450 A, 450 B, 451, and 452. The right hand is on the hip; the left hand is held over the breast with the hand at the shoulder, holding the mantle, which is over the mouth.

Much might be said of the movements in which the dancer uses her tunic during the dance. The ceramic painters made a study of whirling drapery, though they represented it by means of certain conventions (Figs. 346, 347, 348, 349, 357, etc.).

Fig. 448.

Fig. 453: This somewhat lackadaisical person who is enveloped in a mantle, poses on her half-toe, left hand held low and back, right hand under the mantle. She executes the Balance Step (233, 234) with the body bending alternately to the right and left, depending upon which leg carries the weight.

Fig. 449.

Fig. 454: one arm extended forward, enveloped in the mantle.

Fig. 455: much the same, except that an animal's skin replaces the mantle.

Figs. 362, 363, 364, 365, and others show similar gestures with the mantle.

317. The Veil Dancers of Pompeii.—These are airy figures who gracefully fling their veils to the breeze, and who are not bound by the law of equilibrium: this is the one liberty that the artists have taken, and it detracts somewhat from the value of the representations.

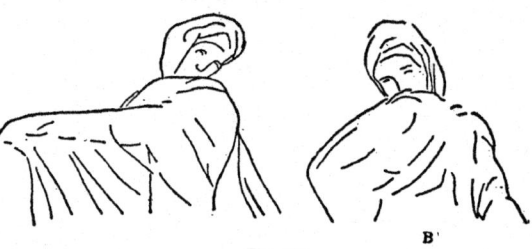

Fig. 450.

182   RECONSTRUCTION OF TEMPOS AND STEPS

But, even with this fantastic misrepresentation, the images prove that the veil was a transparent thing that could be used most coquettishly. The painting has value as a document regard-

Fig. 451.

Fig. 452.

ing decorative painting, but none as an interpretation of the dance.

318. Unfolding the Veil.—The Greek dancers folded and unfolded the material lightly and gracefully. Often they unfurled the veil above the head, making a frame for the face. Indeed, there was a special dance that seems to have been devised for the sole purpose of affording an opportunity to play with the veil.

Fig. 457: the dancer grasps the mantle by its border.

Fig. 458: the arms gesticulate: the feet whirl in IV crossed, on the toes.

Fig. 459: the arms are lifted high, and the veil floats in great folds. The Step is the same as the preceding.

Fig. 453.

The Figs. 107 and 494, B may be interpreted as the end of a

dance with the mantle-play. The fabric is blown by the wind, the wearer catching it in plaits.

The Victory of Pæonios (15, 383) is also a dancer who plays with her veil as she leaps. Similar representations are not at all rare in Greek statuary.

319. Dance with the Joined Hands.—Under this head may be grouped a great number of dancers who cannot be considered solely

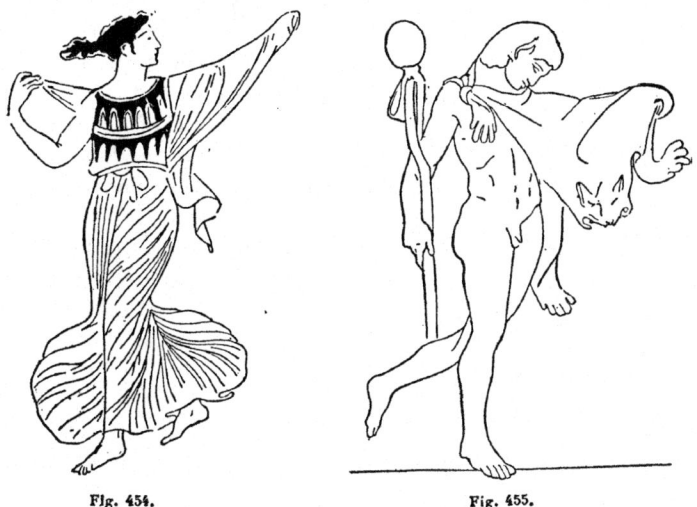

Fig. 454.   Fig. 455.

with reference to the movement of the feet, but who are in a separate class, making the head and hands also dance. They are most often found in character-dances.

The interlacing of the fingers is made in many ways: by reason of the flatness of the relief or the vagueness of drawing, it is often difficult to arrive at an understanding of the details. The series of figures makes description unnecessary.

Mention must be made of statuettes of which the legs are missing, having either been destroyed or never having existed. It may be said that this amputated form has its advantages, because it isolates the gestures of the arms (Fig. 460).

Fig. 461: the dancer's body oscillates in a peculiar manner, better understood by comparing the figure with its opposite in Fig. 462. The dancer walks heavily. This dance was slow, to the music of the lyre, the presence of which usually denotes a dance of solemn character.

Fig. 463: the dancer slides on the half-toe. Compare with Fig. 272.

Fig. 464: the dancer runs on the toes (242). Note that the palms of the hands are turned outward.

Fig. 465: Much like the preceding types and also Fig. 469, a grotesque. This is from a vase of Gallo-Roman origin and is of no value from the art standpoint. It shows the persistence of this traditional pose.

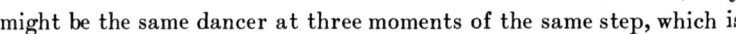

320. The three figures following are arranged in a series: were it not for the difference in sex and costume, they might be the same dancer at three moments of the same step, which is a Separation and Bending,—with a Leap,—and the Descent,—a Jeté.

Fig. 466: Separation of the leg, Bending the left leg for the leap.

Fig. 467: period of suspension of the leap.

Fig. 468: Jeté on the right toe (222): the left leg is held back; Body bends back; Head turns from the side to the back.

Fig. 456.

Fig. 457.

The instantaneous photographs show all of the movements of the Step (Plate V, Images 8, 9, 10, 11, 12, 13, 14).

No. 8: corresponds to Fig. 466.

No. 9: the dancer executes a very small leap.

RECONSTRUCTION OF THE STEPS

No. 10: Jeté on the right leg. The left leg is withdrawn: head turns to the right: backward bend of torso begins.

No. 11: corresponds to Fig. 468 and makes the movements of the left leg, the Head and the Torso which are indicated in the preceding figure.

Fig. 458.

Fig. 459.

No. 12: the left leg descends to position. The head and torso approach the perpendicular.

No. 13: the heel of the right foot is lifted: the leg begins the separation.

No. 14: the same moment as No. 9 and Fig. 466. The right leg is separated in IV crossed. The course of the Step is complete.

321. This strange figure executes a *Jeté crossed*. The left leg crosses on the right leg during the moment of suspension (222).

Figs. 470-473: two essential moments of the Step, opposed (279). Fig. 471 is a reconstruction based on the preceding observations (280, 298).

Figs. 472-473: two moments of another Step, opposed. Fig.

473 is a reconstruction (280, 298). The same is to be said of the tiny dancer (195) who executes the Circles with the legs, alternating the right and left.

Fig. 474: this dancer exaggerates the bending of the torso while making a movement with the legs which would require an erect position. The figure sways the body back and forth with many contortions.

Fig. 460.

Fig. 475: *A tour of the air ?* (264): the appearance is that of pivoting.

322. Between the two dancers A and B, Fig. 476, who are two Amazons, there is a throne upon which their queen is seated. They execute in her honor a step for two: they turn

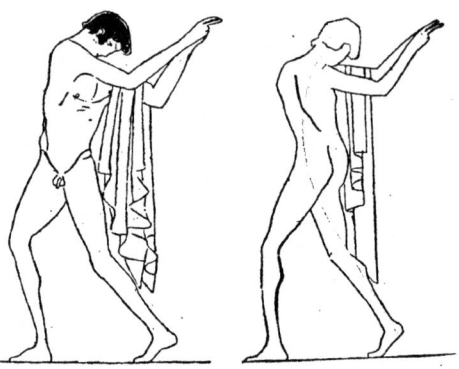

Fig. 461.   Fig. 462.

Fig. 463.   Fig. 464.   Fig. 465.

their sides toward this high seat, facing each other in opposed positions, and showing, by the way that the wind blows their tunics, the direction in which they turn. Dancer A turns from left to right; dancer B turns from right to left.

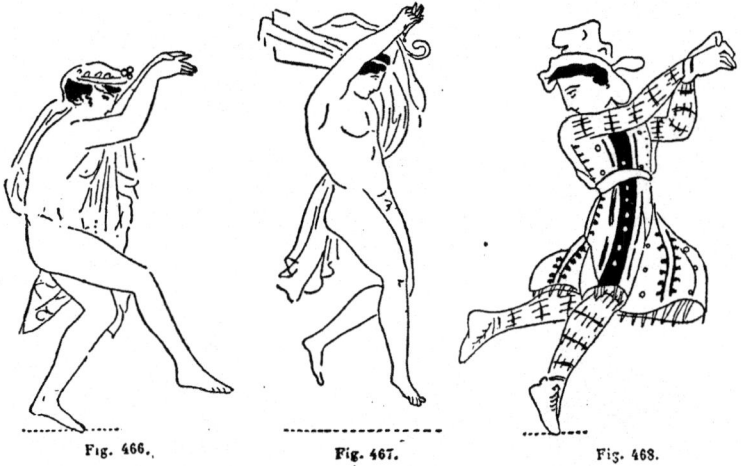

Fig. 466.   Fig. 467.   Fig. 468.

Dancer A executes a turn by stamping on the half toe; dancer B slides upon both toes at the same time (226). More, they accompany the movements of the legs with rhythmic oscillations of the Torso and Head, alternately from right to left.

Fig. 469.

This step for two is nearly identical with one on a famous vase, of which the decoration represents a ceremony in honor of the Indian Dionysos. By an artifice of the painter, the two dancers are separated by a long procession of gods. The votaries are placed in a double line, which, despite the errors of perspective, make two parallel files. At the center of the procession, Dionysos, mounted on a camel, his right arm extended, observes the rhythmic order of the dance (Fig. 477). The procession turns to the right; dancer A (Fig. 478) heads the march; dancer B, apparently going backward, heads the procession.

188 RECONSTRUCTION OF TEMPOS AND STEPS

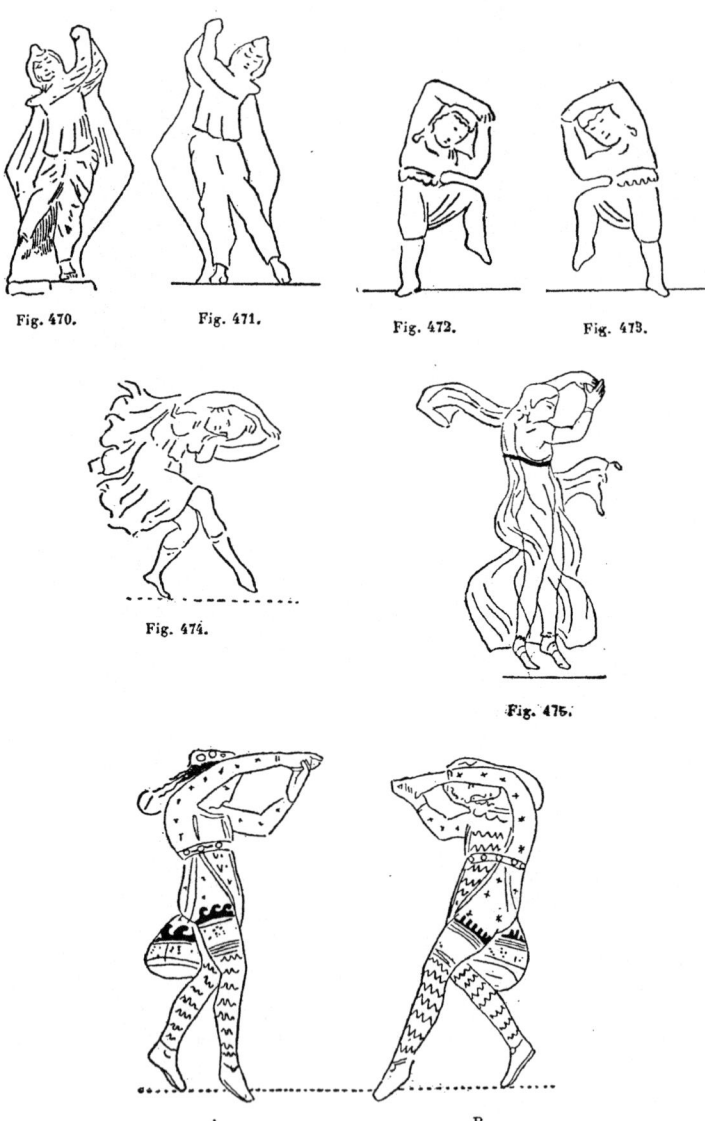

Fig. 470.   Fig. 471.   Fig. 472.   Fig. 473.

Fig. 474.

Fig. 475.

A   B
Fig. 476.

This is much like the effect produced by the two Amazons: compare dancer A (Fig. 478) with the dancers who turn by stamping on the half toe (266), notably Fig. 352, and observe the blowing drapery at the back and left of the tunic, and it becomes plain that the figure is a replica of Amazon A (Fig. 476). Not only are the

Fig. 477.

costumes of the two groups similar, denoting the Asiatic origin of both, but the arrangement and pose are alike.

Dancer B (Fig. 478) executes the slide at the same time on both feet.

An attempt to assign the two dancers to their proper place in the Bacchic procession:—they dance on each side of the god, to honor and amuse him. The ceramist has done his best to show a slide on both feet at each end of the line by these two personages who are on either side of the divinity; this is an artifice of perspective.

Figs. 479, 480: Compare with the above (315).

323. The greater number of the persons who execute the *dance of the joined hands* wear a costume very unlike the Greeks (Figs.

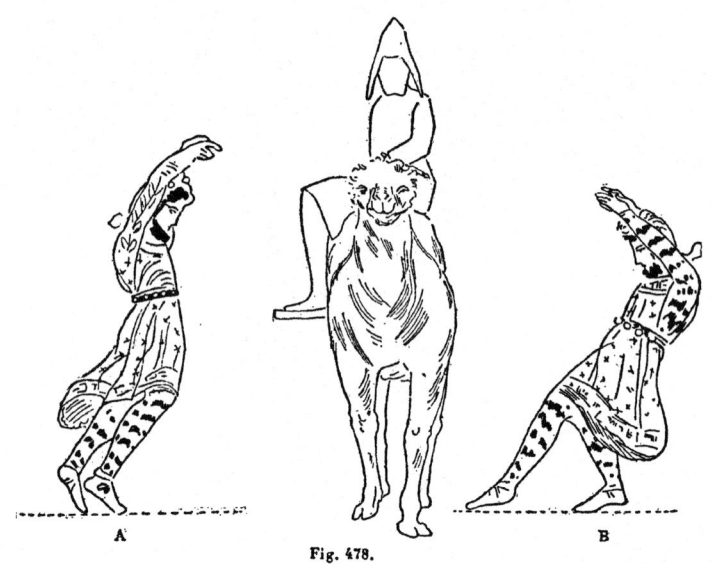

Fig. 478.

460, 464, 469, 470, 472, 474, 478, 479). But the dance itself is of barbaric origin, most likely Asiatic, and, in a happy moment, was

Fig. 479.   Fig. 480.

adopted by the Greeks. The vase in the Louvre, from which Fig. 461 is taken, has red figures, and belongs to the period 450 B. C.

STUDIES OF THE DANCER

324. The Dance Properly So-Called. Its Classes.—*A few words as to the method employed in our schools for the education of the dancer.*

It is necessary to begin the training in childhood. The pupils, boys and girls, enter the classes when from six to eight years old. Then, after a careful medical examination, if they appear to be adapted to the work, they are registered at the school. Their lessons are always given in the morning, and last one and one-half hours.

Only one master instructs the boys, but the girls are under the direction of four teachers.

The first "class" is for girls only, and the work taken up is divided into Petites and Half-Principles. The term of study is from one to two years, after which come the examinations for the next class. The number of pupils accepted is limited: the class is made up of two sections, one of which admits to the second Quadrille, if the applicant is successful. The entrance to the class of coryphees is equally difficult. The result is that many fail, but the high standard is maintained.

In order to develop the muscles in the required manner, the exercises must be practiced perseveringly. The most brilliant artists, both men and women, spend hours every day in the schools, practicing all of the movements which are the indispensable preparation for public representations. The public knows very little of the infinite patience required, of the fatigue suffered, by students of the ballet, who, by this means, educate their bodies to that condition of grace and litheness admired by the public. With our modern dancers, the object is to become great artists, not to hasten through the period of instruction. This, of necessity, means constant toil until the muscles are always capable of vigorous activity and always supple: there is no doubt that dancers truly love their art, else they would never endure the painful discipline necessary to perfect it.

325. *The classes are held in large rooms, the floors of which are built on an incline. Along the walls are arranged the bars which support the students in the "Exercises of the Bar" with which the lessons begin. These are intended to make the body elastic, and form the first third of the lesson. The Bars are on a level with the chest. By posing with the heel on the Bar, the leg is lifted so that it forms an oblique angle with the supporting leg. The Bar aids in holding the body in place, but, as soon as possible, the support is withdrawn and the exercises are taken without any support whatever.*

In order to gain stability the first exercises are the practice of the five fundamental Positions. Holding the feet sidewise is very difficult for most pupils; here the Bar is useful.

The preparatory exercises (Bending, Separating, Striking, Circles with the Legs, First Tempo on the Toes, etc.) are executed with the Bar until the pupil acquires the necessary equilibrium, after which he continues to practice with the Bar for a short time every day, under the eye of a teacher, as the first period of the lesson. The first subjects taken up are the same for every one. All of the dancers use the Bar, standing in a line.

326. **Gradation of Exercises.**—*The method has been indicated above. Everything proceeds in a certain routine: the pupils follow in successive Steps the long course of study, repeating every day the foregoing exercises. The machinery is not allowed to rust,— the dancer must work if he expects to remain a pupil.*

During the first year the classes of Beginners and the Quadrilles study the fundamental Positions in all their variations, their derivatives, and all of the Preparatory Exercises which are regarded as the gymnastics of the dance, Bending and Holding all of the Positions on both feet or on one foot, Separating on the ground, half-high in Principle position II or IV, executing the Battements on the ground, Battement sustained, Grand Battement, Circles of the Legs on the ground, Circles of the Legs held, and Grand Circle of the Legs.

The following are the Exercises for Equilibrium, movements made slowly, in stable Positions held as long as possible. From these are evolved, by Principle II and Principle IV the movements ending in the Attitude and then the Attitude crossed, the Arabesque and the Arabesque crossed, the Preparation and the Tempo of the Pirouette.

Little by little, the pupil practices all of the series of Tempos— Tempos on the ground, Tempos in the air,—Slides, Chassés in all directions, Coupé, Fouettés, Jetés over, under, laterally, Jetés-Ballonnés, Jetés crossed, Cat-leaps, Tempo and Step on the toes, Assemblés, Mutation of the Feet, Battu Steps, Entrechats (Cuts), Jetés-Battus, Slides in turning, Chassés turning, Fouettés turning, Jetés turning, Rising on the toes while turning, Battu steps while turning, whirling steps, Turns in the air, etc.

The class called the Coryphées study different Tempos, Chains,— the course becoming more and more complex,—they execute "Variations," which are mixtures of different steps; these are the superior exercises of the dance. The Coryphée, initiated into the mysteries of the Attitude, *and able to pass through all possible variations of the Steps, possesses the complete technique of the art.*

The plan of exercises for each lesson in the advanced classes is made according to a uniform model. One hour and a half the pupils practice in the following order:—1, Exercises with the Bar; 2, Tempo, Equilibrium and Pirouettes; 3, Tempo and Steps of the Leap; 4, Chains composed of all kinds of Tempos and Steps; Every lesson constitutes a sort of review of all the gymnastics of the dance.

327. The Ballet-Masters.—*The dancers of both sexes, trained in the difficult technique of the dance, directed by their teachers, pass on to the Ballet Masters, with whom they study the rules governing the Grouping, Steps, Assemblés, thus coordinating the various movements already learned. From him they learn the Character-dances, the Steps for Two, for Three, for Four, etc. In a word, the figuration,—the* Choregraphy. *The Ballet-Master is at once the commander and the creator. He decides as to the decoration which makes for perfection, and, on occasion, the arrangement of the rhythms and the evolutions which he dictates to the dancers.*

328. Three figures, 481, 482, and 483, show: the first, the dance of attitude, the other two, the dance of motion.

Fig. 481. Here, to the music of the double flute, the young pupil holds the Attitude (169, 174). The musician who accompanies him is one of the auxiliaries of the Pedotribe (329) of which the long forked rod is the recognized symbol. This piece of pottery has red figures, and belongs to the first half of the fifth century B. C. It is in the Louvre.

Fig. 482. The young dancer is not content with the double flute,

Fig. 481.

and adds the rattle of the castanets, to which she executes her rhythmic movements.

The musician, who is seated, is a professional; therefore, she belongs to a class which acquired an unsavory reputation in Greece. It must be admitted that this scene takes place in one of those mansions of joy where dancers and flute-players found constant occupation.

Of the same world, it would seem, are the teacher and pupil who face one another in Fig. 483. The former leans upon a rod of formidable aspect, which certainly is not intended for use in beating time, as the young girl marks time herself by rattling the castanets. The Step is difficult to recognize; perhaps it is nothing more than a simple sliding walk, with the play of the head and arms forming the principal part of the dance.

329. The Gymnastics of the Dance.—The many exercises, *wrestling, running, discus-throwing, casting the javelin,* etc., were prac-

Fig. 482.

ticed by the children and by the professional athletes. Both used the gymnastics of the dance, which Plato called the mimetic elements of art, and which were intended to make the body supple: they were often very painful.

In fact, the elementary movements of the Greek dance were not essentially different from the other gymnastics in use at the time. With the professionals the children learned the Pyrrhic dances, which is enough to prove that they received the same education. Another proof is given by both Plato and Xenophon, who speak of certain instruction given the professionals as *dance-gymnastics*.

330. An effort to make out a programme of study from the paintings and sculptures, and the texts of writers would read about as follows:

Positions of legs,—equilibrium of the dancer.

Preparatory exercises: Bending, Separating, Battements, Circles with the Legs (?), movements of the Arms, the Hands and the Fingers,—movements of the Body (especially swaying forward and backward)—movements of the Head.

Tempos and Steps: Slides, Jetés, Balances, Assemblés, Mutations

Fig. 483.

of the Feet, Turning by stamping, Whirling on both feet, Pirouettes, Chassés while turning, Jetés while turning, Steps on the half-toe, Steps on the toe.

Kneeling, rising, crouching.

Dances in armour: Pyrrhic dances.

An exercise in which the pupil was obliged to twist his body into a hoop and roll it.

The exercises are many, but are of the same type and all have the same aim—to make the body supple and strong. The Pedotribe did not give all of the instruction necessary for the dance, but they did excel in the Pyrrhic, and gave good training in the difficult mechanism of that dance.

331. The Choregraphy: The Masters of the Dance.—The instruction for the dance was under the direction of a Master of the Dance. Excepting the Pyrrhic, which was under the direction of an officer of the State, all of the characteristic dances were taught in the schools devoted to that purpose. Many Steps were executed by one or more persons disposed in the *Ensemble* that formed the *Chorus*. The mimetic part of the dance had its own especial domain, and was under the charge of the Chorus Master. The dancers were taught to play tragedy in a dignified manner and to play comedy as well; this ability was required of both singers and dancers, who were at once the actors and the stage-decoration. The Orkhestodidaskalos was much like a Ballet-Master in the modern meaning of the term.

There were also *lessons for the citizens*, who, like the dancers, used the gymnastics imposed by the Ballet-Master. He was indeed an important personage and was held in high esteem.

332. The Technique already explained is that of the gymnastic movements of the dance, separating the groups of dancers from the chorus-Ensembles.

The figures, painted and sculptured, give some idea, not only of the solo dancers, but of those who danced in couples, in threes, etc., —even of a multitude dancing together.

Unhappily, the paintings on the vases and the reliefs which represent the *lyric chorus* or the *dramatic chorus*, are rarely in perfect condition. Also, the difficulties connected with a proper understanding of the perspective and depth, are the cause of much confusion.

The Pyrrhic is here considered with the Choregraphy because the professionals found these gymnastics which predominate very important: but they were, at the same time, an "imitation" and had their place in the Ensembles as a very decorative feature.

The figures in painting and sculpture do not give much detail as to the Pyrrhics.

CHOREGRAPHY
The mimic funeral.—The rhythmic games

Plate IV.

2

3 4

STEPS FOR TWO

333. Decorative Contrasts.—The movements executed by two dancers are rarely in symmetry: if they are of the same nature the artist takes care to not represent them at the same *moment;* the result is a decorative contrast always preferred by the Greeks.

Fig. 484 would seem to prove that they had dances in which the performers faced each other, dancing the same step at the same moment. But Fig. 484 is a veritable heresy in decoration. Dancer A is a copy of dancer 2 on Plate I. B represents him in the opposite pose.

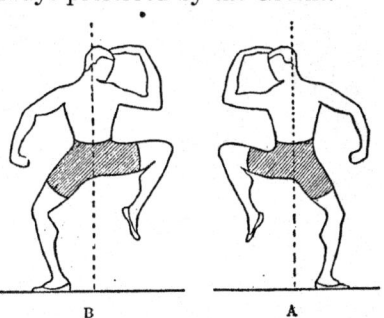

Fig. 484..

334. Two Men.—The two dancers who, in Fig. 128, leap facing each other, the leap being characterized by strongly flexed knees, have their hands moving in unlike manner. Dancer A turns his palms down, holding the hands low. Dancer B holds his hands in the air. This difference in detail destroys the deadly symmetry. The same difference is to be noted in Fig. 407.

Figs. 444-445 are an example of movements that are alike as a whole, but fixed at opposing moments. The turns are also made at different altitudes.

The movements of the two Komos dancers seen facing each other in Fig. 408 are in totally different poses: each dancer has a fantastic step of his own.

Sometimes one of the dancers turns his back completely around, but one must not take these pictures seriously. An illustration of a case of this kind is given in Fig. 485, where one person is twisted at the hips.

An amusingly impossible scene is pictured at Fig. 486. The Satyr hops in place, from one leg to the other, lifting the hip in

an exaggerated fashion: the goat facing him tries to copy the step.

335. The Dance of the Wine-Press was executed by two dancers: it is found only upon the vases of the period when art was at a low ebb. It is shown in a double form.

Fig. 487: The two dancers, with legs interlaced, turn rapidly from right to left or left to right, in such a pose that an oblique line passes from the tops of their heads, through their hands and rear feet. They crush the grapes with their feet as they turn to the accompaniment of a double flute.

Figs. 488 and 489: Two men mark time by an exaggerated lift of the upper leg.

Decorative symmetry is nearly absolute in Fig. 487, which is taken from a terra-cotta bas-relief made in Italy in the first century A. D. Our museums possess a number of sculptures of this nature: it introduces a new style of ornament in which a motif is repeated,—the very thing that the Greek artists avoided. It is well to observe closely the example given, as this kind of decoration is not often found.

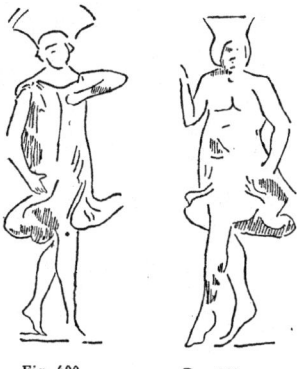

Fig. 490.   Fig. 491.

336. Two Women.—Among the figures from the door of the Heroon of Trysa (15), one dancer turns by stamping on the half-toe, in IV crossed (267); two hierodules (daughters of Zeus) turn in opposite directions. The movements of the legs show both resemblances and differences. The artist has used very strong oppositions of the arms to break up the symmetry, thereby adding to the decoration (Figs. 490, 491).

Fig. 492.

Of the two dancers represented in Fig. 492, one shakes the

castanets, and leaps in place in the manner already described (305); the other, making an exaggerated gesture with her tunic (44) makes a Slide forward on the toe of the left foot. The heads and legs of both women are drawn in profile; the Torsos are in full-

Fig. 493.   Fig. 494.

face. Was this mere clumsiness of design or was it the painter's intention to express the idea of the shoulder turned to the right? (150).

More than charming is the series of dancers grouped two-by-two on a little vase of the fourth century B. C.

Fig. 495.

{ Fig. 493, A: Bending backward; play with mantle;
Fig. 493, B: Slide on both feet (226).

{ Fig. 494, A: One of the forms of the run (82);
{ Fig. 494, B: Play with mantle; backward bend.
{ Fig. 420: Backward bend of the torso (310);
{ Fig. 369: Pirouette on the instep (271).

Figs. 369 and 420 are placed with these so as to make a third group of the same kind.

The contrasting movements practiced by the three groups of dancers who face one another are as evident as they are complete; only a whim of the painter placed them vis-à-vis.

But the whim appears to have a reason when it is noted that, in each case, the dancers relate the rhythm of their work to that of the opposite dancers;

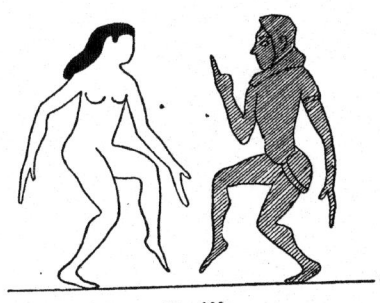

Fig. 496.

each keeping to the common rhythm which is the reason for their association.

When the dancers hold one another's hands—which is seldom—their movements are necessarily more alike. They are always in the position of the dancers of the wine press. Fig. 495 is novel, showing two dancers turning in a small circle on the half-toe, the two women being at opposite extremes of the circle.

Fig. 497.

337. Man and Woman.—When a man and woman are associated in a dance they rarely hold each other's hands, and, in the earlier paintings, are never represented as touching each other in any manner.

In the Greek dance the man and woman are always separated; therefore, their gestures are more mimetic.

On the Corinthian vases of the seventh century B. C. the "Step for Two" is executed with the man and woman facing each other:

the design is very simple. In general, they leap, facing, sometimes in symmetry (Fig. 496).

The vases with black figures show some curious scenes with two dancers, which appear mimetic rather than like a dance in character, if analysed according to modern classifications. Not symmetrical in movement, the figures are always associated in the same way (Fig. 497).

Fig. 498.

The Satyr and Bacchante who turn their backs to each other (Fig. 498) dance an odd step which is not without likeness to the English jig. As in the case of the two Pompeiian dancers (Fig 495), they dance in a circle, keeping their positions at its edges. They remain back to back as they go around, leaping so that the lifted leg is outside the ring, their bodies lightly inclined toward the center.

338. Man and Woman with Arms About Each Other's Necks, or Holding Each Other by the Hand.—The three figures, 499, 500, 501, represent dancers in couples, the first of whom take a step familiar to the student. In Fig. 499 a Satyr playing a double flute precedes the two Bacchants, a young man and a young woman, who, with arms about each other's necks,

Fig. 499.

advance to the same step. The man carries a torch. Behind these dancers Eros Hermaphrodite, shaking the cymbals. The movement of these two persons is nothing more than a cadenced walk,—a joyous departure for Cythera, with instruments. The advance of the two young persons in Fig. 500 is the same, but they are less closely interlaced. The girl carries a candelabrum. Two persons precede them, one playing a flute, the other carries a sacrificial vase and a fillet. The fillet had a religious significance; it was carried in ceremonial processions and swung to the rhythm of the flute. This scene is a dance, in the larger sense of the word.

Fig. 500.

Fig. 501 is a relief from a vase of the third century B. C.—very poor work, as far as the technique goes, but of charming design.

Fig. 501.

The dancer on the left is a young Pan, horned, with the feet of a goat. He leads a young girl by the hand, their arms lifted high, just as was the fashion in France in the elegant days of the seventeenth century. The lovely painting is an allegory,—the story of Echo. The girl is unconsciously pliant; Pan beats the rhythm with his fingers. They advance with small steps on the half-toe. The girl's gesture with the tunic is one of finished elegance.

It is probable that the painter, though dealing with a mythological subject, had the living models before his eyes. When the man and woman hold hands, the work is sure to be of comparatively recent date. Of the more ancient work that served as its prototype, little remains. One exception is to be noted: the motif is not used in work anterior to the third century B. C. nor on the Hellenistic bas-reliefs. It is, therefore, safe to say that men and women did not as a rule touch each other in dancing.

339. The three examples given prove, as exceptions are said to do, the rule.

This sweeping statement does not take into account the flying figures of Pompeii, because they are merely decorative motifs,—images representing scenes of Bacchic loves, and their value is open to doubt. They bear a certain relation to Greek art, but Greek art of a debased period, which inspired the dances of Italy.

Those copyists were quite ignorant of the repugnance of Greek artists toward couples so daringly interlaced: around the earth we may trace the Satyr and Menade executing—*a Boston step!*

STEPS FOR THREE

340. Three Women.—Many works in the Louvre (salon E), present groups of three women who dance in wild disorder. Their move-

Fig. 502.

ments are coarse, rudimentary. They leap in place (299 to 305).

The interpretation of Fig. 502 is somewhat difficult. From the perspective one would suppose that dancer B was farther from the spectator than the other two: by disposing the three in a circle, at equal distances from one another, making the arms of dancers A and C reach out to dancer B, making a kind of broken chain, one gets a clearer idea of what their feet are doing.

341. One Man and Two Women.—Fig. 504: a Satyr leaps in place, between two Menades. They dance with their arms and their gestures, which frame the movements of the person in the center, and which are not rigorously symmetrical.

342. One Woman Between Two Men. —Fig. 505: a Menade between two Satyrs. One leaps in place from one leg to the other: the one on the right Slides on both feet at the same time, but the toe of the right is above the ground. The Menade throws back her head with an orgiastic gesture. The arm-positions of the three are of the fundamental type of Fig. 99, altered by sharp angles of the wrist and elbow.

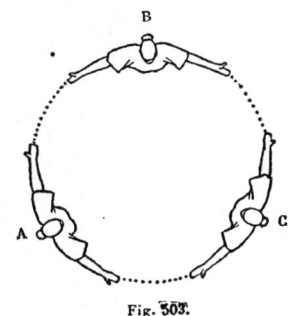

Fig. 505.

Fig. 506: The three Bacchants turn with the same step: the supporting leg is sharply flexed, while the successive leaps are not more accented than in the normal run. This rudimentary Step danced by the three, the grouping being clearly indicated, is remarkable for the simultaneous movements of the legs, the three bounding at the same instant, and descending at the same time, making an ensemble rarely found.

The gesticulation with the arms, grotesque and easy to imagine, is wholly bacchic (142).

THREE DANCERS AND A LEADER

343. Throughout all periods of Greek art there is found a grouping of three female dancers in file or side by side, and preceded by a Leader. The three women may be Nymphs, or Kharites, or the Hours. The person who accompanies them is sometimes Hermes, sometimes Pan or Dionysos;—it is not always possible to say which.

212 CHOREGRAPHY

Fig. 504.

Fig. 505.

2

8

9

Plate V.

6

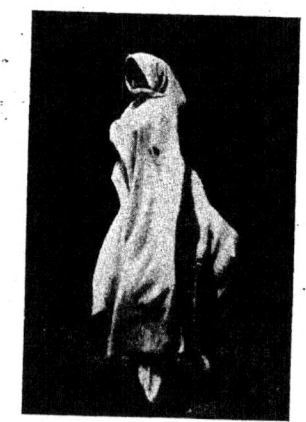

7

13

14

3

4

5

10

11

12

The theme has numberless variants. The three principal types are those following.

Fig. 506.

344. The God Who Leads Precedes Three Women Without Holding Their Hands.—A votive bas-relief discovered on the Acropolis, and belonging to the end of the sixth century B. C., gives a representation of this subject. Hermes, enveloped in an ample cloak, precedes the three women, who step to the music of the double flute. Dressed in Ionian costume, they advance heavily, their feet touching the ground with the whole sole. By a painful effort, the sculptor lifted the left heel of one of them (Fig. 19). Fig. 507 shows the manner in which the women held one another's wrists. The dance is only a rhythmic walk, without character.

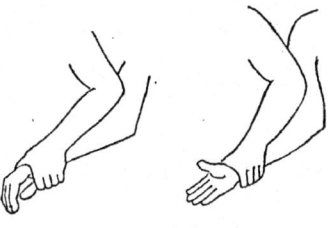

Fig. 507.

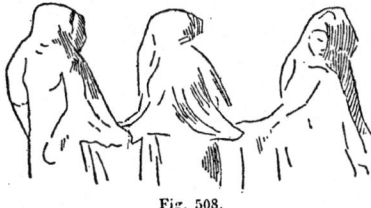

Fig. 508.

On another bas-relief Pan is substituted for Hermes, proving his identity by his cloven hoofs. Playing on the syrinx, he precedes the three Nymphs. The little procession winds toward a bearded river god at the left, whose presence indicates that the three female figures are rightly called Nymphs. They are covered by long cloaks which fall from their shoulders (Fig. 508). The cadenced walk gives a calm and graceful expression to their movement. The presence of Pan does not alter the simplicity of its religious significance of the dance.

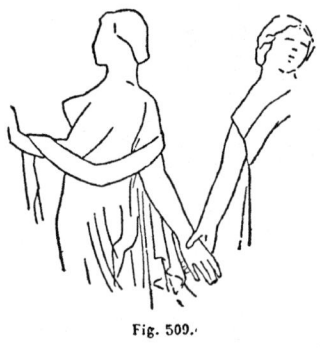
Fig. 509.

For the same reason, when Hermes is the leader, there is an atmosphere of dignity about the cortege. Of the three females who follow the god, the two last hold each other by the hand, the one in front being separated from them. This one lifts the hem of her tunic, from which peep some flowers. All walk on the half-toe, which is the special step for the dancers who figure on the later sculptures (18).

The charming painting reproduced in Fig. 510 is almost a parody on the solemn dances. Three women in file approach a man made up to look like Silenus; the first holds her mantle together with one hand while the other clasps the hand of the next woman, who also holds the hand of the third. The whole

Fig. 510.

scene is replete with gayety, quite in contrast to the austere dance in Fig. 509.

345. The God Who Leads, Holding the Hand of One of the Women.—Fig. 511 is remarkable in that it shows the women with arms entwined. Fig. 512 presents two figures advancing in full face view. These are from the grotto of the Nymphs. The masque of Acheloüs, father of the Nymphs, and the god Pan figure in the decorations. Hermes conducts the three dancers.

346. Three Women Without a Leader.—A terra-cotta from Myrina, shaped like a grotto, shows three dancers aligned in full

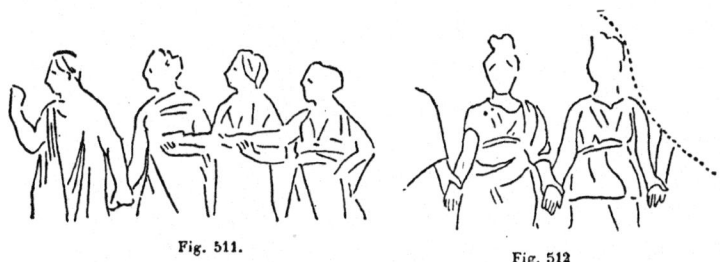

Fig. 511.   Fig. 512

face, without either Pan or Hermes accompanying them. The mask of Pan, suspended from the rock-work, testifies to the symbolic presence of the son of Hermes. The three women come forward in a chain in order to progress more rapidly, playing with their mantles in a dance-movement of the arms, the head turning toward the central figure. Here is a true Step for Three, though some of the details are lost through the mutilation of the terra-cotta. Still, the figures seem very much alive. The feminine trio without a leader is a simple variant of the scene with four persons above mentioned. The absence of the leader is not accounted for, though the mask takes his place.

Many of the later bas-reliefs reproduce the theme of the three women without a leader, walking heavily, as in the primitive work, though this flat-footed walk is an affectation. It is well to inquire what these women represent, who move so stiffly that they appear to be rooted to the ground. The errors in perspective are so great that it is impossible to say whether they are in file or side by side. Often the first and the third, who have one hand free, make the gesture of the veil or tunic: artifices employed by the decorators to give the hands something to do.

Fig. 513.

Fig. 513 is a detail from one of the late bas-reliefs. Fig. 514 exhibits the special characteristics of that conventional kind of art.

347. It is evident that the persistence of the religious symbolism accounts for the noble and stately dance of the three women. This

Fig. 514.

dance, little more than a rhythmic walk, must have been in honor of some of the chaste divinities who inhabited the valleys of earth, and who were worshiped with as elaborate a ceremonial as that by which the Olympic gods were honored.

CHORUS OF THE DANCE

348. The Greek word for Chorus means much more than ours, for it implies a union of the dance and the song. The dance of the Greek chorus, like the dance without words, possessed certain decorative features which were conventions.

The sculptures and paintings are rich in choral representations; but, unhappily, the variety of subjects is limited. The artists, being ignorant of perspective, and unable to suggest depth, were compelled to arrange the figures as though they were in files, or marching toward the spectator. Therefore, we must not demand of these vases that they supply us with information regarding all forms of the Greek dance. It is also very difficult to distinguish whether the chorus is in line, in a circle, or in a square. By reason of the lacunæ, it is impossible to study the choric images with reference to historical divisions. Therefore an artificial classification must be made.

349. Choruses in Which the Dancers Hold One Another by the Hand.—The representation of dancers in Files and Ranks holding one another's hands was greatly favored by painters of a remote period. In a Farandole or in a Circle, the dancer loses all personality and is simply one of a chain. The artists of Dipylon, who present the human figure as an abstract formula, objected to the idea of attempting to show all the complexities and varieties of movement in a dance by one sole figure. On the contrary, they found it easy to dispose many figures around the body and neck of a vase.

The antique representations of the chorus are contemporaneous with the files of soldiers who march with the same step, all holding their weapons in the same attitude, and with the long series of mourners with their hands on their heads or twisted in their hair (Figs. 541, 542). The three subjects—warriors, mourners, dancers in files—seem to have inspired the artists to present them in, as nearly as possible, the same manner.

Reduced, in some cases, to an aspect purely hieroglyphic, these persons dance, their bodies mere triangles, their arms simple zigzags, an opaque silhouette on the ruddy groundwork of the vase. It is sometimes out of the question to guess even at their sex, except to know that the painters put the women on one side and the men on the other, separated by the cytherist who plays for their dance (Fig. 515)—or else there is a file, with all the women in a group, or an ancient version of the Farandole, with the sexes alternating (Fig. 516). The singular disposition is not the result of the artist's clumsy methods, but is intentionally ludicrous. On the left of the dancing chorus is a player on the dulcimer, on the right, two warriors who walk side by side, with swords.

350. The François vase offers a fine specimen of that part of the dance which they attributed to Theseus (Fig. 517). There are shown a long file of men and women alternating, who hold hands. Theseus is the leader. They advance, to the music of the lyre, toward Ariadne in a dignified ceremonial dance. The dancers are none other than the victims intended for the Minotaur, rescued by

Theseus from the death that waits in the labyrinth. They are the very persons who appear on a curious vase of the sixth century B. C. (Louvre), aligned in two rows, immobile and sad, waiting to be given to the monster. Here they are just given back their lives,

Fig. 515.

and they celebrate their deliverance by a dance to the lyre played by their savior. Their happiness is not expressed by joyful bounds; the painter makes them walk on the soles of their feet, with no great lightness of movement. They march with the same step, though the men and women do not take steps of equal length. The splendid Dorian costume which the young ladies of Athens wore made it necessary for them to shorten their steps. Their mien expresses grace and modesty.

The bodies of the dancers are often in three-quarter view, with the head and legs in profile. This does not imply either ignorance or convention. In this dance those taking part do not advance to

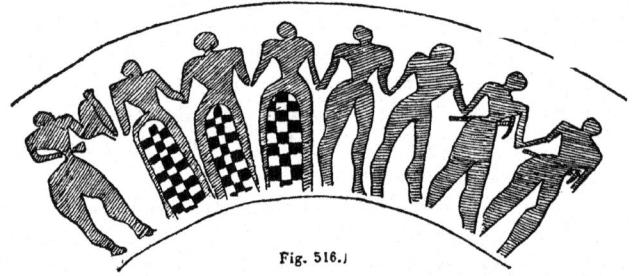
Fig. 516.

the front, consequently, as they hold hands, it results in the torso turning. The ceramists expressed these nuances with wonderful understanding: the perspective is not as good in some other paintings.

The dancers of the François vase are engaged in nothing more than a slow and stately march.

In Fig. 518, a relief from an amphora, may be seen a rapid run,

CHORUS OF THE DANCE 219

arms extended, hands clasped. Here again, the sexes are alternated. The first and last dancers carry wreaths of leaves in their free hands.

351. Fig. 519 reproduces a Farandole, in which the oppositions in

Fig. 517.

attitude are worthy of study. The chain is composed of five women and one man. The oddity of the amusing scene is the reason for mentioning it here.

352. Numberless are the representations of women alone, dancing in chains, throughout all periods of Greek art. Nearly always the dance is accompanied by the dulcimer or cythera and a double

Fig. 518.

flute: sometimes music is absent. The first dancer of the file makes the gesture of the veil with her free hand.

In Fig. 520 the women grasp one another's wrists with violence. Plainly, they are standing still; the Farandole is reduced to an immobile chain.

The Louvre (room XII) possesses a fragment of the frieze of Samothrace, from a temple built in the fourth century B. C., the style being "archaisant." This bas-relief, though badly mutilated, is interesting to the dancer. A long file of women wind along the frieze, two-by-two, walking on the half-toe, with a good deal of hip action.

There are to be found in the Louvre many bas-reliefs of the decadent period, representing chains of dancers; most of them are

Fig. 519.

mediocre decorative compositions, without good drawing, and of little interest to the dancer. The same may be said of many in the Museum of Naples.

353. The Ring.—The Ring may be defined as a chain composed of dancers, all of whom join hands. The Ring is one of the dances that

Fig. 520.

are instinctive, and it appears on the most ancient monuments. The vases of Dipylon furnish many types. The Museum of the Louvre possesses a figurine of clay, one of a series of similar figures, of which the articulations of the legs come below the robe, which, blown by the wind, closely wraps the figure, defining it. With hands hidden, but each clasping that of her neighbor, the women dance in a circle (seventh century B. C.).

A beautiful Corinthian vase is decorated with parallel rows of dancers. The same subject is used on a vase with black figures, to be seen in the Museum of Corneto, and is reproduced (in Greek Vase Paintings) by Miss Harrison.

The Louvre possesses three groups (terra-cotta and limestone) of the decadent period, representing three women executing a circle-

CHORUS OF THE DANCE

dance around the sacred tree, while playing on the flute. There are also some groups, "abridged representations," to use the expression of M. Perrot: the dancers who take part in the circle are many in number. The costume worn is Asiatic.

Examples, of which there are a great number, prove that the Circle was practiced by both the Greeks on the continent and by the insular Greeks. It is certain that the Circle, broken or unbroken, was in favor. There were some varieties of it that are to be considered as figures, where the leader straightens out the line, rolls it up, unfolds it, always preserving its independence, which was dear to the Greek dancer. One had an active roll, with one hand free; this one remained at the head of the line; the others held each other's hands, and were simply links in the chain.

Fig. 521.

354. The Chorus in Which the Dancers, in File, Do Not Hold Hands.—In this case, each dancer preserves her own independence,

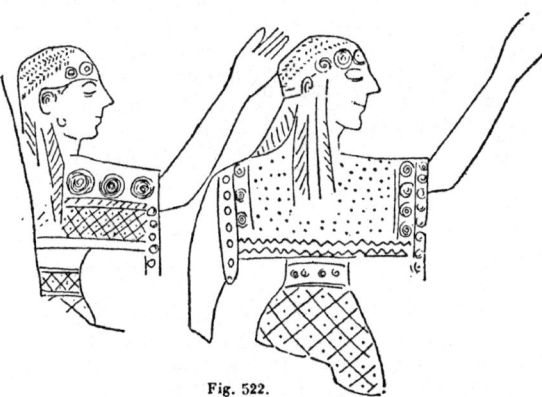

Fig. 522.

although rigorously conforming to the movements and gestures of her companions. This obligation resulted in unity in the Ensemble.

This unity is equally apparent in the files of dancers. It is clearly revealed when the dancers represent the same moment of the Step.

Figs. 521 and 522 are taken from a series in which the same type is uniformly repeated; the two individuals isolated give a correct idea of the whole file. The unity of the whole is even more clearly manifested in Fig. 523. Three Satyrs with ape-like heads simultaneously execute the same movement of the legs (303), but their gestures do not synchronize.

Fig. 523.

The woman is not a part of the dance-Ensemble, she is merely a spectator.

Between the dancers in Fig. 524 there is no relation except the pose of the left arm. Dancer A appears to be running; dancer B to be leaping; the third Slides. By join-

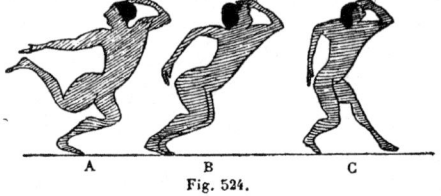

Fig. 524.

ing the gestures of B and C, one gets a gesture even more grotesque than that of the figures in 277.

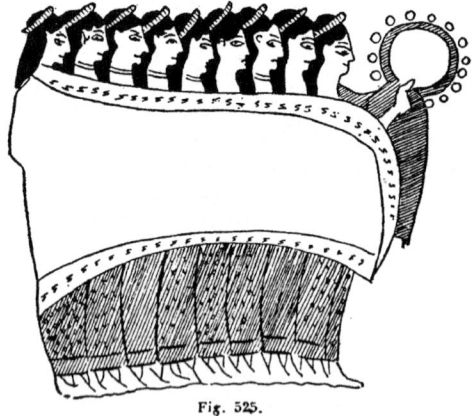

Fig. 525.

The files of dancers, analysed in another paragraph (Figs. 230, 277) and composed of persons represented at differing moments of the same Tempo or the same Step, prove, in many instances, to be exactly alike. The Greek dancers studied to synchronize their movements.

355. Dancers in Ranks.—In the alignment of dancers in ranks the Greeks experienced the same difficulties as in depicting the soldiers in ranks. Being ignorant of the *point of view*, they were, perforce, contented to make the figures lap over one another, without fading

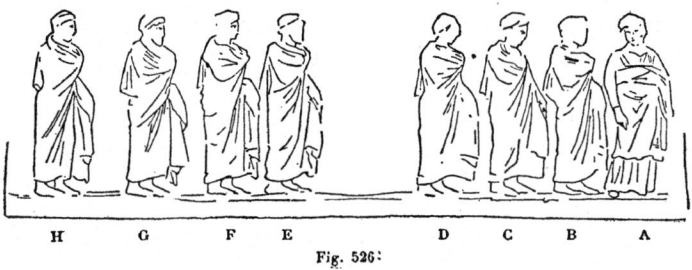

Fig. 526.

in to perspective. The lines remain parallel, and the front is set back from the spectator without any angle-variation.

In Fig. 525 one may see an unexampled piece of primitive awkwardness. With naïve simplicity, the painter has made one cloak cover all nine of the women who compose the rank, hiding the play of the hands. The first holds a crown in her free hand.

It is certain that some of the *files* are to be interpreted as *ranks*. For instance, Fig. 526, which is considered by Beulé to be a fragment of a cyclic Chorus. Person A, who leads the group, may be left in place, disposing the others in three ranks:

```
  *  *  H
  G  F  E
  D  C  B
```

The sculptor, unable to draw three ranks, one behind the other, arranged three groups *in line*.

Examples of Files which were intended to represent Ranks need not be multiplied.

356. The Chorus of the Theatre.—Fig. 527 is exceptionally interesting. It shows warriors mounted upon dolphins, arranged in

Ranks of three, one placed behind the other. The one who leads is a grotesque being who plays on the double flute. These singular persons belong to the *comic chorus* who open the scene. The *comic*

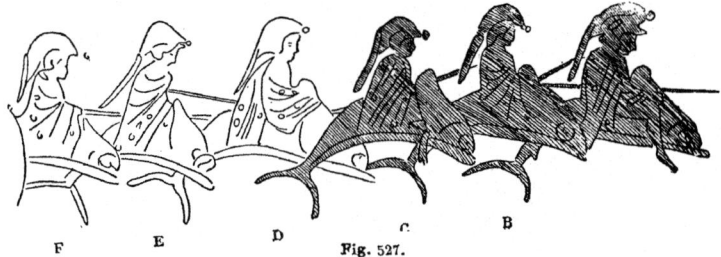

F   E   D   C   B
Fig. 527.

chorus, complete, is composed of twenty-four singers, who are necessary to the burlesque procession.

```
*  *  *  *  *  *  D  A
*  *  *  *  *  *  E  B
*  *  *  *  *  *  F  C
```

Representations like this are rare; the simple juxtaposition of persons in the other perspective, that is, in file.

The comic chorus (Fig. 528) affected strange costumes, imitating

Fig. 528.

the cock or lapwing (78), and playing the double flute, while swinging the arms like bat's wings.

M. Collignon thinks that the creatures with dolphins' heads on the monument of Lysicrate (16) are choristers who compete for victory. Fig. 529 shows five of these metamorphosed persons at the moment of diving head first. The subject of a charming little frieze is the struggle of Dionysos against the buccaneers who endeavor to overcome him and metamorphose him into a porpoise. The billows of the ocean are plainly indicated. One can imagine the singular movement of the ensemble presented when the Chorus fell head over heels, executing the dance at the same time that they simulated being engulfed in—the boards!

The theatrical representations are the subjects of many of the ceramic paintings, which, unhappily, are all but impossible to interpret. These paintings give an abundance of material for the study of the mimetic dance, which, indeed, could not be undertaken without them,—its scenic effects, even though the perspective is faulty and misleading.

Fig. 529.

The chorus-man or chorus-woman, comic or tragic, is at once actor, dancer, and singer. The dance, like a book, must keep its predominant characteristic, being both the "imitation of the word and of the voice."

357. The Tratta.—The Tratta is a dance of the Greece of to-day. It is executed by women who hold each other's hands according to a special formula. Each of them, instead of taking her neighbor, reaches past her to the next dancer on each side and takes her arm, thus making a chain of crossed arms. The skill of the dance consists in balancing the whole chain, producing alternately steps forward and steps backward, usually five forward and three back, executed obliquely (205).

226 CHOREGRAPHY

Next comes a short description of the paintings on a Greek tomb at Ruvo, which shows a striking resemblance between the ancient dance and the modern. There are twenty-seven figures in two groups, each conducted by a man. The presence of the masculine leaders is the only point at which the dance differs from the Tratta, in which only women take part.

The heavy walk on the soles of the feet is an awkward mode of locomotion, but for a long period it was the conventional mode of walking. Notwithstanding its defects, which result in a monotony

Fig. 530.

of parallel lines, it takes on a certain decorative value when there are many figures. The costumes are painted in soft colors, the dress and the tunic in different shades. Few of the ancient paintings give such an impression of life.

358. Dancers in Armour.—These were practiced not only at the solemn festivals, by a great number of dancers, in the presence of a vast audience,—they were also introduced at the close of feasts, when men and women danced the varied movements of the traditional *Pyrrhic* for the amusement of the diners.

If we hold to the letter of Plato's definition of the Pyrrhic, it will be correct to consider the armed figures on the vases and reliefs as Pyrrhic dancers. The Pyrrhic is an exact imitation of the movements of attack and defence; the casting of the javelin, the parade with shields; all of the postures necessary in different exercises, enter into the Pyrrhic dance. In studying it, a knowledge of the military art of the Greeks is necessary. The sculptured figures alone are not enough to give a clear idea of the dances. At the best period the ceramic painters depicted the figures of warriors with all their paraphernalia. The period of Dipylon (8) shows files of soldiers carrying shields and double lances, who, in monotone silhouette, march around the bodies of the vases. There are also, notably on the plates of Rhodes (9), warriors who stand face to face to wrestle, and, on the amphoræ of Corinth, cavaliers arranged in symmetrical ranks on either side of a central motif. For a time these motifs were traditional, and so were presented for ages in the ceramic paintings. It follows that similar representations are often simple decorations which add nothing to our knowledge of these persons.

Fig. 531.

The writers do not distinguish between the two kinds of Pyrrhic, but their descriptions inform us that the dance was sometimes given by a number of performers and sometimes by only one. The figures of the *Pyrrhic en masse* were made up of rhythmic evolutions, complex studies, which excluded the more violent and prolonged individual movements: the *solo Pyrrhic* was an exercise of a mimetic type, made up of running Steps, leaps, Steps in retreat, whirling Steps, crouchings, movements of the arms in infinite variety,—in a word, all the artifices of both dancing and wrestling.

It is better to separate the *Pyrrhics* from the armed men taken from the vases and reliefs.

359. Pyrrhic for One.—The musician who plays on the double flute, beside the Pyrrhic dancer, proves that the exercise really was a dance.

Fig. 531—a youth turns in IV crossed, or, to be more exact,

executes a movement turning from the head, with the left foot as a pivot.

Fig. 532: the warrior, laced in a tightly-fitting costume, turns his head to the side, while the whole body swings to the left, the right hand holding a lance ready to strike.

Fig. 533: the young Pyrrhic dancer, who stands on a sort of

Fig. 532.

low stage, makes a high leap in place, like the crossed Jeté alternating (321). He is represented during the moment of suspension.

The targeteer who creeps (Fig. 534), the persons who kneel (Figs. 535, 536), are figures of combatants during an engagement. They execute the movements and hold the poses which Xenophon and

Fig. 533.

Fig. 534. Fig. 535.

Plato describe as the feints of the Pyrrhic. Often the dancer's left arm is enveloped in the folds of his chalmys, of which he makes a shield.

The Greek amphoræ (10) present many figures of lancers and javelin-throwers who follow the formula described, pausing abruptly, and so changing the movement of the run, while retaining the sense of a force projected. No doubt this is the motive of some of the exercises used by the Pyrrhic dancers.

360. Pyrrhic for Two.—The warriors who face one another on the vases of the seventh and sixth centuries B. C. are the far-off prototypes of the Pyrrhicists who are seen in groups of two on the Hellenistic bas-reliefs (17) and in the Italian bas-reliefs of terra-cotta. In the first case the two duellists with lances often attack one another with fury (Fig. 537), lance lifted, the helmeted

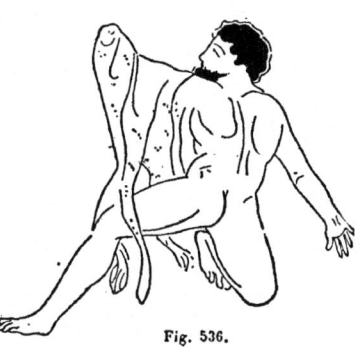

Fig. 536.

dancers giving a realistic imitation of actual combat (Fig. 538). The left arm holds the shield, the right lifts the weapon, the nude body turning by stamping in IV crossed, making a circular track, the dancers always standing on the rim of this circle, its diameter remaining the same, whatever the movement of the dancers. It is

Fig. 537.

probable that at set intervals the warriors struck with the sword or lance (as the figures in 538 would seem to prove) across the shields.

On a marble bowl in the Vatican is sculptured a Satyr between the two Pyrrhic dancers. The presence of this subject of Dionysos between the armed men proves the antiquity of this exercise by which the Spartans—and from their example the Athenians—prepared for combat, though in later times it was altered. The Pyrrhic dancers then came carrying the thyrsus in place of the arrows, brandishing rods and torches as they mingled with the Bacchants in the dances. In this period the transformation is complete and definite.

361. Pyrrhic en Masse.—The same difficulties with perspective which hindered the ceramic painters and the sculptors of the bas-reliefs interfere with a correct representation of the Chorus in ranks and disfigure the Ensemble in the case of the Pyrrhic dancers.

Fig. 538

On the bas-reliefs of the temple of the Nereides (Fig. 539) the warriors advance in ranks, facing, pressed close to each other, overlapping without tapering to give perspective (335). They take wide steps, giving an impression of rapidity; all of the legs on the same side advance at the same moment with military precision, just as our own soldiers do. This *rule of the same step* imposes itself by instinct, therefore the whole band moves with one rhythm, so that the eye has the same impression of rhythm as the ear. It is reasonable to conclude that the Pyrrhic en masse were subject to the same rule. The proof is in the next figure.

Fig. 539.

A bas-relief from the Acropolis (Fig. 540) shows a troop of eight Pyrrhicists in two groups of four, who, without doubt, were really in ranks, one behind the other (355).

H G F E
D C B A

They advance with the same step: with their left arms they hold their shields before them: their right arms, at the sides of their bodies, are held stiffly and somewhat back (113) as though the hand carried some sort of weapon, which is, however, non-existent in the picture. The chorus-leader, in cloak and tunic, walks gravely at the side of the troop. The bas-relief is on a pedestal; an inscription states that the statue it supports is to be consecrated to the victorious Chorus of the Pyrrhic dance.

It is quite within the bounds of possibility that each of the groups

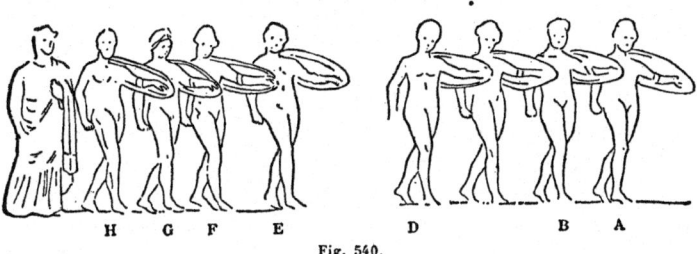

Fig. 540.

of four represent or symbolize a whole chorus, which, at the moment of action, oppose each other, though their movements appear to our eyes to indicate the contrary.

The only positive statement that can be made is that the Pyrrhic en masse, made, at certain moments, certain gestures, in unison; more than this it would be rash to assume.

362. The Pyrrhic dances figure in the Athenian processions. The Parthenon frieze (15) gives an important place to the Athenian cavaliers; but it must be remembered that the heavily-armed soldiers who carry sword and shield are $_{not}$ Pyrrhic dancers. When Athenian civilisation had reached its highest development, the military parades took on a religious character, very different from the armed dances of the Lacedemonians. Spartan in origin, the Pyrrhic preserved for a long time its primitive characteristics: it was like a miniature fight; it was the preparation for actual warfare; it was something more than a gymnastic. Later it became a brilliant spectacle.

MOURNING DANCES

363. Essentially mimetic in type, and their movements and gestures of symbolic import, the Funeral Dances must, in this resume, be treated by reducing them to their component parts, making a study of the origin and changes in the symbolic ritualistic gestures which, from long custom, became the necessary accompaniment of the funeral chants.

The funeral rites, in Attica, were governed by iron rules. With the help of the sculptures, it is possible to get a glimpse of the customs, hallowed by long usage, which governed the ceremony of placing the dead in the tomb.

The *Showing the Dead* was a decree of Solon, though the custom antedated his time. Among the most ancient representations of the human form are the long files of persons shown on the funeral vases of Dipylon (8). They repeat over and over the strange silhouettes (Figs. 541, 542) which permit the student to believe that the scene was governed by set rules and that the gestures of the different persons were made at the same moment. Hired mourners accompanied their lamentations with rhythmic gestures. Sometimes they tore their hair; sometimes they were contented with merely twisting their hands over their heads. The latter gesture was the conventionalized expression of the former.

During the exposition of the dead, the chants did not cease; usually a player on the flute accompanied them, the cadenced gesticulation followed the rhythms indicated by the instrument. The ceremony is, for this reason, called the *Mimic Funeral*. Grouped around the dead, these mourners manifested grief by all of the external signs; they tore their hair, they beat their breasts, they rent their clothing; the women scratched their faces, the men beat their thighs, all spoke to the dead, holding out their arms in their direction, as though they were the cause of their sorrow. Later, the gesticulation became milder, as can be proved by the sculptures.

The funeral lamentations lasted during the *journey to the tomb* and the *burial*. The body, placed on a chariot drawn by horses or carried by bearers on a litter, was escorted by the relatives and hired mourners. The face of the dead was uncovered during the journey. The songs of lamentation and the funeral gestures served to make the ceremony longer.

The representations of the *ekphora*, more rare than the *prothesis*, have their prototype in the great vase of Dipylon (8).

The funeral repast, which followed the shrouding of the dead; *the sacrifices at the tomb* on the third and ninth days, or for thirty days, which, with the Athenians, was the period of mourning; the repast offered to the dead at periods fixed by the survivors: all of these things are shown in the strange ceremonies of the mimic funeral. The *visits to the stelle* (Fig. 550) and the sacrifices presented in great number, gave rise to a kind of gesticulation much like that which accompanied the mournful songs during the exposition of the body and the journey to the tomb.

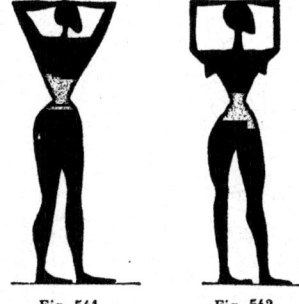

Fig. 541.   Fig. 542.

364. The scenes taken from these rites hold an important place on the vases of Dipylon. These antiques show the dead man on the

Fig. 543.

couch or litter, carried by bearers, or on the funeral chariot, the face uncovered; he is surrounded by women who tear their hair (Figs. 541, 542). Although their sex is not always clearly revealed, there is no doubt about their being women, because the back of the vase explains the gesture. These women are nude, but their nudity is a convention of the painters of that time, being merely a

Fig. 544.

simplification of costume, showing the human figure as an abstract idea.

Fig. 543, from a Corinthian jar of the seventh century B. C., exhibits the violent gestures against which Solon issued an edict,—gestures which are the outward manifestation of great grief. These three women tear their hair by the handful. The one in the center resembles Fig. 542, of which it is an explanation. In many instances the funeral dance is cruelly realistic; this marks the climax before the modification.

365. In the case of the most ancient vases, the women do not beat their breasts or feign to scratch with their nails; the representation of these things was too difficult for the artists of that period. But the vases of the sixth and fifth centuries B. C. (10, 11) present pictures of the ancient practices. The plaques of terra-cotta, painted, and contemporaneous with the black-figured vases, are found to be of much assistance in separating the true gesture from the gesture that is simply figurative,—the brutal movement from the symbolic movement. The fine plaque in the Louvre (Fig. 544) is a true picture; the persons are separated into two groups,—

the chorus of men, the leader of which gives the signal for the threnody (363), and the group of women who press close to the dead (in this case a woman)—all is according to custom. The gestures

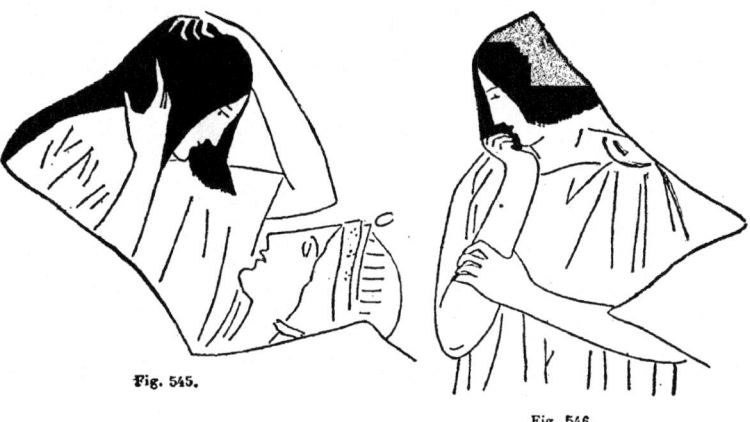

Fig. 545.

Fig. 546.

of the different persons have been described (Figs. 545, 547, 548, etc.).

366. The many fine vases with red figures, of severe style (11), are

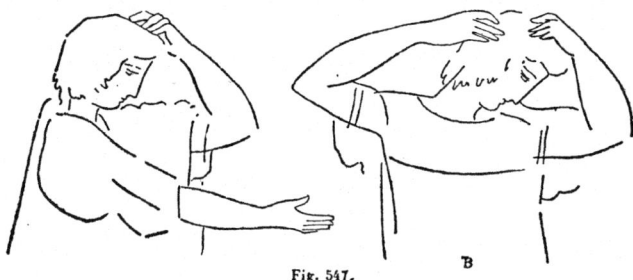

Fig. 547.

ornamented with paintings of funerals, and express in a like manner the same scenes, so it is safe to believe the gestures were made just as represented. Nevertheless, it is probable that the woman in Fig. 545 is not really tearing her hair, and that the other, whose hand is on her head, is not really scratching her face with her nails (Fig. 546).

Yet the vases with the black figures and the painted plaques (Fig. 544) all show the women, and, in some rare cases, men also, lifting their arms in a symmetrical manner and resting the hands on the head, but without tearing the hair. This proves that the practice had been discarded, though the figurative g e s t u r e preserves the tradition.

367. A variant of the type came into use in the sixth century B. C. (10).

The person who takes part in the funeral lamentation holds the hand to the head with a gesture the calmness of which reveals a very noble sense of the dramatic: the other hand is extended in the direction of the dead (Figs. 544, 547, A, 548). The hand of the arm which touches the head is not lifted very high in front,—it is not to be confused with the gesture of adoration, which takes a form not unlike this (Figs. 549, 550).

Fig. 548.

Fig. 549.

Fig. 550.

368. Fig. 551 may be considered the prototype of a funeral gesture that is most decorative: one hand rests on the head; the other arm, instead of being extended in front, is lifted in the unusual manner seen in the illustration. The neck of the vase from which it is taken is shown in Fig. 552. Fig. 553 shows a variation of the same gesture.

MOURNING DANCES

369. It is certain that, on some of the funeral lecythes, the positions of the thumb and index finger have a ritualistic signification, though the disposition of the fingers is not emphasis in the mimic funeral. They express adoration, and there is evidence that they held a place of their own in the cult of the dead.

370. The persistence of the gestures of the funeral ritual is also evident; on one amphora, dating from the third century B. C., is seen a man, who lifts his left arm

Fig. 551.

Fig. 553.

Fig 552.

over his head, approaching a litter upon which the dead is carried (Fig 554). Though the practice of tearing the hair had long been abandoned, the meaning of the gesture had not been lost, but was retained in a symbolic form.

CHOREGRAPHY

Myrina shows a great number of figures of which the type is uniform (Fig. 555). The Siren is winged, the legs terminate in claws; the right hand pretends to tear the thin hair; the left hand rests on the breast. The great wings droop, folding around the monster's body. These figures, which were deposited in the tomb, symbolize grief.

Fig. 554

Fig. 555.

371. The modern Greeks have preserved some of the funeral customs of the ancients. The *myriologues* chanted by the female relatives or friends of the departed, and also by hired mourners, are the variable threnodies with which the ancients reproached the dead for abandoning his friends. The body, richly dressed, is exposed in the death-chamber. The coffin is not closed until the moment of burial.

The funeral gesticulation is not the custom throughout all Greece, it is retained mostly in the villages of the interior. At the beginning of the nineteenth century, funerals were preceded by paid mourners who tore their hair and chanted the songs of the dead.

THE PLAY RHYTHMS

372. Homer, Lucien, and Plutarch, indeed, all of the Greek writers, use the same word to designate the dancers, whether they be the ball players, the acrobats, the women who walk on their hands, or some other type. The word "Dancer" has a wide range of meanings. Everything was considered a dance if it was executed to music, from the exercises of the palestræ to the studied evolutions of the Chorus.

The rowers of the galleys, who swung their oars to the cadences of the flute, or the workers in the arsenal who toiled to the sound of fifes, the orator who spoke his words and timed his gestures to a

THE PLAY RHYTHMS 239

measure,—these were all dancers, in the larger Greek sense of the word. The power of rhythm is universally accepted, therefore the Greek made his oracles speak in verse, and, many times in his

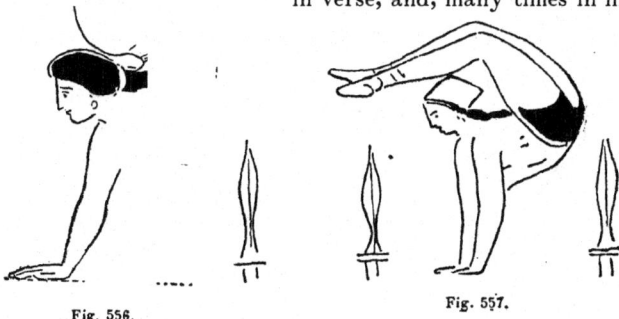

Fig. 556.
Fig. 557.

history, the legend of the lyre of Amphion has been realized. Epaminondas built the walls of Messina to the sound of flutes which played the airs of Sakadas and of Pronomos; Lysander demolished the walls of Piree to the music of the flute.

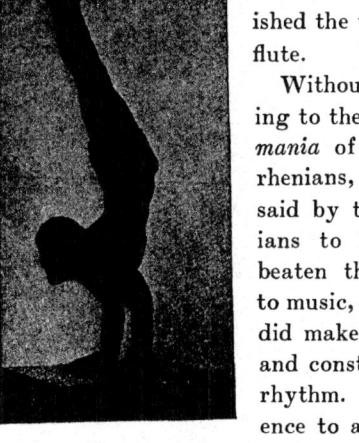

Fig. 558.

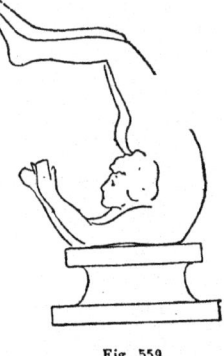

Fig. 559.

Without descending to the *rhythmomania* of the Tyrrhenians, who are said by the Athenians to have even beaten their slaves to music, the Greeks did make a general and constant use of rhythm. In obedience to a racial instinct, they allowed music to permeate their lives. Their philosophers ended by proclaiming the principle of *eurhythmy*, the perfection of rhythm and in rhythm, its more precious and essential quality. The people made it grow into the very fiber of their bodies, a process accomplished by many exercises. The Greeks made their costume, their walk, their language,—all eurhythmic, whether the result was obtained by hard gymnastics or the less violent movements of the dance. They appreciated grace in playing ball, in dancing on a tight-rope, and, even in these things, made eurhythmy perfect.

Fig. 560.

There is a tendency to generalize in speaking of eurhythmy. The word is one that cannot be precisely translated into any modern language.

373. It is not easy to distinguish between the *play-rhythms* and the dances, properly so called. It is quite possible that many mistakes have been made, calling dances games and viceversa.

The ball-games, which the Greek writers call dances, do not hold any such position, if the sculptures may be trusted, and are not so represented in a single instance.

374. The "Kubistétères." —They dance on their hands, head down, and, in this inconvenient posture, perform many exercises. It is enough to look at the representations of acrobatic dancers (Figs.

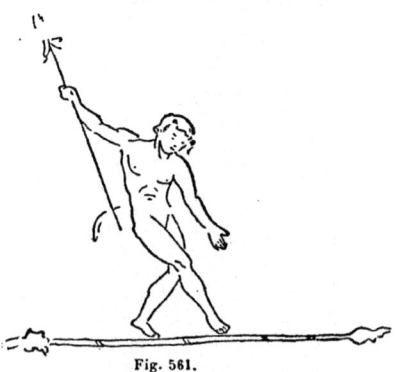

Fig. 561.

556, 557, 558) to reconstruct the feats of these jugglers. Powerful enough to lift the feet, with the weight of the whole body resting on the hands, and, substituting hands for feet, walk and dance on them; in the instance of the kubisteteria reproduced in Fig. 557, the Jeté is made by the dancer on the hands, and who is about to *leap backward on the wrists.*

The British Museum possesses a very singular *kubistétère*, whose hands rest on the back of a crocodile, the dancer's legs, raised vertically, turn toward the animal's tail.

Fig. 559 is interesting because the dancer rests upon the upper arms, leaving the forearms free to make gestures.

In the case of the elegant figurine (Fig. 560) the spectator is puzzled to know whether she combines the play with the hoop with tumbling.

375. Dances on Vases. Kottabe.—The dancers of Komos (415) carry various accessories; sometimes it is simply a drinking-horn holding the sacrificial wine, or a fragile cup. These dancers enlivened the feasts, entertaining the guests with exercise in equilibrium, with the vases of wine (Fig. 120).

Fig. 562.

Fig. 563.

The *Kottabe* play has many variations, but it consisted principally in darting on some object which would fall easily, the remnant of the liquid left at the bottom of the cup. In a painting on one of the vases a judge watches while the dancers, holding the cups, execute the movements. Posed on the left toe, they turn with the cups on the head. The legs obey a certain rhythm, giving the scene the characteristics of the dance. To become a perfect cup-bearer required a complete knowledge of eurhythmy.

376. The Rope-dancers of Pompeii.—The greater number of the rope-dancers of Pompeii are dancers on terra firma, which the fantasy of the painters represent on a stretched cord, and who certainly find it difficult to hold an upright position (Fig. 205). Sometimes they slide lightly along the cord on their toes (Fig. 561).

Some of these young persons who dance are Satyrs; these brandish the thyrses; others play with vases. It would be trespassing on the domain of fiction, which reigns sovereign on these Pompeiian frescos, to pretend to find in them anything that can be treated as a serious contribution to our knowledge of the dance.

377. Excepting the ball games, no outdoor play is represented in painting or sculpture. The writers speak of those games where

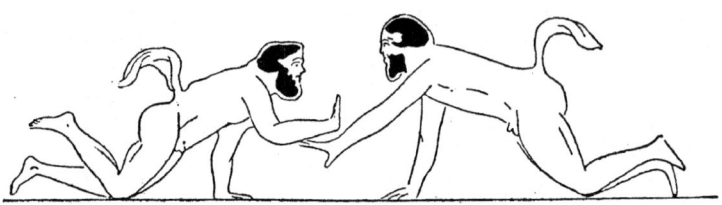

Fig. 561.

the players leaped up and down in an exaggerated manner on a slippery cord, inevitably meeting with misadventures, to the delight of the spectators. A player marked the rhythm to which these leaps were made.

378. **Play-rhythms for Two.**—The aulette was often accompanied by the ephedrismos. It is supposed, from the aspect of the players represented in Figs. 564 and 565, that the rhythm acted as a regulator.

Fig. 565.

Properly speaking, the *ephedrismos* is a wager, the loser being obliged to carry the victor on his back. Representations of it are numerous in all periods of Greek art. Fig. 562 is one of the oldest: this is a youth who carries a younger boy on his back in a sort of game, the point being to throw the person being carried on the ground.

The play takes on another form in Fig. 563. The one who carries the other is motionless, his hands held between his knees; astride his neck is his companion, who beats his hands in time. A flute player marks the rhythm.

Representations analogous to Fig. 562 are frequent. On a cup of the fifth century B. C. (Millin, *Antique Vases*, II, Pl. X) is shown a picture of Hercules carrying Dionysos, who holds a drinking-horn.

Sometimes a man carries a woman (Heuzey, *Figurines of the Louvre*, XXXIII, 2), or one woman on the back of another, one playing with a ball (Pottier, *Figurines of Terra-cotta*, p. 90).

It is not rare to find an intaglio showing one Satyr on the back of another (Cabinet of Medallions).

379. The two Satyrs (Fig. 564) are engaged in a comic wrestling bout. Each is supported on one hand and both knees, trying to force one another backward.

380. A lovely group of Tanagra figurines, in the Louvre (Fig. 565), must have the following comment: the movements are executed by two young girls and may be either simultaneous or successive; they are at the point of departure, or, perhaps, at the end, the expression of the movement being the same.

1. Girl A turns in place from left to right, without letting go the hands of her companion, turning her shoulders and head under the arms. The crossing of the arms is reversed as the game proceeds.

2. The other girl turns at the same time in the opposite direction. This game with the hands crossed goes back to the earliest times.

According to the movements executed simultaneously, or successively, by the two players, they are classed as single or double.

The interpretation given is founded upon the relation existing between the Tanagra group and the play practiced in the Eastern countries.

THE DANCERS

GODS WHO DANCE

381. The writer has endeavored, throughout this study, to keep the personality of the dancers separated from the steps they execute. It has been necessary to consult the Greek authors and enter into their philological discussions in order to be sure of giving the correct names to the dancers and to explain the scenes in which they figure.

The monuments themselves have been interrogated, and the explanations so obtained have been more easy to understand by the presence of explanatory legends on vases and bas-reliefs, and the persistence of traditional types of dancing figures.

382. Sometimes the gods of ancient Greece are themselves the dancers: Zeus, Hera, Demeter, Apollo, Aphrodite, Hermes, Athena, not only preside at the dances of their worshipers,—the poets tell us that these and other gods took part in person. The dignity attributed by the Greeks to this art is nowhere more clearly revealed than in the scenes where the gods of high Olympus honor their favorites by appearing in the dances.

The high gods deigned to play the rôle of leader or accompanist. The dances at which they preside are usually nothing more than a stately walk, which varies but little. The bas-reliefs of Thaos (Louvre) exhibit this type of representation. Apollo accompanies playing on some stringed instrument: Hermes conducts the procession of Nymphs. The feet of the women are not lifted in the same time: an elegant and restrained gesture of the arm is the only symmetrical, dance-like movement of the Ensemble.

Usually, as indicated by the vases, the high gods did little more than assist at the dances of the inferior divinities. Such was the Asiatic Cybele, whose cult evoked the most furious saltation, but who herself advanced with a grave manner which excluded all violent motion, carrying a dulcimer—like her worshipers—to the rhythm of which they whirled in delirium, but which, in her hand, was only a symbol; Cybele comes forward with majesty, as befits the great mother of the gods.

Fig. 566.

Among the secondary divinities, the Charites, the Nymphs, and the Hours are the principal ones. The dance is heavy and clumsy: here the paintings are in direct contradiction to the poets, who speak of the light Step of the gracious goddesses.

The two dancers par excellence are Nike and Eros.

383. Nike the Dancer.—

Fig 567.

Nike is always winged. The personification of Victory, she is also its messenger. In raising the Temple of the Wingless Victory the Athenians tore down this tradition, craftily depriving Victory of her wings so that she might never leave Athens.

The primitive artists were limited to the winged *form;* they were not able to devise for a figure in the air an expression of rapidity of movement, so they were obliged to represent the goddess as running, the wings serving only to give lightness to the figure (Fig. 566). Nike was not slow to adopt the gesture of the tunic, so dear to other running figures: she made the gesture in double form (Fig. 106).

At a later time the artists became more daring and attempted to show her leaping. An amphora in the Louvre, of the middle of the fifth century B. C. shows Nike soaring through the air, her feet parallel, toe down, as though she were leaping over a rope; a curious detail is that the traverse position of the goddess on the body of the vase shows that the painter's only way to give an idea of flight was to incline the wings: the artifice suggested to him the thought of the instability of a body in the air.

Near the end of the fifth century B. C. Pæonios cut from a block of marble a flying Victory (Fig. 567) in high relief, who is suspended in space. The form and direction of her flying draperies show that the Victory of Olympus is nearing the earth. The resistance

Fig. 568.

to the air, produced by the vertical descent, affects likewise the right leg which is covered by the tunic: the left leg, nude, and placed forward to touch the earth, escapes from the folds of the chiton. The veil, blowing about her at the back, is lifted high,—of this only fragments remain, but enough to enable us to reconstruct the movement of the material: it would seem that Pæonios had been inspired by the gracious dancer herself to create this play of the mantle, which combines fullness and flexibility. The dots in Fig. 567 are an indication of the supposed movement of the arms and draperies. The movement is suggested by one of the figures in high relief from the temple of the Nereides.

Of very different aspect are the twelve Victories whose feet rest on the foot of the throne of Olympian Jove,—the work of Phedias. Pausanias, not always alive to details, speaks of the attitude of these dancers. There is little to prove the exact time in the fifth century B. C. Nike adopted the forward dancing movement, and it would be impious to suppose that a human dancer served as a model for Nike as Pæonios has presented her.

Fig. 569.

The Hellenistic "coroplastie," reflecting the great art of the day, did not think of Nike otherwise than as a dancer, and she often holds in her hands the attributes of Dionysos, the castanets, the crowns of leaves; she belongs, like Eros, to that cycle of gods who at all times are associated with Aphrodite. The new Nike is a professional dancer; her poses are elegant, her arms take on the most gracious curves (Figs. 144, 152, 253).

A great number of the figurines were intended to be suspended: there is, in the movement of their legs, a liberty of motion that transcends truth; the modeler, in order to suggest flight, paid no attention to the laws of equilibrium.

The dancers who soar without wings on a charming vase of the fifth century B. C., —see Fig. 568,—show the extent of the convention. The legs are lightly bent at the knees, the feet are close together, the inferior members appear to the eye to be flying. The curve of the whole body, inclined beyond the normal center of gravity, has more elegance than if it obeyed that law. The only indications of dance-movement which remain, in the case of the small paintings, are furnished by the arms of the dancers. The legs are inactive. Thus it is seen that they are similar to the winged Nike intended to be suspended.

Fig. 570.

The flying Victories returned to the ancient traditions in making the double gesture with the tunic (Fig. 569).

384. Eros the Dancer.—In this history of the dance enough has been said of Nike. In the fifth century Eros is winged; though tardy, he at last makes his appearance as a dancer.

In the fifth century B. C. Eros personifies love, leaving all his playfulness behind him. He becomes a melancholy and grave youth. This is the period of the Hellenistic effeminacy, which gives a new interpretation to religious ideas. This period is that of the Eros Hermaphrodite who loves to dance or to lead a dance (Fig. 188) (E. Pottier).

Another type of Eros appears in the fourth century B. C., the winged babies of Tanagra, charming children, full of roguishness. Often they, like the Nikes, are intended to be suspended. It is to be regretted that there is no indication as to the method of suspension, when it is evident that the figures to be seen in the cases of several museums are really *figures in the air*. Posed on the feet, they lose all their individuality and cease to be interesting.

Fig. 511.

Toward the end of the fourth century B. C., all of the Eros, whether young children or youths, take part in the Bacchic ceremonies and carry the attributes of Dionysos. They mingle with the Satyrs and Menades and are as indefatigable in their dancing, though their movements are less violent than those of the Bacchic dancers. They are more joyous than their noisy companions, and are always governed by the law of eurhythmy.

385. Atys Dancer.—Atys is a Phrygian divinity, whose cult was, in a happy hour, introduced into Greece, though the exact time remains a secret of the gods. The lover of the mother of the gods, to whom he is always most tender, he is not at all times to be found among the gods of ancient Greece. Like Sabazios, like Men and Mithras, he is officially looked down upon; yet it is quite certain that his mysteries were celebrated. He presents an Oriental aspect; a Phrygian helmet on his head, he wears a costume of eastern type, a detail of which is the pantaloons that are wrapped around his legs.

This Atys is a dancer. He is not the only winged dancer,—there are Nike, Eros, Psyche. The suspension at the back (Fig. 571) permits this figure to be studied under the conditions which the artist intended.

386. The Curetes (Clashers).—The ancient writers disagree as to the origin of the Pyrrhic, but all are in accord regarding the most ancient of all the dances in armour of which history guards the memory,—the dance of the "Clashers." Their rôle was to play for the infant Zeus. Rhea, the great mother of the gods, married Kronos, and, to prevent the infant from the voracity of her husband, charged the armed men to clash their weapons to drown the sound of his cries. The Clashers acquitted themselves well, clashing their helmets, swords and shields. Their dance, necessarily noisy, is distinguished by disordered movements, made necessary by the essential point of legend.

Fig. 572.

The sculptures which represent their exercises, are, unhappily, nearly all of them, of the lower period of art, and therefore conventional.

These dancers always turn by stamping, on a circular track (Fig. 338). They dance in groups of two or three. They strike their swords against each other's shields, or hurl their shields against those of their companions. Ordinarily the infant Zeus is represented in their midst (Fig. 572).

The scenes in which the Clashers figure are reproduced in the case of Zagreus, who is the son of Zeus and Korah.

387. There is this essential difference between the Pyrrhic and the dance of the Clashers,—the Pyrrhic is a mimetic dance, an imitation of a battle, with varied movements; the dance of the Clashers is not a pretense, it is a noisy clash of brazen shields; it is a dance in the modern acceptance of the word; it is reduced to a gesticulation at once boisterous and mechanical.

The passage from the one form to the other is simple; the Hellenistic artists, in search of new motifs, purposely confused the two. There are represented Pyrrhics for two, executed by two Clashers who can be recognized by their helmets, swords and shields (360).

388. **Dionysos, and the Dionysian Dances.**—Among the gods who dance and in whose honor dances are given, Dionysos holds a place in the first rank. In his character of the god of wine, with which, in a happy moment, legend endowed him, he becomes the incarnation of joyous folly; he does not walk, he dances: flutes and dulcimers accompany him in his processions; there is much noisy music in his honor. If his life be not a perpetual fête, his one care is to banish care,—to fill his days with joy. He loves the mountains, the forests, the rivers; his temple is nature; these places are peopled with gods, men, or beasts, who love the joys of life, and who raise the celebration of his orgies to the dignity of a cult. Silenes and Satyrs, bearded, with bare heads and hairy bodies, are the guests of the forests. Pans, with their cloven hoofs, take their pleasure at the summits of the rocky places; Centaurs roam on the mountains; Nymphs, at the mouths of the rivers, give food to the young god; Naiades and Menades of all ranks form around Dionysos a court of folly, in the etiquette of which dancing holds a unique place.

Though the aspect of these companions of Dionysos underwent important changes as time passed, they are always recognizable.

389. The Silenes and the Satyrs are not of the same mythological origin; though so nearly alike in form that they may be mistaken one for the other. The primitive Silenus is of brutal aspect; he is made more hideous by his dress of the head and skin of some animal (Figs. 523, 415, 578). He may have the feet and tail of a horse (Fig. 386). In this form he is seen on many of the black-figured vases. In the fifth century B. C. the face of the Silenus becomes less

simian, though he still possesses his bestial characteristics (Fig. 164). Little by little this fantastic being loses his grosser symbols; his face becomes human, his feet cease to be hoofs, his tail is shortened. The fourth century B. C. brings in a type of a *young* Silenus, with waving hair and laughing mouth; he is the Satyr who became the Roman faun (Fig. 180). The Hellenistic period did not renounce the old-man type of Silenus, though he did not remain a beast, he was still drunken. Gross of body, hairy, bald-headed, crowned with ivy (Fig. 573), the artists of all periods represented him as an old man but not always a grotesque. He joyously carries the infant Dionysos in his arms, his face expressing paternal tenderness (E. Pottier). Thus there are two distinct types, which are easily distinguishable.

Fig. 573.

390. Pan is the pastoral deity. He lives on the summits of the Arcadian hills and is the genius of the mountains. His legends have nothing in common with those of Dionysos except that they are both rustic in nature.

When he enters the Dionysian procession, it is robbed of its ugliness. He remains goat-like, horned and hoofed (Fig. 501). Often he appears thus in the masques. He is never without the syrinx, the flute of the mountain shepherds, the art of playing which he learned on Mount Olympus.

391. The Menades are the followers of Dionysos. They are hard to classify, being neither gods nor human beings. They take part in the sports of the Silenes and Satyrs, though their gallant enterprises are less startling. They are crowned with leaves, twining the ivy or chains of smilax in their scanty hair: fawn or leopard skins are carelessly draped about their shoulders or carried over their arms. Nearly always they carry serpents in their hands, like living wreaths. Often they brandish the thyrsus or the torch; the torch is the symbol and the accessory of the nocturnal orgies dear to the god. The thyrsus is a staff or rod, terminating in a ball of pine or a bunch of ivy leaves. Often streamers were tied to the shaft.

392. The Menades are, of course, fabulous. At fêtes celebrated by the Hellenic populace in honor of Dionysos they are represented

according to ritualistic tradition by women who are usually called *Bacchants*, but each region has a different name for them.

The *Thyades* were a company composed of women of Athens and Delphos; they roamed through the gorges of Parnassus during the winter nights, screaming as they went. The *Mimallonides* of Macedonia, the *Bassarides* and the *Edonides* of Thrace were noted for the violence of their Bacchic fury

The painters and sculptors made use of the models before their eyes, so that the Menades of fable are represented by real persons. While the Menades are always with the Satyrs, the Bacchants did not admit any masculine dancers among them; the celebration of the orgiastic fêtes was confined to women.

' The artists, taking for models the living women who danced, also painted the scenes of the dances, always violent, often obscene, which were part of the satyric drama.

393. Satyrs and Menades, both of whom modern custom calls Bacchants, carry the same insignia. The thyrsus and the torch have been mentioned (391); the *vase* is to Dionysos what the shield is to Mars, and by this word Aristotle explains the presence in his hand and the hands of his worshipers of utensils which might contain the divine beverage. The *canthare*, a jug with a long handle; the *keras*, a drinking-horn; the *ryton*, a small vase of characteristic form from which one drank by throwing back the head and pouring the liquid down the throat; and amphoræ of various shapes. Sometimes the Satyrs play together a game with a large bowl which stands on the ground. The companions of Komos (415), imitating this as they did other customs, dance around the jars containing wine.

All of the musical instruments, except the lyre, which belongs to Apollo, are seen in the hands of the Bacchants: *castanets, cymbals, tambourines, the double flute, the lateral flute* (rare), *syrinx*, or flute of Pan, much like the flute played by the goat-herds, and bells attached to the clothing of the Bacchants,—compose an orchestra quite noisy enough. When to this were added the cries of furious play, the clapping of hands and stamping of feet of the dancers, one can imagine how strange a concert announced to the ears of the populace the coming of the Bacchants.

394. Among other accessories, *comic masks* were suspended from

the trees; baskets (round, covered ones) from which the mystic serpents escaped; the litter, cradle of the infant Dionysos, and symbol of purification, always filled with fruit; paniers of all kinds, containing the offerings used in the Dionysian ceremonies. The serpents often had a part in the fête. Plutarch is authority for the statement that Olympia, mother of Alexander, was one of the most zealous of the Mimallonides, and most barbarous in the expression of bacchic frenzy, appearing in the *thiases* and training the great serpents, which slid out of the mystic vases and among the ivy, rolling through the procession, to the fright of the people.

The presence of the panther among the Dionysians, the Satyrs and the Menades is symbolic; the panther was dear to Dionysos, because he is the most ardent of all animals.

395. The word *Bacchanales*, which serves to distinguish the Dionysian scenes, is Roman, and usage gives it a certain value. It is impossible to establish any classification of the dances of the Bacchants, which the paintings present in endless variety. The absence of symmetry,—the systematic disorder, were the rule.

The modern method of rules for the dance is essentially different. It insists upon a rigorous *simultaneity* of *identical movements*, executed by all of the dancers, and the *symmetrical disposition* of the groups of dancers. The Greeks, on the contrary, evidently cared little for the simultaneity and repetition of Ensemble movements. The arts purely Greek were, during the classic age, opposed to the juxtaposition of like forms. When symmetry was imposed by conditions, the artists bent all their efforts toward minimizing it.

It is possible the dance en masse, especially the dance of the Bacchants, was inspired by the same principle as the arts of design. The painters not only conformed to the laws of their own art, but to the art of the dance. The apparent disorder is really conformity to rule. That very thing, to us, spells ruin; we cannot understand concerted movement without perceptible symmetry. The very thing that, to our ears, loses all sense of melodic nuances and rhythmic combinations, the Greeks found full of charm. Where our eyes see but confusion of movement, theirs found an Ensemble ruled by perfect order. They had eyes and ears keener than ours, therefore they could see unity where we get only an impression of complexity.

396. The absence of symmetry from the Bacchanales does not preclude groupings. They are found throughout the entire list, like *part dances*, composed of two, three, or a greater number. Sometimes the whole band is separated into groups which reform to include all the dancers. But in this case, the movements are executed differently by the different groups.

The Bacchanales also present the simple forms of procession dances, with the dancers all going in the same direction. The dancers who are associated advance with the same step, which, indeed, only adds to the irregularity which marks the progress.

397. The mimetic dances, the dramatic scenes, have a prominent place in the Bacchanales,—Satyrs pursue Menades, Bacchants, drunk and frenzied, shaking with orgiastic fury,—a mêlée of dancers who manage to keep to the rhythm. It is a ritual of order in seeming disorder.

398. Representations of the god himself and of the Bacchants figure in vast numbers in dance and legend, which tells of many places where Satyrs and Menades mingle together.

Hermes precedes the cortèges of Nymphs, or presides with Dionysos at the gambols of the Bacchants. He may also be seen, seated on a rock, accompanying the dance of the Satyrs with the lyre of Apollo in his hands. It must be explained how it happens that the instrument of Apollo is used as the music for a dance of Satyrs. The god of Delphos does not refuse to make merry with the Dionysians. A few vases show Menades shaking the castanets as they dance around Apollo.

The chaste Athena herself did not fear being led into joyous company; she is seen among the Bacchants, beside Apollo and Dionysos.

Dionysos on Olympus is the god of fire, Hephaistos having been exiled by Zeus. The banished one may not be reinstated in grace, and Hera is left wearily waiting on the golden throne, while he forges the invisible bonds. Dionysos has recourse to a ruse. He makes the lame god drunk, and gives him into the hands of the Satyrs, and he is held prisoner at the doors of Olympus. This singular ceremony is one of the favorite subjects of the painters.

Nowhere are the worshipers of Dionysos shown in a more wonderful way than where associated with this legend. In the marriage of Ariadne or the mysteries of Korah, the Satyrs and Menades have the same office, and their tireless dance forever frames the loves of their master. There are so many mythic scenes in which they have part. They are the guard of honor when the god goes abroad, and they carry arms in combat. Together with Dionysos they fight with the Tyrrhenian pirates and against the Amazons: they faithfully follow in the triumphal marches of India: they throw away the thyrsus and, arming themselves, lead murderous charges.

399. In the Hellenistic period, when the religion changed, becoming more sensual, losing the stern character of the sixth century B. C., all of the gods enrolled under the banner of Dionysos. They adopted the bacchic insignia, they wore the crown of the Bacchants; the movements of the dances became more exaggerated until they reached a point that can be explained only by pathologists. The backward bending of the body, the bizarre contortions, the mad whirling, became more and more habitual with the dancers.

DANCES IN HONOR OF THE GODS

400. Originally all of these dances were in honor of the gods, a religious practice of worship by means of rhythmic movements.

Strabo speaks of the sacrifices accompanied by frenzy thus: "Frenzy is a kind of celestial inspiration." It is a saintly fury, manifested by visible signs.

Its ritual included the *orgiastic* dances. It is not confined to the worship of Dionysos; the cult of Rhea, and the mysteries of Orpheus evoked a dance that was strangely violent, which transformed its adepts into frantic maniacs. It is possible that the cult of Apollo had its place in the orgiastic dances: the frenzy, according to Strabo, extended to prophecy, as is proved by the contortions of the Pythonesses. There is a likeness between their ecstatic poses and the movements of a great number of the dancers who figure in the paintings and reliefs.

401. The dance of the Clashers (386) is derived from the ritualistic dance belonging to the cult of Rhea. It is reasonable to sup-

DANCES IN HONOR OF THE GODS 259

pose that the adorers of the Great Mother of the gods executed the whirling Steps which are related to those used by the protectors of the infant Zeus. The priests of Rhea were mad, they stamped their feet and uttered inarticulate sounds, while making crazy motions as to which the texts are rather obscure, but which appear to have been something like those of the whirling dervishes.

402. The practices of the Omophagie, where blood was spilled, and to which some monuments are consecrated, cannot be regarded as altogether fictitious. Without doubt the menade who holds a human foot in her hand, and, with backward bent head, executes an orgiastic dance, is

Fig. 574.

to be accepted as purely symbolic. This recalls the legend of Dionysos Zagreus and the Titans. But this "cult of raw flesh"—reduced

Fig. 575.

to the laceration of the body, was practiced in the nocturnal ceremonies in honor of Zagreus. The initiates partook of the raw flesh of a bull. The ceremony is not to be described.

Fig. 578 is taken from a vase with red figures of the fifth century B. C. and shows a Dionysian hacking a head to pieces and throwing the débris about.

The Menade of Scopas (Fig. 575) shows that the sole idea of the dances was to use movements so violent that they lost all eurhythmy.

403. Persons of all ranks, ages, and sexes participated in the *phallic dances*, —citizens of the capital and inhabitants of the villages: these dances were of a nature not to be described. It is enough to say that the grossness of the urban Phallus worshipers

260 THE DANCERS

was copied by the rural population. In that period the thiase of Bacchic legend became a reality, and the obscene gambols pictured on the vases were copied from life.

404. The Dionysian dance is one of the forms of the Bacchic cult and, on the whole, may be considered as a part of the ritual of

Fig. 576.

frenzy of the Bacchants. It is not rare to find the sacrifice arranged in their midst; the religious character is evident. Figs. 273, 352, 438, 439, 576, 577 and 578, taken from paintings on vases, show

Fig. 577.

the altar beside which are the Bacchants. The only difference between these scenes and the Bacchanales is the presence of the altar.

405. What were the movements peculiar to the Bacchic dances, and used by all of the dancers who took part in the orgiastic ceremonies? The distinguishing mark is not the essential form of the dance, but the *exaggeration* of the movements. The dancers who worked themselves into frenzy in honor of Dionysos, of Rhea, or Atys, present, fundamentally, the same movements and gestures common to all Greek dances, though, in their liturgical delirium, they amplified all

DANCES IN HONOR OF THE GODS   261

of these motions until the original characteristics were lost in the heaped-up exaggerations, which, at last, became grotesque (Fig. 579), losing all likeness to nature.

They were distinguished by the backward bend of the Head and Torso (156, 163), by bending the head and Torso forward (162, 155), four Positions so easy to exaggerate (Figs. 111, 118, 132, 171, 180, 189, 193, 352, 369, 411, 413, 420, 438, 439, 455, 494, B, 505, 575, 577, 579, etc.). In sharp contrast are the types of religious orgiastic dances from which the *frenzy* was excluded.

406. To the second category belongs the symbolic dance by three women who may or may not be preceded by a leader: the decency and gravity of these dances is traditional: all contortions are excluded.

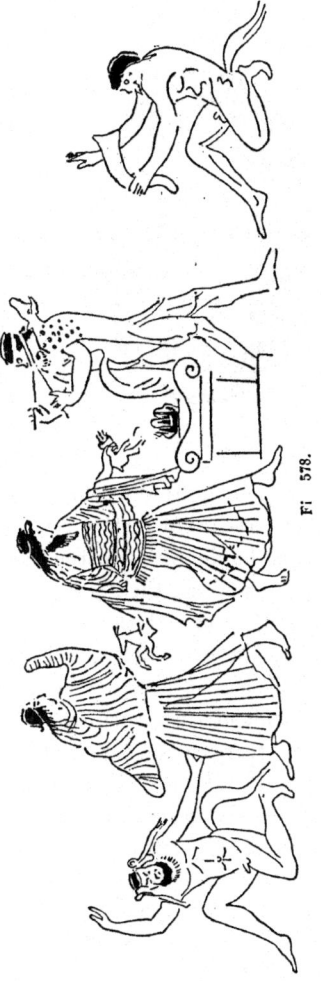

Fi 578.

The funeral dances in the later form, decreed by Solon, were reduced to a mimetic form which was nobly expressive, founded as they were partly on the religious dance, and notable for their dignity of pose and gesture, which was governed by strict rules.

The same kind of dance is seen in the pose of the majestic priestess who faces a crouching figure (Fig. 580). It should be explained that the scene, so far as it concerns the woman's gesture, is a religious rite; the right elbow rests on the left hand, as though the arm had been raised a long time.

In the interior of the sanctuary there was an altar against the wall from which the fillets were suspended. This altar was in the form of an Ionic capital, and the sacred fire burned on it (Fig. 581).

Fig. 579.

With arms hidden in her cloak, a woman executes a lively dance to the music of a double flute. The painter naïvely represents the dance as more like a run, there being no indication of a true dance-step. Incapable of depicting the details of the step, the artist confined his attention to the ritualistic side of the subject. The dancer, chastely draped, head and torso turned to the side, moves without exaggeration, dancing in honor of the deity. Certainly there is no *frenzy* here. The whole movement, while it possesses a sort of dignity, verges upon the grotesque.

407. The dancers represented by Figs. 582 to 593 are the *hierodules*, or daughters of Zeus, consecrated to the service of a god whose identity is unknown. The presence of certain remarkable accessories and details of costume leaves no doubt as to the nature of their functions.

All wear on their heads the *kalathos*, a kind of diadem, large at the top, and in shape much like a basket of which the head forms the bottom. Sometimes it is like a large fillet, sometimes it is a trellis of rush-work, or of willow or palm leaves. The terra-cotta figurines often wear a heavy-striped *kalathos* (Figs. 586 and 587). The bas-reliefs transform this into a crown of twigs and leaves (Fig. 589 and following).

The tunics of the *hierodules* are very short, leaving the upper leg bare. Sometimes the breasts are uncovered, the scanty drapery falling only from the hips.

Fig. 580.

All of these dancers are posed on the half-toe, or the toe (102, 215, 216), this being prescribed by rule.

DANCES IN HONOR OF THE GODS

One may judge from the following enumeration of the varieties of movement and gesture executed by the *hierodules*.

Figs. 582 and 583. Whirling Steps.

Fig. 581.

Fig. 584. Gesture of the Pourer (52) which is here adapted to the dance.

Fig. 585. Whirling Step, gesture like the preceding.

Fig. 586. IV crossed on the half-toe (108), gesture of the Pourer (52) made with the castanets.

Fig. 587. IV outward, on the half-toe (95); the dancer shakes the castanets.

Fig. 588. Small running Steps on the toes (242), double gesture with the tunic (44).

Fig. 589. IV crossed (109); the dancer turns by stamping (267); gesture of Adoration (40).

Fig. 582. Fig. 583.

Fig. 590. I on the half-toe (106) turning, gesture identical with Fig. 584.

Fig. 591. IV on the half-toe (108); gesture of supplication. Between the two *hierodules* is a statue of Athena.

Fig. 592. IV on the half-toe: plays with the mantle, with the right hand. Makes an offering to a divinity.

Fig. 593. IV on the half-toe; gesture of Adoration (40). At one side of the *hierodule* there is a rustic altar on which burns the sacred fire.

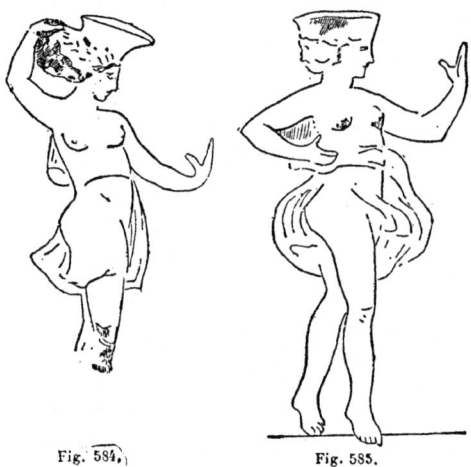

Fig. 584. Fig. 585.

These examples are, of course, not all taken from one dance, but from a group of dances of the same type, which is to say that they celebrate the same rite. The *hierodules* have one particular dance, varied, but of which the important element is the

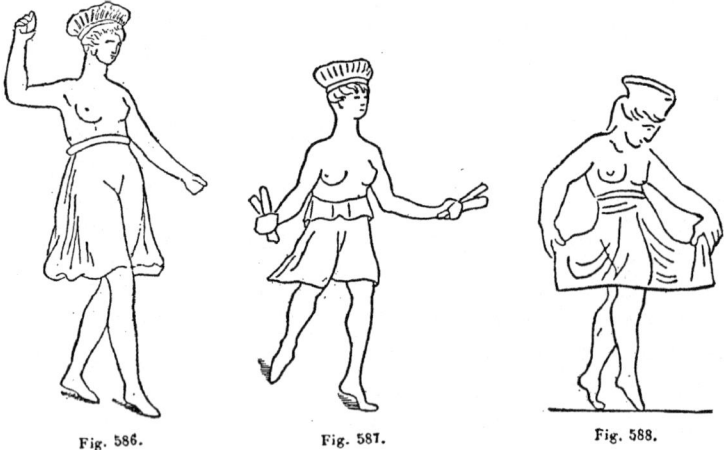

Fig. 586. Fig. 587. Fig. 588.

mimetic. They abstain from exaggeration in their poses and movements. They let their heads incline, and their torsos always turn to the right. Their knees do not bend; there is no leap; they seem to slide on the ground, lightly, and with short steps.

From all this we do not get the Tempo (207). They execute the Step of running on the toes (242), during which the arms join

Fig. 589. Fig. 590.

above the head in a special form of the *dance of the joined hands* (319, 322). In the numerous forms of the character-dances, the movements are varied and many in number. The *hierodule* does not always conform to the customs of the dance, but the divergence is slight, and there is none of the unnatural movement that characterizes the other *dances with joined hands*.

The series of dancers who wear the *kalothos* is an ensemble most valuable in the study of the homogeneity of the

Fig. 591.

dance; the absence of the gymnastic forms dear to the Bacchants and their like prove that the dance of the *hierodules* is the expression of a cult without frenzy.

408. Religious Processions.—There are a great number of processions with which the dance is connected by the music; in the solemn processions the attributes of the god were carried; the hymns were sung as an accompaniment to the march, the metrical form of

Fig. 592.   Fig. 593.

them being ruled by tradition. Whatever the rhythm of the processional may be, the aspect of the dancers is the same.

The painters could not resist the temptation to systematize the

Fig. 594.   Fig. 595.

representations of the processions: they followed one of two forms for every occasion, in order not to destroy the decorative effect. The only exceptions are the Dionysian processions, where the rule

DANCES IN HONOR OF THE GODS

is disorder, and which were composed of persons dancing, each to suit his own fancy. But in all other ceremonies the dance is a simple rhythmic movement, which, in the sculptures, is always presented in the same way.

Sometimes the persons advance in files, one-and-one; sometimes, but more rarely, they march two-and-two. The boldness of the artists never went beyond this.

409. Fig. 594 is taken from the temple of the Harpies (14): it is an abridged cortege, three young women in file. Their walk is slow and their steps short; their bodies are too stiff to be graceful; they do not make the same gestures. This remark applies also to the cortege of nymphs (Fig. 595) from a bas-relief of Thasos (14). In these two examples it is easy to see, as in the case of the Parthenon frieze, a convention peculiar to the bas-relief (29), which consists in making the walker whose weight is on the right foot turn to the left and vice versa.

410. The Parthenon Frieze.—In applying the same formula to the people on this frieze, Phidias escaped from the monotony which results from the uniformly forward movement. He broke up the symmetry; the persons who walk with the same step are unequally distant from each other; they are presented at different angles: some turn the head to the side, others look backward (Fig. 596).

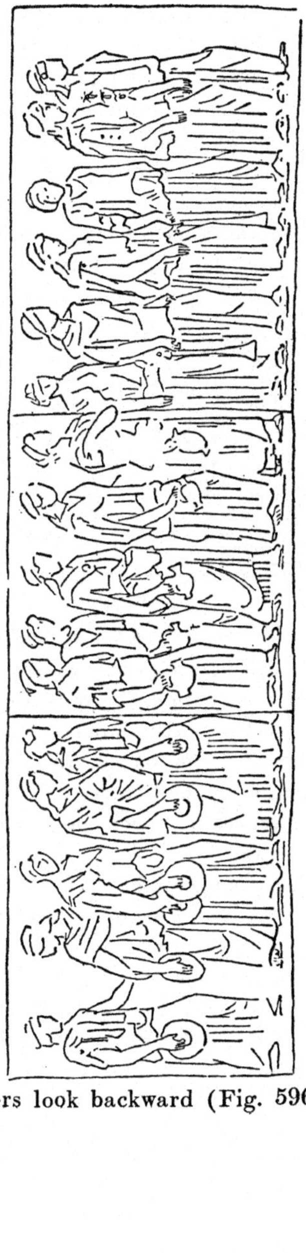

Fig. 596.

All of those who carry phials hold the vase in the right hand, which is the direction in which they march. By a convention, the choice of the arm which supports the vase is determined by the direction in which the step is made.

The women whose hands are empty lightly lift the arms at the elbow, without any stiffness, the fingers being well grouped.

The groups of two persons are irregular, and are introduced to give variety.

Men and women file past slowly, without lifting the heels. Their walk is a compromise between movement and immobility.

Fig. 596 bis.

The Parthenon frieze is not to be accepted as a literal copy of one of the *panathenian* processions; Phidias, in planning it as a decoration, took considerable liberty in disposing the motifs. Even the gods who appear amid the groups of mortals are made to conform to the scheme of decoration. It is a scene of sacrifice; the portresses carry the sacred baskets, etc. The men, armed, dance the Pyrrhic, this dance having a prominent place. The Athenian cavalry is also important. They executed, in these processions, a sort of *hippic* dance, which does not appear on the frieze. It is surprising to find traces of *ranks* among the cavaliers, which are to be interpreted as conventions of perspective. The chariots follow the cavalry.

There is no doubt that all this is ordered according to the sculptor's fancy. For the same reason he has not brought different subjects into juxtaposition, and has not abridged the unique ceremony. Nor has he clung to facts: he makes the gods descend to earth among their worshipers. These liberties presuppose others.

411. Religious Processions on the Painted Vases.—The form of the procession cannot be definitely learned from the painted vases because of the faults of perspective. Only in the sixth century

B. C. did the painters break away from the conventions and permit their figures to walk in couples (Fig. 597). It is an artifice, and a first attempt at perspective, but it is not to be confused with the rules for true perspective; this was long before the sculptors of the bas-reliefs ventured on any such innovation.

412. The greater part of the decorative convention concerns itself with the representations of processions, which accounts for the monotony of the poses and the gestures, one figure being a copy of

Fig. 597.

the others. The opposition,—the contrasts,—even the disorder, which exist in the Bacchic processions, composed of true Greek dancers, show their dislike of synchronism of movement by a great number of persons (395, 396). But the grand ceremonials in honor of the high gods, made up of cadenced marches, embellished with a gesticulation both dramatic and dignified, were instinct with eurhythmy. They followed the rule of contrast and did not tire the spectator with their monotony.

It may be said that, in a simple procession, the marchers timed their steps to a song, the forward movement being uniform. This *rule of the same step* is not a decorative simplification, designed by the painters and sculptors; it was a rule used by the Greeks for the same reason that it is used by moderns.

PRIVATE OR SOCIAL DANCES

413. The private dances were at all times held in high esteem by the Greeks. From the Iliad of Homer to the Banquet of the Sages, —from the vases of the seventh century B. C. to the latest products of ceramic art, proof of this may be found.

As they were not executed by professionals, the dances varied. The ability to dance was encouraged; even Socrates practiced the art to keep his body in condition.

The artists copied the movements of the dancers from life; in the case of Nike, Eros, etc., living dancers at least served as the inspiration.

Not all of the representations were of a public character; the citizens in their own homes were taught to take part in the dance, and derived much pleasure from it.

The professional dancers, like the musicians, were recruited from the ranks of slaves. The dancers who entertained the guests at dinner parties were not of the courtesan class.

414. Often the men are represented as nude; this is an artistic convention, used because it was not easy, otherwise, to mark certain figures as Satyrs: the definite sign is the tail. On the vases with red figures, they are generally young, beardless men (fifth, fourth, third centuries B. C.). The black figured vases often show them bearded.

The citizen dancers are always represented as purely human, never as animals (Plate I, Figs. 128, 131, 132, 136, 158, 159, 178, 189, 230, 277, 278, 407, 408, 409, 410, 453, 461, 466, 467, 496, 515, 516, 517, 518, 524, 562). The figures 496 and 499, of which the nudity is a convention, are to be considered private dancers, or, as we would say, *social dancers*.

There is less certainty about Figs. 448, 449, 450, 451, 452, 457. One may well doubt if they were professional dancers; the modest costume, the moderation of their movements, the style of their work, all indicate that they belong to a high class. Similar examples are not wanting. It is likely that women of free birth often figure among the dancers on the vases, but, with the exception of the

PRIVATE OR SOCIAL DANCES 271

hierodules and the young women who take part in the religious processions, it is not always easy to decide as to their social status.

415. The Komos Dances.—The private dances executed by men alone were, according to all tradition, *Komos* dances.

The Greeks drank little wine with their meals; it was after meals that the wine appeared. At the close of the repast the dancers and musicians came in, and the slaves again filled the cups. With the Komos, there was feasting, joyous drinking, which the courtesans, players of the flute, dancers, actors, and buffoons little by little changed from a concert to an orgy.

Fig. 598.

During the seventh century B. C. the representations of Komos figures was much affected by the painters of vases, and the fashion spread over the whole Hellenic world. Originally these dances were a part of the Dionysian rites and are always to be found connected with the Bacchic cult. The companions of Komos, the *Komastai* are sometimes regarded as substitutes for the Satyrs in real life. The likeness between the two is indicated by the name "Komos" which is always given to the Satyrs of the bacchic *thiase*.

Fig. 599.

In the ancient figures of Komos dancers, the whipping legs seem alway to be on the point of losing their equilibrium; in the case of the large vases, the contents are often indicated by the figures with knees bent, which is the rule of their kind; they half crouch, as though about to leap. The artist does not hurl these figures into space: they are at the beginning or the end of the leap, which renders the flexion of the knees necessary. The humorous intention is evident; the joyous *Komastai* have lost all idea of stability. The Bacchic enthusiasm which the Satyrs express in their exaggerated movements is here exhibited with a facility that suggests play rather than dancing.

The name Komos is applied not only to the bacchic follies which followed the feasts in the homes of the rich, but to bands of hilarious  dancers who roamed the streets in noisy processions. Sometimes they would stop a sober citizen and insist upon serenading him; they even invaded houses and took part in the diversions of the company. Certain of the Komos customs were used in the Phallic processions. The Komostai were made up of the most important citizens and the most ignorant peasants, all of whom were worshipers of Dionysos, and the wine-god's dance made one as good as another. In all this fantastic play there was one rule of dancing that held: each dancer danced to please himself, without regard for the step of any other. The result was chaos, of which the disorder of the Bacchanales is only an imitation.

Fig. 600.

416. That the simple citizens were not among the habitual dancers is proved by the way they execute any Tempos that are at all complicated. See Figs. 366, 367 and others classed as character-Steps (Figs. 461, 466, 467). Enough would volunteer to make up the Step for Two (Figs. 128, 408, 485).

Sometimes the Ensemble of the Komostai is ruled as are other dances (Figs. 230, 277). The texts of the Greek writers confirm these deductions. Their anecdotes give the names of certain amateur devotees of the dance, who were trained under the direction of special teachers (331) in all of the different parts of the mechanism of the art, and who attained such perfection in it that their performances gave great pleasure to their friends.

The private dances of the Greeks were wonderful exercises for the body and the mind. They were the means of displaying talent for these things. They did not resemble our modern social dances.

CONCLUSION

417. Results Acquired.—What, with the Greeks, were the modes of dance-movement? That is the question which this book has sought to answer. The problem of the Antique Greek Dance has been reduced to its constituent elements by means of the paintings and the sculptures. The results accomplished are here presented.

Positions

Legs. 1. Holding the *feet sidewise* (97). The invariable rule of the modern French dance was practiced by the Greek dancers.

2. For our *First Position*, the Greek dancer substituted a position excluded from our dance, which may be seen in Figs. 75, 76, 77, 101.

3. The *Fourth crossed* had three forms, which correspond to a triple position of the feet IV crossed on the sole of the foot (Fig. 84) IV crossed on the half-toe (Fig. 85): IV crossed on the toe (Fig. 86) is one of the favorite Positions of the Greek dancers.

Arms. 4. In our dance, the Carriage of the Arms is a decorative detail. The forms are numerous and simple and are expressed in geometrical figures, which give elegant curves (Figs. 88 to 99). The Greek dancer did not always curve the arms. Sometimes he even uses arm positions that are stiff and full of abrupt angles (Figs. 110, 111, 112, 113, 114, 119, 120, 126, 127, 145, etc.).

Hands. 5. The hand is always active. Also, the Positions it takes have great variety from the way the fingers are held (Figs. 161 to 181); with modern dancers, the hand is content to sometimes play a passive rôle, merely adding finish to the arm. The hand expressions play a principal rôle in the Greek dance.

Body; Head. 6. The *Torso bent forward*, and the *Torso bent backward* (Figs. 185, 186) are seldom employed by our dancers, and on the rare occasions when they are used are so attenuated that they do not greatly resemble the exaggerated form so often met in the Greek dance (155, 156).

7. The same observations apply to the *forward and backward inclinations of the head* (Figs. 197, 198) which the Greeks introduced into their dances (162, 163, 164).

8. They practiced the *Attitudes* (Figs. 206, 207, 208).

9. Their ideas of *Oppositions* were the ideas of Noverre and Blasis (171).

Preparatory Exercises

10. The Greek dancers, like the French, never deviated from the rule of the *Toe held down.* Neither permitted the sole of the foot to be seen by the spectators (180).

11. The Greek dancers executed the *Bending,* the *Separation,* the *Battement,* and *the Circles with the Legs* (178, 181, 189, 195).

12. The movements of their arms, instead of being reduced to a gymnastic formula, intended merely to be decorative, as is the case with our dancers (199), were used in expressive *gestures* (55). The activity of the hand is constant, and the fingers maintained their independence of action. The Greek dancer made the dance into a pantomime.

13. Contrary to the custom of our dancers, they indulged in violent movements of the *head and body,* producing oppositions between the Head and Torso in these exaggerated movements.

14. In one word, the Greek dancer achieved eurhythmy while engaged in much freer action than our dancers attempt.

Tempos and Steps

15. The Greek dancers, like ours, posed sometimes on the sole, sometimes on the half-toe, and sometimes on the toe (214 to 216).

16. The *Tempos and Steps were identical with ours.* The Greek dancers employed the *Slide* (226), the *Fouetté* (227), the *Jeté* (229), the *Balance* (234); they used the *tempos and steps on the*

toe (240, 241), the *Cat-leap* (290), the *Assemblé* (254), the *Mutation of the Feet* (254), the *Entrechat* (255), the *Preparation and Execution of the Pirouette* (269 to 271).

17. *Tempos and steps characteristic of the Greek dance: their special mechanism.*

Slides made on both feet at the same time (Figs. 273, 274, 275, 276).

Leaping in place from one foot to the other (Fig. 404).

Upper leg lifted (Figs. 405, 406, 407).

Leaping in place while the body is bent forward (Figs. 411, 412, 413).

Lateral kick (Fig. 414).

Crouching dance similar to the little Russian (Figs. 415 to 418).

Dances bending forward or back (Figs. 420 to 439).

Turning by stamping on the sole of the foot (Figs. 346 to 348).

Turning by stamping on the half-toe (Figs. 349 to 353).

Turning by stamping in IV crossed on the sole of the foot, on the half-toe, or on the toe (Figs. 354 to 359).

Dances with the mantle (Figs. 447 to 459).

Dances with the hands joined (Figs. 460 to 480).

Choregraphy

18. The movements executed by two dancers facing each other are not always alike, and when of the same nature, are rarely simultaneous. The dancers are concerned with making their movements harmonize with those of their companions (333).

19. It may be stated that as a rule *the two dancers do not touch one another*. Whether of the same sex or not, they do not hold one another by the hand or by the waist.

20. In the Steps for Two and in the Steps for Three, contrast rather than symmetry is the rule.

21. The traditional group of *Three Dancers* (with or without a leader) escapes from the conventions of the preceding. Usually the women hold each other by the wrist, the hand, or the border of the tunic: the result is that their movements are simultaneous (343 to 347).

22. **Ensembles.**—Simultaneous movement is seen in the Farandole (files of dancers holding each other by the hand [349, 350]); in the rare representations of the choric scenes (356); in the paintings of Ruvo (Tratta [357]); on a bas-relief from the Acropolis, which furnishes an example of the Pyrrhic en masse (361). The *rule of the same step* is in these instances uniformly applied.

23. On the contrary, in the Ensembles composed of Dionysian dancers, the *absence of all symmetry*, the *systematic disorder*, is the rule.

24. The *Farandole* is one of the most ancient and the most persistent of the forms of popular dance (348 to 352).

25. The *dances in armour* were founded on the principle of imitation, but, in time, they were transformed into mere spectacles of a decorative nature.

26. **The Funeral Dances.**—These were reduced to symbolic gesticulation, from practices that were originally barbarous, such as tearing the hair, scratching the face with the finger-nails, etc., all of which Solon suppressed (364). The gestures are seen on the most ancient vases and on the amphoræ of the decadent period (370). Those dating from the fifth century B. C. indicate nothing more than symbols of the more ancient practices; by this means the tradition was perpetuated.

418. **Technique and Esthetics.**—Though it is certain that the Greek dancers used a great number of Tempos and Steps identical with those of the modern dance, it would be rash to conclude that the mechanism of their dance was the same as ours. Our dancers boast a precision which is acquired only by long practice; their ideal consists in realizing in its whole perfection certain forms of movement rigorously fixed. With them, for example, the Pirouette in II, made in the Attitude is one of the varieties of gyratory movement of which the amplitude, the liveliness, and the successive phases are determined with astonishing exactness.

The Greek dancer did not have as much experience. Without doubt, there was a grammar, a formula of Tempos and Steps, but the dancer was free to commit as many solecisms as he liked. Fantasy was the first rule, and it permeated all kinds of plays. Our dancers misprize the childish play often shown in the ancient work, the grotesque exaggerations of the movements of the walk, the run, the leaps in place, turning by stamping, abrupt inflections and violent twists of the body forward, backward, sidewise, etc. The poorest dancer was the one who lacked flexibility.

The Greek dance is, in effect, a singular mélange of exercises, complicated and difficult, like the Steps on the toes, Entrechats, Pirouettes, which were slowly acquired, and of coarser, rudimentary movements; the Greek dance differs from ours in that theirs was free expression, while ours rules out the unexpected. Except for this one great difference, the arts are essentially the same.

419. One—ours—tends to show the body in perfection of form and grace of movement. Though it presents unusual methods of locomotion, it may be called natural. The movements are transformed in using. It imposes on all of the movements certain contortions of which the reason is esthetic, and the purpose a glorification of the body. Our dance has become less a language than an idealized decorative gymnastic. Therefore, our dancers and our actors do not consider their arts as one; the mimetic scenes and the dance scenes are differently interpreted.

On the contrary, in the Greek dance the expressive gesture belongs to both acting and dancing. The Greek dancer speaks with his body, and addresses the spectator through the eyes. He must, for instance, make it understood that he dances in honor of a god. Tragic dance or comic dance, must each affirm its rôle by the character of its movements, which are always free. The Pyrrhic mimics actual warfare; the Bacchanale inflames the emotions by a ritual of contortions that in truth suggest the god of wine. All movements were delicate or rude, according to need, made in graceful chains, or broken abruptly. The goal was *expression*, and there was no question about choosing the means.

The Greek dance is superior to ours in that it addresses the mind as well as the eyes. Though the mechanism may be inferior to ours, it far surpasses ours in dramatic value.

420. Whence came the sense of *eurhythmy* which enabled the Greek to secure perfection of movement?

The Greek writers often speak of eurhythmy as an essential quality, to which they attached the highest value. Unhappily, their definition is not explicit; there is no doubt that the word expressed a real thing which had a real existence, but we are left in doubt regarding it.

But, if it is impossible to define with exactness the quality that they called *eurhythmy*, we need have no fear as to our ability to understand the general meaning of the word, if we refer to such figures as 151, 152, 155, 161, 188, 452, 453, 457, 463, 468, 501, etc. The principle of Opposition, as our old ballet-masters understood it, meant nearly the same thing that we see in these representations which delight the eye with their harmony in contrast. The perfect type of dance shows a high sense of the ideal form which was held by the antique Greek dancer.

It is to be noted that the images are not for the most part the products of the industrial arts, but the work of the great artists. Phidias sculptured Nike dancing on the steps of the throne of Olympian Zeus (383). The Lacedemonian dancers, bronzes of Callimaque,—the chorus of young women attending Diana,—these are not the only figures of which the historian of the dance deplores the loss. The Flute Player, the famous bronze of Lysippus, the Courtesan of Praxiteles, were probably modeled from the dance. The same supposition holds good with regard to the Satyrs of Lysippus and of Praxiteles, the Silenus of Praxiteles, and many others.

We have reason to believe that the most precious documents regarding the dance have vanished with these works of art. We may, it is true, search and find traces of the influence of the dance in the existing statues or the copies of them preserved in our museums which, from custom, are known as Nike, Aphrodite, or Eros. But it is slippery ground, and the field for conjecture is large.

421. Returning to the vases and the terra-cotta figurines, there are many surprises—and deceptions, if one is to take the word of the poets, which do not prove the dance an art "divine," "irreproachable." Note the corrections to be made in the awkwardness of design, errors of perspective,—taking into account the exaggerations which verge on the grotesque, the sculptured figures exhibit to us the bizarre movements, contortions and violent twists. If eurhythmy is a quality of such figures as those enumerated in a preceding paragraph, *arrhythmy* is the only word that expresses the character of the following examples: 118, 119, 128, 160, 171, 189, 193, 275, 352, 353, 407, 408, 410, 411, 413, 420, 469, 474, 492, 494, B, 575. Never do our dancers show the same kind of brusqueness: they are very careful as to the limits of the movement of Head and Body (150, 200). Sometimes bending Head or Torso forward or back, they stop on the safe side of the grotesque or the ungraceful in the fear that their art might degenerate into the mere acrobatic exercises. The Greek dancer was not deterred by these scruples; he did not object to nearly dislocating his members. This is not to be taken as advice to copy the outlandish movements permitted to the Bacchants and justified only by the ritual of frenzy which they encouraged. A vase in the Louvre, belonging to the fifth century B. C., and of the best style of that period, reveals to our eyes a dance of the Nymphs; the form is identical with that of the Dionysian dance; the moving heads show the delirium of the Menades; the legs of dancer A and the whole pose of the body is much like that of the Satyr in Fig. 375,—the dancer C resembling, in the backward tilt and stamping step, Fig. 352, which is taken from a bacchic scene. The fanatics of Dionysos did not have a monopoly of the violent dances, and it is therefore reasonable to conclude that the Greek dancer did not always obey the law of eurhythmy, assuming the meaning of the word to be inapplicable to movements that lack order.

One other conclusion is inevitable—the improvised gambols which the Greek dancer felt free to introduce made him a sorry figure, at times, compared with the modern dancer whose Steps are governed by the most rigid rules.

422. It is true that, in saying that the Greek dance was mechanically less perfect than ours, it is to be remembered that it was less conventional than ours. The liberty taken in the choice and the execution of the movements permits him to indulge his fancy. It is enough to regard the series of painted vases as showing their independence. They reveal an art which the painters have faithfully reproduced. If they have not slavishly followed the traditional formulas, they have observed fundamentals, and embroidered them with variations of their own which are easy to detect.

Our artists find it difficult to escape from the mold of the school:

the modern dance is a science as well as an art, and no liberty is allowed in the execution or choice as to the smallest detail. The formula is inflexible; the least infraction of the conventions establishes a bad reputation. The Greek dancer was hampered by no such restrictions, and cannot be judged by the same standards.

423. In a word, he was more an actor and less a dancer. The Greek language has but one word for both.

The actor-dancer did not need so rigorous a gymnastic training. The mechanical forms which make up the lessons of our dancing-masters are at once the signs and the interpretation of the language. The Greeks had all the nuances of dramatic expression; the modifications were left to the taste of the dancer.

This justifies the childish play (418), the exaggerations (421), of which much has been said. Through the dramatic element, the dancer played a double rôle, and his audience was quick to see its excellence.

If one may judge the Greek dance by the representations, painted and plastic, which have come down to us, it is indispensable that one should keep in mind the complexities of the two rôles assumed by the performers.

424. The Greek dancer did not sacrifice his independence by following a common rule except to obtain a symmetrical Ensemble; otherwise, he was free.

The dance for two,—a man and a woman,—was not at all like that practiced in our ball-rooms. We transform the couple into one hybrid person, and expect that one to perform movements and make gestures. In our social dances, the man and woman are more or less closely enlaced, each of the dancers preserving the freedom of motion in the legs, the upper part of the body being motionless. The movement of the legs is limited to a certain point which reduces it to a monotonous repetition of a single set of motions.

The independence which was the right of the Greek dancer extended so far as to leave each—man and woman—free from even a restraining hand-clasp. They danced facing, not caring to make their movements simultaneous. In the Bacchanales there are frequently found groups of two or three dancers who execute Steps that imitate an erotic scene. In this mimicry the searcher will find the reason for the grouping, the amorous comedy that is played is, at the same time, the *dance*.

Always, always the Greek dancer acted.

425. Here the study ends. Its science is modest, its word-dress mediocre. It is not an attempt to induce our dancers to spend five or twenty years in preparation, but to show that the dance of the Greeks, though its technique was inferior to ours, yet has its revenge in that it was dramatically superior to the French dance.

•

FINIS

I
LIST OF FIGURES

INDICATING THE ORIGIN AND APPROXIMATE DATE OF THE AN-
TIQUE SCULPTURES FROM WHICH THÉY ARE TAKEN

PLATES FROM TEXT

PLATE I.—Vase in the form of a psyctere (190), from the latter part of the VI century B. C. Museum of the Louvre.—Six joyous companions of Komos, who follow, two by two, executing various dance-exercises. (Photographs by M. J. Bompard.)

PLATE II.—Analysis by means of instantaneous photographs of a *Grand Battement in fourth, open, held, and on the ground*, M. Demeny, arranged by Dr. Marey.

PLATE III.—Analysis by means of instantaneous photographs of an *Entrechat in four*, by M. Demeny.

PLATES IV AND V.—Figures taken from several photographic analyses by Dr. Marey. Reconstructions of steps.

FIGURES FROM THE TEXT

Abbreviations used in the following list:

    v. B. F. = vase with black figures.
    v. R. F. = vase with red figures.
    T. C. F. = Terra-cotta figurine.

The dates given are those of the centuries preceding the Christian era.

Some of the figures are shown reversed in order to facilitate the comparison of the movements.

Among the antique sculptures and paintings mentioned in this volume, but *not published,* are the following: The vase from the Louvre, part of which is shown in Plate I; the vases from the Louvre, partly reproduced in figures 127, 131, 135, 159, 160, 404, 405, 408, 409, 410, 485, 496, 504, 505, 506, 521, 543, 598; the vases from the Louvre, with red figures, from which are taken the figures 206, 366, 367, 414, 461, 481, 486, 531, 552; the terra-cotta figurines, also from the Louvre, from which figures 190, 192, 359, 559, 565 are constructed; the statuettes of bronze from the Cabinet de Medailles (figure 579).

LIST OF FIGURES

1. VENUS DE MEDICI, from the Museum of Florence, the work of Cleomenes of Athens. Marble, of the I century B. C.; the type is a derivation from that of the IV century.
2. WORSHIPPER. Museum of Berlin, bronze, Greco-Roman.
3. LATONA, Museum of the Louvre, bas-relief, "archaisant," of the I century.
4. APHRODITE, Museum of the Louvre, T. C. F., from Marina, III or II century.
5. WOMAN IN DRAPERY, reposing, Louvre Museum, T. C. F. of Tanagra, IV century.
6. ATHLETE, pouring oil over his body, T. C. F. from Marina, III or II century.
7. DIADUMENE (copy of the work of Polycetus), National Library, Cabinet of Medals, a small bronze of the V century type.
8. WOUNDED AMAZON, Berlin Museum, marble, of the V century.
9. APHRODITE ANADYOMENE, British Museum, small bronze in the Hellenistic style.
10. THE POURER (one of the Lare gods?), *Museo Borbonico*, XII, xxv, bronze, from Pompeii.
11. NOTATION OF THE WALK, after Marey, *the Movement*, figure 4.
12-13. Figures constructed after the photographs of Marey, showing the phases of the walk.
14. Walker at different moments of the step. Reproduction in line from a photograph on plate. Marey, *the Movement*, figure 117.
15. Man and woman dancing. *Unpublished Matter of the Institute*, IV, lvi, French vase, v. B. F., from first half VI century.
16. MENADES, of Luynes, *Painted Vases*, V, v. B. F., VI century.
17. DANCER, Inghirami, *Etruscan Vases*, II, cx, v. B. F., VI century.
18. HUNTER, Collignon, *Greek Sculpture*, I, fig. 49, archaic bronze plaque.
19. DANCERS, Museums of Athens, archaic bas-relief (Hermes and the Kharites), VI century.
20. MENADE, Millingen, C*oghill Collection*, xxxix, v. B. F., VI century.
21-22. MARCHERS, from the Parthenon Frieze, fragment in the Louvre, marble bas-relief, V century.
23. TWO WOMEN FACING, Gerhard, *Auserlesene Vasenbilder*, I, xxxvi, v. B. F., VI century.
24. TWO WOMEN FACING, Lenormant and de Witte, *Elite Ceramographique*, II, lxxvii, v. B. F., VI century.
25. NOTATION OF THE RUN, after Marey, *the Movement*, fig. 4.
26. RUNNER, Linair reproduction of photograph from plate, Marey, *the Movement*, fig. 118.
27-30. RUNNER, Reproduction from photograph, by Marey.
31-32. JUMPER, Marey, *the Movement*, fig. 96, Two figures from the plate.
33. WOMAN RUNNING, making the gesture of the tunic, Collignon, *Greek Sculpture*, I, fig. 165, archaic bronze, VI century.
34. WOMAN RUNNING, *Bulletino archeologico napolitano*, V, vii, v. F. R., from the end of the V century to the beginning of the IV.
35. PERSEUS RUNNING, *Archaeologische Zeitung*, 1881, 3, 4, v. B. F., VI century.

36. WINGED GENII RUNNING, Gerhard, *Auserlesene Vasenbilder*, IV, cclv, v. B. F., VI century.
37. NIKE RUNNING, called the Nike of Delos, marble, beginning of the VI century.
38. LEAPER, after a photograph by Marey.
39. FLYING NEREIDES, Museum of the Louvre, bas-relief of Assos, VI century.
40. DANCER, Stackelberg, *die Graeber der Hellenen*, x, v. B. F., VI century.
41. ATHLETIC RUNNERS, Saglio, *Dictionary of the Antique Greeks and Romans;* Gerhard, *Etruskische und Kampanische Vasenbilder*, amphora, panatheniac, of the VI or V century.
42. SATYR, Furtwaengler, *Collection Sabouroff*, I, lvi, v. B. F., one of the V century.
43. MENADE, Clarac, *Musee de Sculpture*, pl. 138, bas-relief of the Roman period,' after the type of the IV or the III centuries.
44. SATYR PURSUING A MENADE, Heydemann, *Griechische Vasenbilder*, v. B. F., end of the V century.
45. WOMAN DANCING (before an altar), Stackelberg, *die Graeber der Hellenen*, xxxv, v. B. F.
46. DANCING KOMOSTES, *Unpublished Matter of the Institute*, X, lii, v. B. F., beginning of the VI century.
47. KOMOSTES DANCING, psyctere of the Louvre (plate I), v. R. F., incised about the head, latter part of the VI century or beginning of the V.
48. DANCING KOMOSTES, Millen, *Paintings on Antique Vases*, xxvii, v. R. F., IV century.
49. DANCING MENADE, Stackelberg, *die Graeber der Hellenen*, v. R. F., end of the V century.
50. MENADE DANCING, Lenormant and de Witte, *Elite ceramographique*, II, xliii, v. R. F., end of the IV century or the III.
51. HERMES RUNNING, Gerhard, *Antique Bildwerke*, xxxii, v. R. F., V century.
52-68. Representations of the legs in different Positions, designs from nature and from photographs.
69-70. KOMOSTI, psyctere from the Louvre (plate I), v. R. F., incised about the head, end of the VI or beginning of the V century.
71. SATYR, Lenormant and de Witte, *Elite ceramographique*, IV, xxxi, v. R. F., IV century.
72. DANCING HETAIRE, Dumont and Chaplain, *Ceramique de la Grece propre*, x, 2, figure of terra-cotta, Hellenistic period.
73-74. HIERODULES DANCING, Heroon of Ghieul-Baschi (Trysa), bas-reliefs decorations of the end of the V century.
75. Representation of turns of the feet.
76. DANCER, Carapanos, *Dodone*, XII, feet from a mirror, of bronze, VI century.
77. DANCER, Clarac, *Musee de Sculpture*, pl. 456, a bronze from Herculaneum.
78. WOMAN STANDING, foot of a mirror of bronze, Louvre Museum, V century.
79. DANCER, from Herculaneum, Museum of Naples, bronze, in the style of the V century.
80. MENADE, la Borde, *Collection Lamberg*, v. F. R., end of the IV or beginning of the III century.

LIST OF FIGURES

81. SATYR, Millin, *Vases Antiques*, xxviii, v. R. F., III century.
82. HIERODULE, Winkelmann, *Monumenti antichi inediti*, xlvii, bas-relief on the base of a candelabrum, of the Hellenistic period.
83. HIERODULE, Dumont and Chaplain, *Ceramique de la Grece propre*, x, I, terra-cotta figurine, Hellenistic period.
84. PYRRHIC DANCER, coupe, R. F., Louvre Museum, V century.
85. SATYR, called the Borghese Faun, marble, Hellenistic period.
86. DANCER, *Compte rendu de la Commission imperiale de Saint-Petersbourg*, 1880, pl. v, terra-cotta, of not later than the end of the IV century.
87. KOMASTES, Benndorf, *Griechische und Sicilsche Vasenbilder*, xliv, v. R. F., III century.
88-101. Representations of the principal positions of the arms.
102. DANCER, making the double gesture of the tunic, Kekule, *Terracotten von Sicilen*, p. 23, T. C. F., Hellenistic period, after a more ancient type.
103. NIKE, flying, dancing, and making the double gesture of the tunic, Furtwaengler, *Collection Sabouroff*, II, cxlv, small terra-cotta plaque, gilded, of the Hellenistic period.
104. DANCER, Clarac, *Musee de Sculpture*, pl. 456, a bronze from Herculaneum.
105. DANCER, making the double gesture of the tunic, *Museo Borbonico*, X, vi., v. R. F., painting from Herculaneum.
106. NIKE DANCING, of Luynes, *Vases peints*, xxx, v. R. F., V century.
107. NIKE DANCING, a suspended figure, *Gazette archeologique*, 1884, pl. 25, bronze of the decadent period.
108. DANCER (vaulting), Stackelberg, *die Graeber der Hellenen*, XXIII, v. R. F., IV century.
109. PSYCHE DANCING, small figurine accompanying the Eros, called the Eros of Magare, Louvre Museum, terra-cotta figurine, Hellenistic period.
110. INFANT DANCING, Heydemann, *Griechische Vasenbilder*, XII, v. R. F., IV century.
111. MENADE DANCING, *Monumenti inediti dell'Instituto*, 1891, supplement, XXIV, v. R. F., first half of the V century.
112. DANCING INFANT, Stackelberg, *die Graeber der Hellenen*, XVII, v. R. F., IV century.
113. KOMASTES, Stackelberg, *die Graeber der Hellenen*, v. R. F., VI century.
114. KOMASTES, psyctere of the Louvre (plate I), v. R. F., incised about the head, end of the VI or commencement of the V century.
115. MENADE, Museum of Naples, marble bas-relief, of the Hellenistic period.
116. DANCER (vaulting), Stackelberg, *die Graeber der Hellenen*, XXIII, v. R. F., IV century.
117-118. MENADES, Gerhard, *Trinkschalen und Gefaesse . . . zu Berlin*, VII, v. R. F., end of the V century.
119. SATYR, Conze and Benndorf, *Vorlege Blaetter*, series D, taf. IV, v. R. F., V century.
120. HETAIRE DANCING, *Compte rendu de la Commission imperiale archeologistique de Saint-Petersbourg*, 1869, p. 161, v. R. F., IV or III century.
121. SATYR, Gerhard, *Trinkschalen und Gefaesse . . . zu Berlin*, X, v. R. F., III century.

LIST OF FIGURES 289

122. BACCHANTE (?), *Antiquites du Bosphore Cimmerien,* LXX, terra-cotta figurine, Hellenistic.
123. WOMAN DANCING (Step for Three), Millingen, *Coghill Collection,* I, v. R. F., IV century.
124. MENADE, Borghese vase, in the Louvre, bas-relief, I century.
125. ITHYPHALLIC KOMASTES, Gerhard, *Antike Bildwerke,* LXXII, v. R. F., III century.
126. SATYR, Conze and Benndorf, *Vorlege Blaetter,* series D, taf. IV, v. R. F., V century.
127. KOMASTES, Corinthian, in the Louvre Museum, v. B. F., beginning of the VI century.
128. Two KOMASTAE (Step for Two), Dumont and Chaplain, *Ceramique de la Grece propre,* p. 239, archaic Corinthian vase, beginning of VI century.
129. MAN DANCING, Dumont and Chaplain, *Ceramique de la Grece propre,* XXXII, foot of a bronze mirror, V century.
130. DANCER, of Herculaneum, in Museum of Naples, bronze, style of V century.
131. KOMASTES, Corinthian, Museum of the Louvre, v. B. F., beginning of the VI century.
132. KOMASTES, Gerhard, *Auserlesene Vasenbilder,* CCLXXXVI, v. B. F., VI century.
133. HIERODULE, Winkelmann, *Monumenti antichi inediti,* XLIX, bas-relief on the base of a candelabrum, of the Hellenistic period.
134. DANCER (vaulting), Stackelberg, *die Graeber der Hellenen,* XXIII, v. R. F., IV century.
135. MENADES, amphora of Nicosthenes, Louvre Museum, v. R. F., VI century.
136. EPHEBE DANCING, Gerhard, *Auserlesene Vasenbilder,* CCVI, v. R. F., V century.
137. SATYR, Carapanos *Dodone,* IX, bronze statuette, VI century.
138. DANCER OF HERCULANEUM, Museum of Naples, style of V century.
139. A dance scene with many persons (?), *Journal of Hellenic Studies,* 1890, XI, v. R. F., V century, second half.
140. SATYR, Gerhard, *Auserlesene Vasenbilder,* CCLXXXVI, v. B. F., VI century.
141. DANCER HOLDING A DULCIMER, Millin, *Peintures de Vases antiques,* II, liii, v. R. F., end of the IV or III century.
142. INFANT EROS (flying), suspended figure, Furtwaengler, *Collection Sabouroff,* II, cxxiv, terra-cotta figurine, IV century.
143. DANCER, Clarac, *Musee de Sculpture,* pl. 776, terra-cotta figurine, Hellenistic.
144. NIKE DANCING, Pottier and Reynach, *Necrepole de Myrina,* XXI, 2, figurine of terra-cotta, III or II century.
145. HETAIRE DANCING, and playing on the tambourine, Scheene, *Griechische Reliefs aus athenischen Sammlungen,* XXXV, bas-relief of terra-cotta, first half of V century.
146. Two SATYRS (Step for Two), v. B. F., VI century.
147. KOMASTES, psyctere in the Louvre Museum, v. R. F., incised about the head, end of the VI or beginning of the V century.
148. MENADE, Gerhard, *Auserlesene Vasenbilder,* II, cxlii, v. B. F., VI century.

149. MENADE, Inghirami, *Vasi Etruschi*, III, cclxx, v. B. F., IV century.
150. BACCHANTE, Stackelberg, *die Graeber der Hellenen*, XXIV, v. R. F., IV century.
151. INFANT EROS, Rayet, *Monuments de l'Art antique*, fig. T. C., Tanagren, IV century.
152. NIKE (winged), dancing, Stackelberg, *die Graeber der Hellenen*, LX, fig. T. C., Hellenistic.
153. NIKE (winged), dancing, Pottier and Reinach, *Necropole de Myrina*, XXI, 1 fig. T. C., III or II century.
154. BACCHANTE, *Antike Denkmaeler von kaiserlich deutschen Archeologischen Institut*, 1888, Band I, dritte Heft, taf. 36, v. R. F., IV century.
155. DANCER OF HERCULANEUM, Museum of Naples, bronze, style of V century.
156. DANCER, Heuzey, *Figurines antiques, du Louvre*, XXVIII, 4, fig. T. C., IV or III century.
157. KOMASTES, Millin, *Peintures de Vases antiques*, II, xlii, v. R. F., IV century.
158. KOMASTES, *Monumenti inediti dell'Instituto*, X, lii, v. B. F., beginning of the VI century.
159. KOMASTES, Corinthian, Louvre Museum, v. B. F., beginning of the VI century.
160. MENADE BEWEEN Two SATYRS, Corinthian vase in the Louvre, v. B. F., beginning of the VI century.
161. DANCER OF HERCULANEUM, Museum of Naples, bronze, style of the V century.
162. SATYR, *Monumenti inediti dell'Instituto*, VIII, xlii, v. R. F., end of the V century.
163. Two SATYRS, Lenormant and de Witte, *Elite ceramographique*, III, xc, v. R. F., IV century.
164. SATYR, Millingen, *Coghill Collection*, XXIX, v. R. F., V century.
165. SATYR, Millingen, *Vases peints*, XXXVI, v. R. F., IV century.
166-169. MENADE, KOMASTES, SATYRS, Millin, *Peintures de Vases antiques*, II, xxxvi and xxxviii, v. R. F., end of the IV century or beginning of the III century.
170. YOUNG GIRL, Lenormant and de Witte, *Elite ceramographique*, III, xxvi, v. R. F., IV century.
171. SILENUS (?), *Museo Borbonico*, VII, xxx, candelabrum in bronze, Roman period.
172. SATYR, Millingen, *Collection Coghill*, XXIX, v. R. F., V century.
173. SATYR, Lenormant and de Witte, *Elite ceramographique*, IV, xxxi, v. R. F., IV century.
174-175. SATYR, MENADE, Millin, *Peintures de Vases antiques*, II, xxxvi, *bis*, vol. I, v. R. F., end of IV century.
176. HIERODULE, Winkelmann, *Monumenti antichi inediti*, XLVIII, bas-relief, on the base of a candelabrum, Hellenistic period.
177. SATYR, Babelon, *le Cabinet des Antiques a la Bibliotheque, Nationale*, XXXI, bronze of Hellenistic period.
178. KOMASTES, Furtwaengler, *Collection Sabouroff*, I, xlvii, v. B. F., beginning of the VI century.

LIST OF FIGURES 291

179. HIERODULE, Visconti, *Museo Pio Clementino,* III, terra-cotta bas-relief, Hellenistic period.
180. SATYR, called the Faun of Pompeii, Museum of Naples, bronze, Hellenistic.
181. SATYR, *Antiquites d'Herculaneum,* VII, cxlix, bronze, Roman period.
182-186. Representations of positions of body.
187. MENADE, Millingen, *Collection Coghill,* XXXIX, v. B. F., VI century.
188. EROS DANCING, holding Bacchic symbol, Pottier and Reynach, *Necropole de Myrina,* XI, terra-cotta figurine, III or II century.
189. KOMASTES, or SATYR, Chabouillet, *Cabinet Fould,* XVIII, v. R. F., III century.
190. BACCHANTE (?), Louvre Museum, terra-cotta figurine, Italio-Greek, II century.
191. DANCER BENDING, Gerhard, *Antike Bildwerke,* C.* I., holding a bronze vase,· V century.
192. BACCHANTE (?), Museum of Medals, terra-cotta figurine, II century.
193. MENADE, Baumeister, *Denkmaeler des Klassischen Alterthums,* p. 848, Hellenistic bas-relief.
194-198. Representations of positions of the head.
199. DANCING NYMPHS, *Monuments grecs,* published by the Association for Encouraging the Study of the Greeks, Nos. 17 and 18, v. R. F., end of V century.
200-203. Representations of the Attitude and Arabesque, from life.
204. INFANT EROS, Rayet, *Monuments de l'Art antique,* terra-cotta figurine, Tanagra, IV century.
205. SATYR ROPE DANCER, *Museo Borbonico,* VII, li, Pompeian painting, I century.
206. CHILD (learning to dance), Louvre Museum, R. F., first half of V century.
207. DANCER IN THE ATTITUDE, Museum of Medals, bronze, Hellenistic period.
208. BACCHANTE, Clarac, *Musee de Sculpture,* pl. 776, terra-cotta figurine, Hellenistic period.
209-214. Representations of bending Positions.
215. KOMASTES, Corinthian bowl, from the Louvre, v. B. F., beginning of VI century.
216. SATYR (Ityphallic), preceding the train of chariots of the centaurs, in which are a grotesque Hercules and Nike. *Monuments Grecs,* published by the Association to Encourage the Study of the Greeks. No. 5, pl. III, v. R. F., IV century.
217. Representations of a Battement on the ground.
218. Representation of a Battement held.
219-220. KOMASTES, psyctere from the Louvre (plate I), v. R. F., incised about the head, end of VI or beginning of the V century.
221. Representation of the "Rond de jambe" (circles with the legs), on the ground.
222-228. Photographic analysis of the circle with the leg, held.
229. Representation of the "Rond de jambe," theory of construction.
230. KOMASTI, *Archaelogische Zeitung,* 1881, III, iv. v. B. F., VI century.
231. Representation of the Directions.
232. Representations of the step in the ordinary walk (A), and the step in the dance-walk (B).

233. The feet with and without the heel, theoretical construction.
234. SATYR, v. B. F., VI century.
235. MENADE, Inghirami, *Vasi Etruschi*, III, cclxx, v. B. F., VI century.
236. MENADE, *Museo Borbonico*, III, xxix, v, R. F., beginning of the IV century.
237. SATYR, called the Faun of Pompeii, Museum of Naples, bronze, Hellenistic.
238. Outline representation of the feet in the Classe.
239-243. Photographic analyses of the Coupé under, with the left leg.
244-247. Photographic analysis of the Coupé over with the left leg.
248-251. Photographic analysis of a Fouetté backwards with the left leg.
252-256. Photographic analysis of a Jeté over with the right leg.
257-261. Photographic analysis of a Jeté over with the left leg.
262-265. Photographic analysis of a Jeté over to the left.
266-269. Photographic analysis of a Jeté over to the right.
270. SATYR, Millin, *Vases antiques*, XXVIII, v. R. F., end of IV or beginning of III century.
271. MENADE, playing with castanets, Gerhard, *Auserlesene Vasenbilder*, CCXXXVI, v. B. F., VI century.
272. SATYR, Gerhard, *Apulloche Vasenbilder*, III, v. R. F., end of the IV or III century.
273. BACCHANTE, Lenormant and de Witte, *Elite ceramographique*, IV, lxi, v. R. F., III century.
274. Reconstruction.
275. SATYR, de Witte, *Hotel Lambert*, XXVIII, v. R. F., end of V century.
276. Reconstruction.
277-278. KOMASTAI, *Jahrbuch des Kaiserlich deutschen Archaeologischer Instituts*, 1890, p. 244, v. B. F., VI century.
279. SATYR, *Monumenti inediti dell'Instituto*, IV, x., v. R. F., end of IV century or beginning of III.
280. KOMASTES, Millin, *Peintures de Vases antiques*, II, xlii, v. R. F., end of IV century.
281. SATYR, Inghirami, *Vasi Etruschi*, I, xcix, v. R. F., V century.
282. SATYR, *Museo Borbonico*, III, xxix, v. R. F., beginning of the IV century.
283. SATYR, Borghese vase, Louvre Museum, bas-relief, I century.
284. Representations of the Satyr called the Faun of Pompeii.
285. Reconstruction.
286. DANCER, playing with castanets, Pottier and Reynach, *Necropole de Myrina*, XXXIV, 2, figurine of terra-cotta, III or II century.
287-293. Photographic analysis of an Eschappe in II on the toes.
294-302. Photographic analysis of a rise on the toes.
303. HIERODULE, *Compte rendu de la Commission imperiale archeologique de Saint-Petersbourg*, 1866, small gold plaque, an ornament on the costume of a priestess of Demeter, Hellenistic period.
304. BACCHANTE, *Compte rendu* (see preceding figure), 1862, V, v. R. F., end of IV century or III century.
305. SATYR, Millin, *Peintures de Vases antiques*, I, lxvii, v. R. F., end of IV century or III century.
306-309. Photographic analysis of small steps on the toes.
310-311. HIERODULES (see fig. 303), Hellenistic period.

LIST OF FIGURES

312. Outline and plans of the Assemblé.
313. Outlines and plans of the change of the feet.
314-316. Outlines and plans of the three forms of the Entrechat-three.
317. Outlines and plans of the Entrechat-four.
318. BACCHANTE, Chabouillet, *Cabinet Fould*, XVIII, v. R. F., III century.
319. Representation of the Preparation for the Pirouette.
320. Representation of the Execution of the Pirouette outward.
321. Representation of the Execution of the Pirouette inward.
322-345. Photographic analysis of the Preparation and Execution of the Pirouette.
346. HETAIRE DANCING, Dumont and Chaplain, *Ceramique de la Grece propre*, X, 2, terra-cotta figurine, Hellenistic.
347-348. HIERODULES DANCING, Heroon of Ghient-Baschi (Tyrsa), decorative bas-reliefs of the end of the V century.
349. MENADE, la Borde, *Collection Lamberg*, end of IV century or III century.
350. CURETE DANCING, bas-relief from Campana, Louvre Museum, terra-cotta, I century.
350. (Cont'd), CURETES DANCING (the infant Zeus, nursed by Amalthee, is found between two gods), Saglio, *Dictionnaire des Antiquitis greques et romaines*, article on Amalthee, bas-relief in terra-cotta, I century.
351. BACCHANTE, Dumont and Chaplain, *Ceramique de la Grece propre*, XII, xii, v. R. F., V century.
352. BACCHANTE, Lenormant and de Witte, *Elite ceramographique*, IV, lxi, v. R. F., III century.
353. BACCHANTE, Millingen, *Collection Coghill*, XX, v. R. F., end of IV century or III century.
354. SATYR, Lenormant and de Witte, *Elite ceramographique*, II, xlv, v. R. R.
355. SATYR, called the Borghese Faun, marble, Hellenistic period.
356. HIERODULE DANCING (see 348), decorative bas-relief, end of V century.
357. DANCER, *Compte rendu de la Commission imperiale archeologique de Saint-Petersbourg*, 1880, pl. V, terra-cotta, supposed to be of the end of the IV century.
358. DANCER, Heusey, *Figurines antiques du Musee du Louvre*, pl. 47, terra-cotta figure, Cyrenian, in style of IV century.
359. DANCER, Louvre Museum, Tanagra figurine of terra-cotta, IV century.
360. KOMASTES, psyctere, in the Louvre (plate 1), v. R. F., incised about the head, end of the VI or beginning of the V century.
361. MENADE, Conze and Beundorf, *Vorlege Blaetter*, 1891, Vol. VII, v. R. F., V century.
362. DANCER (see 358), terra-cotta figurine, style of IV century.
363. HETAIRE DANCING, Inghisami, *Vasi Etruschi*, III, cclxxiii, v. R. F., IV century.
364. MENADE, *Archaeologische Zeitung*, 1872, p. 70, v. R. F., IV century.
365. WOMAN DANCING, Stackelberg, *die Graeber der Hellenen*, XXVI, v. R. F., IV century.
366-367. KOMASTI (see fig. 360), v. R. F., end of VI century.
368. Vase in form of a dancer. Treu, *Programm zum Winkelmannfeste*, terra-cotta figurine, III or II century.
369. BACCHANTE, Stackelberg, *die Graeber der Hellene*, XXIV, xxiv, v. R. F., IV century.

370-375. Photographic analysis of a very simple chain; Coupé and Fouetté.
376. Representation of Battement, alternating on the ground, from life.
377-384. Photographic analysis of alternating Jeté over.
385. Representation of two contrasting movements.
386. SATYRS, Lenormant and de Witte, *Elite ceramographique*, III, xc, v. R. F., IV century.
387-398. Photographic analysis of the "cat-leap."
399. NYMPH DANCING, and playing the cymbals, *Monuments grecs*, published by the Association for the Encouragement of the Study of the Greeks in France, Nos. 17 and 18, v. R. F., end of the V century.
400. BACCHANTE, Stackelberg, *die Graeber der Hellenen*, XXIV, v. R. F., IV century.
401. Representation of the line of equilibrium.
402-403. Representation of the vertical line of balance.
404-405. KOMASTI, taken from two Corinthian vases in the Louvre, v. R. F., beginning of VI century.
406. SATYR, Hergard, *Auserlesene Vasenbilder*, I, lii, v. R. F., VI century.
407. KOMASTI (step for two), Dumont and Chaplain, *Ceramique de la Grece propre*, p. 239, v. B. F., beginning of VI century.
408-410. KOMASTI (see figs. 404, 405), v. B. F., beginning of VI century.
411. SATYR, Gerhard, *Auserlesene Vasenbilder*, II, cxlii, v. B. F., VI century.
412. Reconstruction.
413. SATYR, Heydemann, *Griechische Vasenbilder*, II, v. R. F., V century.
414. SATYR, Skyphos, in the Louvre Museum, v. R. F., IV century.
415. SATYR (see fig. 411), v. B. F., VI century.
416. SATYR, Stackelberg, *die Graeber der Hellenen*, XXV, 4, v. R. F., V century.
417-418. SATYR, *Museo Borbonico*, VII, painting from Pompeii, I century.
419. DANCE OF LITTLE RUSSIA, from an instantaneous photograph.
420. BACCHANTE, Stackelberg, *die Graeber der Hellenen*, XXIV, v. R. F., IV century.
421-426. Photographic analysis of the steps indicated in the preceding figure.
427. MENADE AND SATYR, Baumeister, *Denkmaeler des Klassichen Alterthums*, p. 848, Hellenistic bas-relief.
428-437. Photographic analysis of a reconstructed step.
438-439. BACCHANTES, Gerhard, *Trinkschalen und Gefaesse*, . . . *zu Berlin*, W., v. R. F., ascribed to Heiron, beginning of the V century.
440. SATYR, Gerhard, *Auserlesene Vasenbilder*, IV, ccli, v. B. F., VI century.
441. Person of Asiatic appearance, *Antiquites de Bosphore Cimmerien*, LXX, a, figurine in terra-cotta, Hellenistic period.
442. Reconstruction.
443. SCYTHE (?), DANCING, *Antiques du Bosphore Cimmerien*, LXIV, terracotta figurine, Hellenistic.
444. SATYR, *Museo Borbonico*, XV, xv, v. R. F., IV century.
445. Reconstruction.
446. SATYR, Gerhard, *Auserlesene Vasenbilder*, LX, v. R. F., V century.
447. WOMEN DANCING, v. R. F., IV century.

LIST OF FIGURES 295

448. WOMAN IN DRAPERY, DANCING, Stackelberg, *die Graeber der Hellenen*, LXVII, terra-cotta figurine, IV century.
449. WOMAN IN DRAPERY, DANCING, *Collection Lécuyer*, S., 2, figurine of terra-cotta, style of IV century.
450. WOMEN IN DRAPERY, DANCING, *Revue archeologique*, 1868, III, engraved mirror, Hellenistic period.
451. WOMAN IN DRAPERY, DANCING, *Bulletin de Correspondance hellenique*, 1892, pl. IV, terra-cotta figurine, style between that of Tanagra and the Hellenic, end of IV century.
452. WOMAN IN DRAPERY, DANCING, Louvre Museum, terra-cotta figurine of Tanagra, IV century.
453. DANCER, *Collection Lécuyer*, Z., terra-cotta figure, Hellenistic.
454. BACCHANTE, Inghirami, *Vasi Etruschi*, II, cl., v. R. F., III century.
455. SATYR, Museum of Naples, Hellenistic bas-relief.
456. Figure in the air, *Museo Borbonico*, VII, xxxviii, decorative painting from Pompeii, I century.
457. DANCER IN DRAPERY, about to fling her mantle, Museum of Athens, bas-relief from the Theatre of Dionysos, of the Hellenistic period.
458. Dancer flinging her veil, *Collection Lécuyer*, P. 2, terra-cotta figurine, Hellenistic period.
459. Dancer flinging her veil, *Compte rendu de la Commission imperiale archeologique de Saint-Petersbourg*, 1880, terra-cotta figure, Hellenistic period.
460. ASIATIC DANCER, Panofka, *Terracotten—des Koeniglichen Museum zu Berlin*, terra-cotta, Hellenistic.
461. KOMASTES (?), Museum of the Louvre, v. R. F., middle of V century.
462. Reconstruction.
463. DANCER, Heydemann, *4th Hallisches Winckelmannsprogramm*, 1879, v. R. F., end of IV or III century.
464. HIERODULE, *Compte rendu de la Commission imperiale archeologique de Saint-Petersbourg*, 1866, III.
465. GROTESQUE DANCER, Frohner, *Musees de France*, XVIII, bronze vase, Fallo-Roman, of the worst period.
466. KOMASTES, *Compte rendu*— (see fig. 459), 1868, v. R. F., end of V or beginning of IV century.
467. KOMASTES, la Borde, *Collection Lemberg*, I, xxi, v. R. F., end of IV or III century.
468. DANCER IN ORIENTAL COSTUME, Dumont and Chaplain, *Ceramique de la Grece propre*, XXVII, v. R. F., IV century.
469. DANCER IN ORIENTAL COSTUME, Inghirami, *Vasi Etruschi*, II, clxxxiv, v. R. F., II century.
470. DANCER IN ASIATIC COSTUME, Pottier and Reynach, *Necropole de Myrina*, XXVIII, 3, terra-cotta figure, III or II century.
471. Reconstruction.
472. DANCER IN ASIATIC COSTUME, Hensey, *Figurines antiques du Muses du Louvre*, XXXVII, terra-cotta figurine, Hellenistic period.
473. Reconstruction.
474. DANCER IN ASIATIC COSTUME, Kekule, *Terracotten von Sicilien*, LVIII, Hellenistic bas-relief.

475. BACCHANTE, Chabouillet, *Cabinet Fould*, XVIII, v. R. F., III century.
476. AMAZONS (?), Dancing in Oriental Costume, *Monumenti inediti dell'Instituto*, IV, xliii, v. R. F., IV century.
477. DIONYSOS (in the centre of an Oriental procession), *Monumenti inediti dell'Instituto*, I, l, v. R. F., IV century.
478. DANCERS AT EACH SIDE OF THE GOD (see preceding figure).
479. Person of Asiatic appearance, *Antiques du Bosphore Cimmerien*, LXX, a, terra-cotta figurine, Hellenistic.
480. SCYTHE (?), DANCING, *Antiques du Bosphore Cimmerien*, LXIV, terra-cotta figurine of Hellenistic period.
481. DANCING-LESSON, cup from Museum of the Louvre, first half of the V century.
482. DANCING-LESSON, Conze and Beundorf, *Vorlege Blaetter*, Series C, fig. V, cup with red figures, first half of V century.
483. DANCING-LESSON, Gerhard, *Antike Bildwerke*, LXVI, v. R. F.
484. Representation constructed from figure 2 of the psyctere in the Louvre (plate 1).
485. KOMASTAI, from Corinthian piece in the Louvre, v. B. R., beginning of VI century.
486. SATYR facing a goat, Museum of the Louvre, v. R. F., III century.
487. SATYRS pressing grapes, Panofka, *Terracotten—zu Berlin*, XLIII, bas-relief of terra-cotta, I century.
488. WINE-PRESSERS, *Museo Borbonico*, VIII, xxxii, from a bronze harness, Roman period.
489. WINE-PRESSERS, *Bulletino della Commissione archeologica Communale di Roma*, 1874, II-IV, bronze seat, Roman period.
490-491. HIERODULES DANCING, on each side of the entrance-gate of the Heroon of Ghieul-Baschi (Trysa), decorative bas-relief of the end of V century.
492. HETAIRES DANCING (and playing the castanets), *Compte rendu de la Commission imperiale archeologique de Saint-Petersbourg*, 1869, P. 173, v. B. F., VI century.
493-494. BACCHANTES, Stackelberg, *die Graeber der Hellenen*, XXIV, v. R. F., IV century.
495. DANCE BY TWO WOMEN, *Museo Borbonico*, VII, xxxiii, decorative painting from Pompeii, I century.
496. MAN AND WOMAN WITH A KOMAS, dancing vis-à-vis, from a Corinthian cup in the Louvre, B. F., beginning of VI century.
497. SATYR AND MENADE, Gerhard, *Auserlesene Vasenbilder*, CCLXXXVI, v. B. F., VI century.
498. SATYR AND MENADE, Gerhard, *Auserlesene Vasenbilder*, CCCXV, v. B. F., VI century.
499. MAN AND WOMAN WITH KOMAS, *Monumenti dell'Instituto*, XXXI, v. R. F., end of IV century.
500. YOUNG MAN AND YOUNG WOMAN, arms entwined, Panofka, *Musee Blacas*, XXX, v. R. F., end of IV or III century.
501. PAN AND YOUNG GIRL (THE NYMPH ECHO?), Panofka, *Musee Blacas*, XXXIII, a yellow figure, end of V century.

502. STEP FOR THREE WOMEN, Millingen, *Collection Coghill*, I, v. R. F., IV century.
503. Representation, on horizontal plane of the preceding.
504-505. SATYRS AND MENADES, Louvre Museum, Amphore attributed to Nikosthenes, latter part of VI century.
506. MENADE BETWEEN TWO SATYRS, Corinthian vase in the Louvre, B. F., beginning of VI century.
507. Details taken from a bas-relief in the Museum of Athens (Hermes and the Kharites), VI century.
508. THREE NYMPHS (advancing before Pan), *Bulletine de Correspondance hellenique*, 1881, Pl. 7, votive bas-relief, IV century.
509. (Dionysos following the three), DANCERS, Louvre Museum, bas-relief in "archaisant" style, I century.
510. OLD MAN AND THREE WOMEN, Stackelberg, *die Graeber der Hellenen*, XXIII, v. R. F., IV century.
511. HERMES AND THREE NYMPHS, Furtwaengler, *Collection Sabouroff*, I, xxviii, votive bas-relief of marble, IV century.
512. HERMES AND THREE NYMPHS, Baumeister, *Denkmaeler des Klassischen Alterthums*, p. 1032, votive bas-relief, IV or III century.
513. Detail taken from an "archaisant" called the Kharos of Socrates, I century.
514. THREE KHARITES, Louvre Museum, from an "archaisant" marble, called "the altar of the twelve Gods," I century.
515. CHORUS, *Yahrbuch des K. deutschen Archaeologischen Instituts*, 1887, Vol. II, vase in geometric style, VIII or VII century.
516. FUNERAL CHORUS, *Monumenti inediti dell'Instituto*, IX, xxxix, vase from Dipylon, geometric style, VIII or VII century.
517. FARANDOLE (conducted by Theseus), *Monumenti inediti dell'Instituto*, the French vase, B. F., early part of VI century.
518. FARANDOLE, *Museo Borbonico*, VIII, lviii, v. R. F., end of IV or III century.
519. FARANDOLE, Frohner, *Musees de France*, XIII, v. B. F., VI century.
520. CHORUS, Inghirami, *Vasi Etruschi*, II, ccliv, v. R. F., V century.
521. SATYR AND MENADE, Louvre Museum, v. B. F., VI century.
522. Two WOMEN, taking part in a chorus, *Monuments grecs*, published by the Association for the Encouragement of the Study of the Greeks, in France, Nos. 14-16, fragment of an archaic vase decorated with bas-reliefs, VI century.
523. SATYRS AND MENADE, *Bulletin de Correspondance hellenique*, 1893, v. B. F., VI century.
524. KOMASTI, *Bulletin de Correspondance hellenique*, 1893, v. B. F., VI century.
525. CHORUS, Furtwaengler, *Collection Sabouroff*, I, li, v. B. F., VI century.
526. CHORUS OF MEN, Beule, *Aeropole*, bas-relief belonging to a pedestal, IV century.
527. COMIC CHORUS, *Bulletino archeologico napolitano*, year V, v. B. F., VI century.
528. COMIC CHORUS, *Journal of Hellenic Studies*, II, xiv, v. B. F., VI century.
529. CHORUS (?), Frieze of a choragic monument of Lyricratus, Athens, decorative bas-relief, IV century.

530. TRATTA, Raoul Rochette, *Peintures antiques inedites*, XV, painting on a Greek tomb at Ruvo, III century.
531. PYRRHIC DANCER AND AULETE, Louvre Museum, bowl of V century, red figures.
532. WOMAN PYRRHIC DANCER, Stackelberg, *die Graeber der Hellennen*, XXII, v. R. F., V century.
533. PYRRHIC DANCER, Lenormant and de Witte, *Elite ceramographique*, II, lxxx, v. R. F., latter part of V century.
534. TARGETEER, Stackelberg, *die Graeber der Hellenen*, XXXVIII, v. R. F.
535. WARRIOR ON THE DEFENSIVE, Millengen (Ed. Raynach), Painted vase, V, v. R. F., IV century.
536. WARRIOR ON THE DEFENSIVE, *Monuments grecs* (see fig. 522), No. 4, v. R. F., beginning of IV century.
537. WARRIOR ON THE OFFENSIVE, de Lyunes, *Vases peints*, I, v. B. F., VI century.
538. PYRRHIC DANCERS (?), Visconti, *Museo Pio Clementino*, IV, ix, marble bas-relief, Hellenistic period.
539. Rank of Warriors advancing with the same step, *Monumenti inediti dell'Instituto*, X, cv, bas-relief from the monument of the Nereides, end of the V century
540. PYRRHIC DANCERS, Beule, *Acropole*, bas-relief belonging to a pedestal, IV century.
541-542. MOURNERS, *Monumenti inediti dell'Instituto*, IX, xxxix, vase from Dipylon, geometrical style, VIII or VII century.
543. MOURNERS, Corinthian Hydra, Museum of the Louvre, v. B. F., beginning of VI century.
544. EXPOSITION OF THE DEAD, painted plaque from the Louvre Museum, black figure showing the white ground, work in parts of the figure.
545-546. MOURNERS, *Monumenti inediti dell'Instituto*, VIII, v, v. R. F., first half of the V century.
547. FUNERAL LAMENTATIONS, Beundorf, *Griechische und Sicilische Vasen*, XXIII, funeral lecythe, polychrome, IV century.
548. FUNERAL LAMENTATION, Beundorf, *Griechische und Sicilische Vasen*, XVII, painting in red outline on a white ground, funeral lecythe, IV century.
549. MOURNERS, Rayet, *Monuments de l'Art antique*, LXXV, v. B. F., VI century.
550. VISIT TO A STELE (see fig. 548), lecythe, IV century.
551. FUNERAL GESTURES OF LAMENTATION, *Monumenti inediti dell'Instituto*, VIII, iv, v. B. F., VI century
552. FUNERAL GESTURES OF LAMENTATION, loutrophore from the Louvre Museum, v. R. F., early part of V century.
553. MOURNERS, *Monumenti inediti dell'Instituto*, III, lx, v. B. F., VI century.
554. Person making the funeral gestures, Inghirami, *Vasi Etruschi*, IV, ccclxxi, v. R. F., end of IV or III century.
555. SYREN, Pottier and Reynach, *Necropole de Myrina*, XXVII, terra-cotta figurine, III or II century.
556. KUBISTETERIA, Inghirami, *Vase Etruschi*, I, lxxxvii, v. R. F., III century.
557. KUBISTETERIA, Baumeister, *Denkmaeler des klassischen Altherthums*, p. 585, v. R. F., II century.

558. KUBISTETERE, Museum of Medals, small bronze piece, Hellenistic or Roman period.
559. ACROBATIC DANCER, Louvre, terra-cotta figurine, Hellenistic.
560. ACROBATIC DANCER, *Collection Lécuyer*, O, terra-cotta figurine, IV or III century.
561. TIGHT-ROPE DANCER, *Museo Borbonico*, VII, decorative painting from Pompeii, I century.
562. WRESTLING GAME, *Monumenti inediti dell'Instituto*, I, v. B. F., VI century.
563. WRESTLING GAME, *Journal of Hellenic Studies*, 1890, XII, v. R. F., V century.
564. TWO SATYRS AT PLAY, Millingen, *Collection Coghill*, v. R. F., end of V century or IV century.
565. TWO YOUNG GIRLS AT PLAY, Louvre Museum, terra-cotta figurine, Tanagra, IV century.
566. NIKE RUNNING (Nike of Delos), Collignon, *Histcire de la Sculpture grecque*, I, fig. 58, marble, VI century.
567. NIKE of Paeonios (indication in arms and drapery that the statue was taken from the temple of Nereides), marble statue of the V century.
568. DANCERS LEAPING, Stackelberg, *die Graeber der Hellenen*, XXIII, v. R. F., IV century.
569. NIKE DANCING, figure suspended, Furtwaengler, *Collection Sabouroff*, II, cxlv, small terra-cotta plaque, gilded, Hellenistic period.
570. EROS DANCING, figure suspended, Furtwaengler, *Collection Sabouroff*, II, cxxiv, figurine of terra-cotta, Tanagra, IV century.
571. ATYS DANCING, *Yahrbuch des K. deutschen Archaeologischen Instituts*, 1889, Beiblatt, 90, figurine of terra-cotta, III or II century.
572. DANCE OF THE CURETES (Clashers), around the infant Zeus, *Annali dell'Instituto de correspondenza archæologica*, 1840, bas-relief of terra-cotta, I century.
573. SILENE, Museum of the Louvre, Hellenistic bas-relief.
574. MENADE, *Gazette archeologique*, 1879, v. R. F., end of IV or III century.
575. MENADE, tearing a kid in pieces (said to be the work of Scopas), bas-relief from the Capitoline Museum, Hellenistic period.
576. DIONYSIAN ALTAR and BACCHANTES, *Museo Borbonico*, XII, v. R. F., latter part of V century.
577. MENADE, Conze and Beundorf, *Vorlege Blaetter*, 1891, VII, v. R. F., V century.
578. DIONYSOS, tearing a kid to pieces, SATYRS AND MENADES, Panofka, *Musee Blacas*, XV, v. R. F., V century.
579. SATYR, Museum of Medals, Cameo, Roman period.
580. PRIESTESS, de Witte, *Hotel Lambert*, XXII, v. R. F., V century.
581. DANCE OF SACRIFICE, Stackelberg, *die Graeber der Hellenen*, XXXV, v. R. F., end of V century.
582-583. HIERODULES (see figs. 490, 491), decorative bas-relief, end of V century.
584-585. HIERODULES, *Yahrbuch des K.* (see fig. 511), 1893, pages 76 and 77, marble bas-relief, IV century.

586. HIERODULE, Dumont and Chaplain, *Ceramique de la Grece propre,* X, i, terra-cotta figurine, Hellenistic period.
587. HIERODULE, Louvre Museum, terra-cotta figurine, Hellenistic.
588. HIERODULE, *Compte rendu de la Commission imperiale archeologique de Saint-Petersbourg,* 1866, small gold plaque, an ornament on the costume of a priestess of Demeter, Hellenistic period.
589-590. HIERODULES, Clarac, *Musee de Sculpture,* pl. 167-168, bas-reliefs on the base of a candelabrum, Hellenistic period.
591. HIERODULES (the statue of Athena between the two), Muller-Wieseler, *Denkmaeler,* Vol. II, chap. xx, bas-relief, terra-cotta, I century.
592-593. HIERODULES, Winckelmann, *Monumenti antichi inediti,* XLVII, xlix, bas-reliefs on the base of a candelabrum, Hellenistic period.
594. PROCESSION, from the temple of the Harpies, bas-relief, end of VI century.
595. PROCESSION OF NYMPHS, Museum of the Louvre, bas-relief of Thasos, beginning of the V century.
596. PROCESSION OF YOUNG GIRLS, from the Parthenon frieze, bas-relief, V century.
596. (Cont'd), PROCESSION OF YOUNG GIRLS, Parthenon frieze, bas-relief, V century.
597. HERMES AND SIX WOMEN (who play on the lyre and the contents), Gerhard, *Auserlesene Vasenbilder,* I, xxi, v. B. F., VI century.
598. KOMASTAI, Corinthian cup, from the Louvre, v. B. F., beginning of the VI century.
599. KOMASTES, *Monumenti inediti dell'Instituto,* X, lii, v. B. F., beginning of the VI century.
600. KOMASTES, Gerhard, *Auserlesene Vasenbilder,* CLXXXVIII, v. R. F., first half of V century.

ALPHABETICAL REPERTORY OF THE TERMS OF THE DANCE AND OF TECHNICAL WORDS

[The numbers refer to the paragraphs.]

I signifies the First Position of the legs.
II signifies the Second Position of the legs.
III signifies the Third Position of the legs.
IV signifies the Fourth Position of the legs.
V signifies the Fifth Position of the legs.

A

Alternating movements (275)
Analytic series (291)
Arabesque (170)
Arms (divisions of the) (197)
Arms held (113)
Arms (positions of the) (112)
Assemblé (243)
Attitude (169)
 (dances of) (326)

B

Backward bending body (150)
Balance steps (233)
Bar (325)
Battement held (185)
Beating steps (battus) (247)
Bending (177)

C

Cabrioles (247)
Chains of movement (273)
Character dances (327)
Characteristic moments (283)
Chassé forward, Chassé to the side (219)
Choregraphy (327)
Circle of the leg held (193)
Circle of the leg outward, inward (191)
Circles on the ground (192)
Circles with the leg (191)
Contrasting positions (115)
Contrasting positions of the arm (115)
Coupé (220)
Coupé over, Coupé under (220)
Cuts (Three) (250)
Cuts (Four) 251)
Cuts (Five, Six, Seven, Eight) (203)

D

Dances of character (327)
Decorative contrasts (333)
Determining moments of the movement (313)

E

Entrechat (248)
Equilibrium (326)
Eurhythmy (372, 395)
Exercises at the bar (325, 326)
Exercises of the bar (325, 326)
Expressive movements (55)
Extreme moments (284)

F

Figuration choregraphy (327)
Figures in series (289)
Five, or V, abbreviation of Fifth Position (219)
Fouetté (221)
Fouetté forward, Fouetté backward (221)
Fouetté in turning (256)
Fundamental positions of the legs (89)
Fundamental positions on the soles of the feet (89)
Fourth crossed (95)
Fourth open (95)
Fourth, or IV, abbreviation for Fourth Position

G

Gradation of exercises (326)
Grand battement (186)
Grand circle of the leg (194)

ALPHABETICAL REPERTORY

H
Half-toe (102)
Heels of shoes (213)
Horizontal projection of the movements (243)

I
Intermediate moments (313)

J
Jeté (222)
Jeté ballonné (272)
Jeté battu (272)
Jeté crossed (321)
Jeté in turning (256)
Jeté over (222)
Jeté under (222)
Jeté with circles of the legs (272)

K
Kubistetere (374)

L
Leap (its mechanism and form) (73-74)
Leaving II on the toes (237)
Limit positions (175, 200, 313)
Line of equilibrium (298)

M
Marking the steps (205)
Mechanical movements (54)
Mechanism of the run (69)
Mechanism of the walk (62)
Moments essential (284)
Moments of opposition (233, 234, 277)
Movements (282)
Movements in opposition (277)
Movements on the ground and in the air (209)
Mutation of the feet (245)

O
Oppositions of the dance (167)
Oppositions of the walk (63)
Oppositions simple, Oppositions double (277)
Orchestric movements (57, 86)

P
Period of suspension (69-72)
Pirouettes (258)
Pirouettes and strikes (263)
Pirouettes in attitude, Pirouettes in Arabesque (263)
Pirouettes in II (263)
Pirouettes on the instep (263)
Pirouettes outward, Pirouettes inward (259)
Pirouettes with circle of the leg (263)
Positions of the arms (102, 112)
Positions of the body (150)
Positions of the feet on the horizontal plane (90)
Positions of the head (158)
Positions on the half-toe (102)
Preparation (237-250)
Preparation for the pirouette (260)
Preparatory exercises (176)
Principle II, abbreviation for Second Principal Position
Principle IV, abbreviation for Fourth Principal Position

R
Repeated movements (274)
Ring (353)
Rising on the toes (238)
Rule of the same step (261)
Running steps on the toes (242)

S
Second, or II, abbreviation for Second Position
Secondary moments (285)
Separating (179)
Separating in II or in IV (179)
Separating on the ground (179)
Steps (206)
Steps for two (327)
Steps for three (327)
Steps for four (327)
Steps upon the toes (236-239)
Striking the ground (184)
Superposition of movements (272)
Symmetrical positions (114)
Symmetry (395)

T
Tempos and steps on the toes (236)
Tour in the air (264)
Turning by stamping (267, 268, 310)
Turning movements (256)

V
Variations (326)
Vertical axis of equilibrium (298)

W
Whirling steps (257)

TABLE OF CONTENTS

	PAGE
ABRIDGED INDEX	xxiii

SCULPTURES AND PAINTINGS

SOURCES	3
PAINTED VASES	6
HIGH AND LOW RELIEFS	11
INTERPRETATION OF THE FIGURES	16
TRADITIONAL GESTURES	23

MOVEMENTS IN GENERAL

THE WALK	35
THE RUN	43

TECHNIQUE OF THE DANCE

I.—The Positions

LEGS	56
ARMS	64
TORSO	84
HEAD	87

II.—Preparatory Exercises   95

III.—Tempos and Steps

POSTURES OF THE FEET	113
DESCRIPTION OF TEMPOS AND STEPS	117

RECONSTRUCTION OF THE TEMPOS AND STEPS
From the antique paintings and statues

COÖRDINATION OF MOVEMENTS	151
FIXATION OF MOVEMENTS FROM VASES	157
RECONSTRUCTION OF TEMPOS	160
RECONSTRUCTION OF STEPS	164

CHOREGRAPHY

	PAGE
STEPS FOR TWO	203
STEPS FOR THREE	210
THREE DANCERS AND A LEADER	211
CHORUS OF THE DANCE	216
FUNERAL DANCES	232
RHYTHMIC GAMES	238

THE DANCERS

GODS WHO DANCE	247
DANCES IN HONOR OF THE GODS	258
PRIVATE DANCES	270

CONCLUSION

LIST OF FIGURES	285
ALPHABETICAL REPERTORY	301

RETURN TO ➡ CIRCULATION DEPARTMENT
202 Main Library

LOAN PERIOD 1 **HOME USE**	2	3
4	5	6

ALL BOOKS MAY BE RECALLED AFTER 7 DAYS
1-month loans may be renewed by calling 642-3405
6-month loans may be recharged by bringing books to Circulation Desk
Renewals and recharges may be made 4 days prior to due date

DUE AS STAMPED BELOW

NOV 10 1979

AUG 28 1983
REC CIR AUG 12 '83

MAR 12 1999

UNIVERSITY OF CALIFORNIA, BERKELEY
FORM NO. DD6, 60m, 11/78   BERKELEY, CA 94720

LD 21A-60m-4,'64
(E4555s10)476B

General Library
University of California
Berkeley

CPSIA information can be obtained
at www.ICGtesting.com
Printed in the USA
BVOW11s1409150316

440418BV00019B/142/P